D1596183

The Wilsonian Impulse

The Wilsonian Impulse

U.S. Foreign Policy, the Alliance, and German Unification

Mary N. Hampton

Westport, Connecticut
London

Library of Congress Cataloging-in-Publication Data

Hampton, Mary N.
   The Wilsonian impulse : U.S. foreign policy, the alliance, and
German unification / Mary N. Hampton.
      p.   cm.
   Includes bibliographical references and index.
   ISBN 0–275–95505–2 (alk. paper)
   1. United States—Foreign relations—Germany (West)   2. Germany
(West)—Foreign relations—United States.   3. German reunification
question (1949–1990)   4. Wilson, Woodrow, 1856–1924—Influence.
5. United States—Foreign relations—1945–1989.   I. Title.
E183.8.G3H24   1996
327.73043—dc20   95–45418

British Library Cataloguing in Publication Data is available.

Library of Congress Catalog Card Number: 95–45418
ISBN: 0–275–95505–2

First published in 1996

Praeger Publishers, 88 Post Road West, Westport, CT 06881
An imprint of Greenwood Publishing Group, Inc.

Printed in the United States of America

The paper used in this book complies with the
Permanent Paper Standard issued by the National
Information Standards Organization (Z39.48–1984).

10 9 8 7 6 5 4 3 2 1

For my mother,
Mary Nelle Feathers Hampton,
and in memory of my father,
James Webb Hampton

CONTENTS

Preface   ix

Introduction   1

1 The Historical Origins of the Wilsonian Impulse
   and the Western Alliance   7

2 The Eisenhower Administration and the Wilsonian Impulse   35

3 The Kennedy Administration and the
   Long Wilsonian Shadow   65

4 Restoring the Atlantic Community Under Johnson   93

5 From Ostpolitik to Unification: The Legacy of the
   Wilsonian Impulse and the Versailles Remedial   127

6 Conclusions   157

Bibliography   163

Index   177

PREFACE

I started research for this book some time before the seismic changes that began occurring in international politics in 1989. I sought to explain why realism, the dominant approach in international relations theory, overlooked crucial aspects of the Western Alliance that allowed West Germany so much influence on American and Western security policy. As the events of 1989 and 1990 unfolded, it became evident that fifty years of Allied relations had helped clear the way for the peaceful unification of Germany. How and why the Alliance was so important to that event, and why the role of U.S. foreign policy has been critical to the success of the German quest for unity, are the focus of this book.

In preparing this book, I have had tremendous help. I am grateful to a number of people who have helped me during the course of the research project. First and foremost I would like to thank Ronald Rogowski, whose constant support and insightful comments have been crucial throughout the course of my research and the many incarnations of this project. I would like to thank the following people for their helpful comments on earlier versions of the work: Jeffrey Frieden, David Cattell, Hans Schulhammer, Scott Sagan, David Calleo, Robert O. Keohane, Lilly Gardner-Feldman, Anne-Marie Burley, and Richard Eichenberg. Most recently, I thank Robert O. Keohane, Robert Putnam, Celeste Wallander, Chris Kruegler, Gillian Price, Lawrence Broz, Phil Williams, B. George Thomas, Steve Jones, Mary Reddick, and Robert Paarlberg for their excellent suggestions.

I am grateful to the Fulbright Commission for awarding me a Fulbright Fellowship in Bonn, Germany during 1984–85. During my stay in Germany, the Konrad Adenauer and Friedrich Ebert Stiftungs were of great help. I also thank the approximately fifty current and former West German policymakers and academics who allowed me to interview them. I have used these interviews in the work, often as background. I appreciate as well the participation of the handful of former American foreign policymakers who engaged in written interviews with me.

Also crucial to my work was the assistance of the staff people at the Dwight D. Eisenhower, John F. Kennedy, and Lyndon Baines Johnson Libraries. The people at the Kennedy Library have repeated their help on three research trips.

My department at the University of Utah has been especially supportive. In particular, I thank the chair, Don Hanson, and Lori Sather.

I also acknowledge *Security Studies*, where an earlier version of the ideas in this book was published in spring of 1995. I especially thank the reviewers and the editor, Benjamin Frankel.

Finally, I thank the Center for International Affairs (CFIA) at Harvard University, where I have twice been able to spend time working on versions of this manuscript, first as a Ford Fellow and most recently as an Associate of the Center.

INTRODUCTION

In 1990, in an unprecedented historic moment, Germany reunited in peace and at peace with its neighbors. The factors that contributed to the successful completion of that event were many. Central among them was the influence of U.S. foreign policy, through what I call the Wilsonian impulse. The impact of the specific set of American political beliefs that constituted the Wilsonian impulse was decisive for trans-Atlantic relations and allowed West German policymakers to gain much advantage for their own national interests, including an Allied guarantee to promote German reunification.[1] The Allied pledge to "the achievement through peaceful means of a fully free and unified Germany" played a more significant role in constraining American security policy through the Cold War years than is usually acknowledged.[2]

A component of the Wilsonian impulse, what I call the Versailles remedial, directly informed U.S. postwar policy toward Germany. As I will develop later, the remedial reflected the widespread belief of American policymakers that Germany must not be treated as harshly after WWII as it had been at Versailles in 1919.

The influence of the Wilsonian impulse and Versailles remedial constituted a prism through which American policymakers viewed and acted on their security interests. Beliefs were therefore a causal force in the evolution of Allied relations. An important result was the enhancement of West German leverage in Allied and East-West relations. Thus, in this study, I answer in the affirmative the question posed by Robert Keohane and Judith Goldstein: "Do ideas have an impact on political outcomes, and if so, under what conditions?"[3]

I focus heavily on the early years of the Alliance. As the clearly predominant power at the close of World War II, the United States was able in large part to specify the design of the postwar system, or at least of its Western half. The study shows that the Western Alliance evolved in ways that do not conform to the realist understanding of alliances.[4] While all alliances may serve the minimal function of collective defense, they are not necessarily limited to that function and the realist concern with it, nor have they all been created for that purpose exclusively. The Wilsonian impulse and Versailles remedial constructed American beliefs and expectations concerning the Western Alliance in ways that the Munich lesson and realism overlook. Realism has emphasized the lessons learned by postwar American policymakers concerning the West's appeasement of Hitler in 1938. These lessons, it has been argued, directly influenced the American approach to the Soviet Union, and to potential aggression by dictators around the world. I argue that the Wilsonian impulse presented an alternative set of beliefs regarding international relations, specifically concerning Europe.

The American-led international order that evolved reflected American ideological as well as material interests. As Stephen Krasner has argued, the power capabilities achieved by the United States after World War II allowed it to go beyond pursuing narrowly defined particularistic interests and enabled it to focus as well on projecting its ideological preferences into the world.[5] G. John Ikenberry and Charles A. Kupchan have written insightfully on the phenomenon of emerging hegemons creating their own normative orders in the international system and the socialization process of secondary powers that this process entails.[6] At the moment of American hegemonic innovation, the role of historical learning was pivotal in creating American expectations concerning the postwar international system.

Much has already been written by analysts of international political economy concerning the lessons learned from the economic consequences of American isolationism after World War I. These are in large part Keynesian lessons. Aside from the Munich analogy, there has been little systematic treatment concerning American responses to the security and political lessons that followed the Versailles and interwar experiences. That is the focus of what I call the Wilsonian impulse and the accompanying Versailles remedial.

In defining the Wilsonian impulse, I emphasize three aspects. First, Wilsonians make a number of assumptions concerning the nature of international politics and the kind of behavior that states ought to pursue because of it. To be brief, such beliefs include the rejection of traditional balance of power alliances and the behavior they produce. Second, the real historical experiences of leading American foreign policymakers in the immediate postwar period lent a cognitive predisposition to view the particular context of West Germany and the Western Alliance through the eyes of the failed Wilsonian experience at the end of World War I. My study confirms the significance of the cognitive approach to international relations. Third, the institutionalization of the Wilsonian impulse guaranteed its longevity. The power of the Wilsonian impulse and Versailles remedial were bolstered by the fact that they resonated with the American historical tradition and quickly became institutionalized into the American policymaking process, especially at the State Department.[7] This process assured that the policy prescriptions would remain a significant force over time. Subsequent American policymakers who sought to change course, such as President John F. Kennedy, were eventually constrained by it.

The Versailles remedial demanded the successful socialization of West Germany into the Alliance. West German policymakers influenced heavily the direction and concerns of American security objectives and the substance of Allied security policy through their persistent appeal to American Wilsonianism. This phenomenon confirms the observation of G. John Ikenberry and Charles A. Kupchan that "socialization is a two-way process."[8]

The U.S. interest in establishing a trans-Atlantic community that included a peaceful Germany preceded the American drive to balance against the Soviet threat. While the widely recognized Munich lesson may have influenced the U.S. disposition toward the Soviet Union once that threat perception clearly emerged, the distinctly Wilsonian lessons of Versailles 1919 and the chaotic interwar years were even more operative and immediately so for early postwar American decisionmakers. Therefore, the realist claim regarding balancing behavior explains only a part of the American push to create the Western Alliance. That is, while it is true that the emergence of the Soviet threat galvanized American foreign policy and the Western community in a way that the initial expression of the Wilsonian impulse did not, it is not true that the threat created the drive for Western unity and German rehabilitation.

Further, I will show that the Wilsonian impulse is better at explaining the evolution of Allied relations over time than is a strict realist reading that remains focused on U.S.–Soviet relations. That West Germany's enhanced position far exceeded its role as a so-called junior partner was largely a product of that influence. The Versailles remedial led key American policymakers to look through the lens of 1919 at the failed Wilsonian project they experienced. The influence of the Federal Republic of Germany (FRG) became especially pronounced as the political goal of Alliance cohesion often dominated narrowly defined military objectives for Washington. The FRG would also directly influence the East-West relationship.

I will also examine throughout the study the policy choices of West German decisionmakers and show how their menu was largely constructed by the Wilsonian bargain. The findings are important because they transcend the tautological realist position that West Germany increased its influence in the relationship because it was an important player. My argument is that the manner in which Bonn chose to enhance its influence abroad and consider options domestically was colored heavily by the Wilsonian impulse and produced historically important outcomes both in intra-Allied affairs and in international relations generally. I will argue that the Wilsonian impulse led the West Germans to choose undermining the Cold War system peacefully and from within the Alliance in order to achieve unity. The consequence was monumental: The international system was radically altered by 1990, no systemic war ensued, and the Alliance still stood.

CHAPTER OUTLINE

I concentrate first on the historical origins of the Wilsonian impulse and its influence on the formation of the Alliance. I define in more detail the constituent elements of the impulse and the Versailles remedial.

The second chapter focuses on the Eisenhower administration's approach to West Germany and the Alliance. Specifically, I examine the unification issue and the nuclear sharing idea. John Foster Dulles and his relationship with Konrad Adenauer, the first and perhaps most important of West Germany's postwar leaders, play a prominent role in this section.

As a comparison, I then focus on John F. Kennedy and his tendency to ride roughshod over the American–West German relationship established in the previous administrations. In part, this change represented Kennedy's generational and personal deviation from the Wilsonian past, a deviation that had tremendous implications for the West German perception of its relations with Washington. More important, he was more predisposed to follow the lessons of Munich than the paradigm reflecting the Wilsonian impulse. His outlook tended to conform to a realist reading of U.S.–West German and East-West relations. Because the Wilsonian impulse was already institutionalized at State, still resonated with the public, and was continuously promoted by Adenauer, he would be constrained in his ability to forge change.

Chapter four examines the Johnson administration's efforts to repair relations between the two countries. Through its acceptance in 1967 of the West German–inspired Harmel Report, the United States allowed the consequences of the Wilsonian impulse to be codified into the Alliance. The institutionalization therefore continued. It represented an important turning point both in Western and in East-West relations, and paved the way for the sea-changes in international relations that started in 1989.

In the final chapter, I trace the influence of the Wilsonian impulse through to German reunification. From Ostpolitik onward, West Germans were able to undermine the Cold War order legitimately and peacefully from within the Alliance. By adhering to its Wilsonian bargain with Bonn, the United States nurtured the demise of the bipolar order it had led. I place my claims within the context of the ongoing debate concerning the "long peace" of the last half century. My work specifically addresses realist arguments like John Mearsheimer's. He claims that "bipolarity, an equal military balance, and nuclear weapons have fostered peace in Europe over the past 45 years."[9] I argue instead that a set of ideas that guided American and West German foreign policy, and that were separate from bipolar considerations, contributed immensely to the peace.

NOTES

1. A number of recent and important works concerning the impact of beliefs on policy include Judy Goldstein and Robert O. Keohane, eds., *Ideas and Foreign Policy: Beliefs, Institutions and Political Change* (Ithaca, N.Y.: Cornell University Press, 1993), esp. their "Ideas and Foreign Policy: An Analytical Framework," pp. 3–30, and G. John Ikenberry, "Creating Yesterday's New World Order: Keynesian 'New Thinking' and the Anglo-American Postwar Settlement," pp. 57–86; Judith Goldstein, *Ideas, Interests, and American Trade Policy* (Ithaca, N.Y.: Cornell University Press, 1993); Tony Smith, *America's Mission: The United States and the Worldwide Struggle for Democracy in the Twentieth Century* (Princeton, N.J.: Princeton University Press, 1994); David Fromkin, *In the Time of the Americans: The Generation That Changed America's Role in the World* (New York: Alfred A. Knopf, 1995). For works on the importance of domestic politics to foreign policy, see Robert O. Keohane, *International Institutions and State Power* (Boulder, Colo.: Westview Press, 1989); David A. Lake, *Power, Protection, and Free Trade: International Sources of U.S. Commercial Strategy, 1887–1939* (Ithaca, N.Y.: Cornell University Press, 1988); G. John Ikenberry, David A. Lake, and Michael Mastanduno, eds., *The State and American Foreign Economic Policy* (Ithaca, N.Y.: Cornell University Press, 1988); Robert D. Putnam, "Diplomacy and Domestic Politics: The Logic of Two-Level Games," *International Organization* 42 (Summer 1987), pp. 427–61; Peter B. Evans, Harold K. Jacobson, and Robert D. Putnam, eds., *Double-Edged Diplomacy: International Bargaining and Domestic Politics* (Berkeley: University of California Press, 1993).

2. This pledge was given in the Final Act of the 1954 London Conference that prepared the way for West German entry into NATO. Department of State, Documents on Germany, cited in Dennis L. Bark and David R. Gress, *A History of Germany*, Vol. 1, *From Shadow to Substance 1945–1963*, 2d ed (Cambridge: Blackwell, 1993), p. 331.

3. Keohane and Goldstein, "Ideas and Foreign Policy," pp. 3–30, quotation on p. 11.

4. For an excellent review of the alliance literature, see Stephen M. Walt, *The Origins of Alliances* (Ithaca, N.Y.: Cornell University Press, 1987), esp. the Introduction. For a sophisticated recent discussion, see also Arthur A. Stein, *Why Nations*

Cooperate: Circumstance and Choice in International Relations (Ithaca, N.Y.: Cornell University Press, 1990), ch. 6; an insightful examination of the realist interpretation of alliances is found in John Mearsheimer, "Back to the Future: Instability in Europe After the Cold War," *International Security* 15 (Summer 1990), pp. 5–56.

5. Stephen D. Krasner, *Defending the National Interest: Raw Materials Investments and U.S. Foreign Policy* (Princeton, N.J.: Princeton University Press, 1978), esp. p. 15. See also John Gerard Ruggie, "Multilateralism: The Anatomy of an Institution," in his edited volume, *Multilateralism Matters: The Theory and Praxis of an Institutional Form* (New York: Columbia University Press, 1993), pp. 3–47. On p. 8, Ruggies says of the postwar creative moment that "it was less the fact of American *hegemony* . . . than of *American* hegemony."

6. G. John Ikenberry and Charles A. Kupchan, "Socialization and Hegemonic Power," *International Organization* 44 (Summer 1990), pp. 283–315, esp. p. 284.

7. I especially thank B. George Thomas for his help and suggestions in developing these points. On the importance of institutionalizing ideas, see Goldstein, *Ideas, Interests and American Trade Policy*, and Ikenberry, "Creating Yesterday's New World Order." Regarding the Wilsonian impulse's resonance with the American public, Ninkovich observes that "Wilsonian ideology became 'sedimented' as part of American political culture." Frank Ninkovich, *Modernity and Power: A History of the Domino Theory in the Twentieth Century* (Chicago: University of Chicago Press, 1994), p. 67.

8. Ikenberry and Kupchan, "Socialization and Hegemonic Power," p. 293.

9. Mearsheimer, "Back to the Future," p. 187.

Chapter 1 ————————————————

THE HISTORICAL ORIGINS OF THE WILSONIAN IMPULSE AND THE WESTERN ALLIANCE

America's outward projection of the set of political beliefs that constituted the Wilsonian impulse during its hegemonic moment at the end of World War II heavily influenced the evolution of Washington's most important security relationship, the Western Alliance. The result was not a traditional alliance as understood by realist balance of power thinking, but something quite distinct. As will be shown, the interjection of bipolar Cold War hostilities that informed American containment policy did not destroy the American Wilsonian pursuit; it regionalized it to the Western Alliance.[1]

Further, in addressing realism, I argue that rather than creating America's desire to build a Western community that included an equal and democratic Germany, the Soviet threat galvanized the effort. The Western Alliance therefore evolved as a hybrid between a collective defense pact that targeted the external Soviet threat and a Wilsonian collective security community, wherein interstate relations among the Allies became more domesticated, interdependent, and routinized. The Alliance was highly successful in developing the political culture of a security community, although only partially so in handling the important issue of managing community conflicts. I will focus on the former in the study and return in the conclusion to consider the latter.

THE WILSONIAN IMPULSE: BELIEFS MATTER

In defining Wilsonian beliefs here as an impulse, I take that set of beliefs to have induced a certain kind of behavior or set of responses. Similar to J. David Greenstone's definition of persuasion, I take the term *impulse* to be a set of beliefs shared by a group that "at a given social moment . . . acquire a compelling importance."[2] The ideas that shaped the Wilsonian impulse were derived from the historical experiences of Versailles and the interwar years. As Yuen Foong Khong has pointed out, when behavior is influenced by reasoning based on historical lessons or analogies, the lessons or analogies may "exert their impact on the decision-making process" and "make certain options more attractive and others less so."[3]

Insofar as the Wilsonian impulse produced a set of ordering principles concerning international relations that followed from a historical lesson, it helped shape decisions and thereby played a causal role. The idea that policymakers responded to external reality according to these ordering principles is illuminated especially by the Wilsonian guideposts that so influenced prominent members of the Roosevelt, Truman, and Eisenhower administrations, who were Wilsonians both in outlook and by experience.[4] In David Fromkin's insightful study that focuses on this generation of policymakers, he argues that "their encounter with Woodrow Wilson" and the experiences of World War I and the interwar years "left a decisive impression on them."[5]

The Wilsonian impulse therefore provided the lens through which many leading postwar American policy makers viewed the U.S.–West German–Allied relationship and competed with the lessons of Munich. The Wilsonian impulse presented to those policymakers a limited range of available alternatives. It then proved enduring over time by becoming institutionalized at the State Department.

The Wilsonian Experience and Wilsonian Assumptions

The first component of the impulse was the actual historical experience of the failed Wilsonian vision. The harsh victors' peace of 1919, the chaos of the 1920s, and the repetition of world war in Europe during the following decade confirmed many of Wilson's warnings regarding the effects of the European balance of power system, the treatment of defeated Germany, and American isolationism.

As Frank Ninkovich argues, Wilson's rejection of the European balance of power system arose from his progressive roots and was "based not so much on idealism as on a historical understanding" of that system.[6] The devastation and unlimited nature of World War I were pivotal to Wilson's analysis and the set of ideas and beliefs that emerged as the Wilsonian impulse. From this experience, Wilson determined: "There must be something substituted for the balance of power."[7] In order to avoid the horror of another world war based on the dysfunctional and outmoded balance of power system, the time had arrived for building a community of nations.

His critique of balance of power behavior that was dominated by the great powers in international politics reflected Wilson's criticism of laissez-faire and monopolistic tendencies in the American context.[8] Wilson and his political descendants favored a jointly managed or regulated international system that emphasized "the values of community and individualism."[9] An objective in international politics was therefore to build a transnational community, or to construct a "healthy society. . . through the moral, regulated pursuit of individual interests," and according to universally accepted principles and rules.[10] Entailed are the domestication and routinization of international politics. Economic interdependence and advances in technology were necessary components in making this process possible, although they were by themselves not sufficient for establishing the community.

To this end, a shared culture needed to evolve.[11] Ninkovich states of the Wilsonian position: "With the destruction of traditional mentalities, the construction of genuinely human values was for the first time becoming politically feasible."[12] The collective security community concept emphasized shared values and agreed-upon rules that would help establish a common political culture. First and foremost was the recognition that for historical reasons, such as the advances in technology and communication, great power war had become an anachronistic institution and could no longer be supported as a means for settling differences among states—especially among democratic states. Obviously, many of the ideas had progenitors other than Wilson. However, he constructed them into a set of assumptions that addressed a particular set of historical circumstances. Current analyses in international relations continue to emphasize these ideas. John Mueller's argument that war is now obsolete as a power management resource among the great powers is one example.[13] The body of literature claiming that democracies do not go to war against one another is yet another.[14]

For Wilsonians, the process of community-building was also to help establish the appropriate pool of world public opinion so important to their conception of democracy. Although Wilson intended to include a diversity of cultures and political systems in his global vision, it is also clear that he accepted the possibility that the West might be the first to create such a community.[15] Tony Smith argues persuasively that in other regional contexts during the Cold War, American Wilsonianism was often unsuccessful.[16] As will be discussed in the next chapter, regionalization of the impulse in fact occurred with success in the Western Alliance.

Akin to the advocacy of greater cooperation through regulatory politics of the modern American state under progressivism, more institutionalization and management of international security relations were foreseen and encouraged through the Wilsonian impulse in contrast to the ad hoc competitive security relations reflective of balance of power behavior.[17] Traditionally, alliances were thought to serve the function of coordinating policies among balancing states should conflict erupt. In pursuing collective security as an alternative to European balance of power politics, Wilson envisioned a new kind of international system where "states would cooperate in the common cause of guaranteeing security and justice to all . . . and in which coercion would serve the common peace and order."[18] Herein lies the idea that security is all for one and one for all—it is indivisible.[19] The presumption in international relations as in domestic relations is therefore toward inclusiveness. As Inis Claude persuasively argues, this aspect of Wilsonian security thinking is contrary to the necessary exclusiveness that inheres in balance of power and alliance behavior.[20]

In defining the security relationship envisioned by the Wilsonian impulse, Wilson's own understanding of a collective security community shares features of Karl Deutsch's idea of a pluralistic security community. For Deutsch, a pluralistic security community is one in which sovereign states integrate by attaining a "'sense of community'" in which "common social problems" are resolved peacefully and "normally by institutionalized procedures."[21] For both, the emphasis is on the development of interdependence and the institutionalized management of relations among member states wherein agreed-upon norms, values, and rules establish the habits of cooperation and shared expectations. Both concepts emphasize the joint coordination and management of interstate relations along wide-ranging issues and clearly lead to a shared political culture.[22] They both assume cooperation as the norm, although the collective security idea deals with potential conflict by promoting overwhelming community condemnation of the likely aggressor through political, moral, and economic sanctions, and only as a last resort by military means. Finally, then, both assume that long-term expectations of political cooperation among members have replaced the short-term strategic calculations typical of traditional military alliances. The creation of this shared political culture will then shape each member's policy choices on a wide range of issues differently from what would happen under a traditional defense pact.

Wilsonians promoted security community-building wherein all are to be beholden to what Robert Keohane calls "diffuse" as opposed to specific reciprocal understandings.[23] Rather than establishing a security relationship typical of past alliances, where "the simultaneous balancing of specific quid pro quos by each party with every other at all times" was focused on narrowly defined military goals, the security community includes political and economic understandings that "yield a rough equivalence of benefits in the aggregate and over time."[24] Thus, expectations regarding political, economic, and military policies are constructed differently. In short, the security community emphasizes shared values more than it does shared threats.

Wilsonian assumptions compare with those of the European Concert model.[25] As with the nineteenth-century concert, members compete with one another but according to a regulated set of understandings that are established to avoid outright conflict. Similar again to both is the idea that security is indivisible. On the other hand, the institutionalization and encouragement of shared values of the Wilsonian concept go far beyond the older version.[26] While the concert sought regulation of behavior at the interstate level among the great powers, the Wilsonian concept assumes a congruency of values as well as interests. Also important, the Wilsonian impulse seeks to democratize international politics by asserting such universal principles as equality of status. Wilson stated in 1918: "It is not contemplated by this that nations should always be equal, but that they shall receive equal opportunity."[27] Wilson assumed that a community of democracies would be best able to maintain a community of shared values.

Finally, it was assumed by Wilsonians that the United States would be the international leader in the community-building process. Wilson had said of the need for American leadership regarding the League of Nations that the United States was "'the only country in the world whose leadership and guidance will be accepted.'"[28] Most Wilsonians of the post–World War II period were equally prone to believe that the United States would necessarily lead. This was far from naive, and as Ninkovich observes, Wilson himself and many Wilsonians understood the link between ideology and power.[29] To a great extent, many analysts in international relations today have adopted such a view, from those that discuss the benefits of American hegemonic leadership to those that emphasize the "soft power" base of American leadership abroad.[30]

The failure of the Allies in 1919 to deal effectively with the German problem or to rehabilitate Germany as a great power was to be avoided at all costs. In his admonishments, Wilson warned of the costs of failing to integrate the vanquished German nation into the fold. This belief is the *Versailles remedial* component of the Wilsonian impulse. Thomas Alan Schwartz observes similarly that "the lesson of Weimar was that the West must reward peaceful democracies."[31] Appropriately, Tony Smith notes that Wilson's view of community-building in Europe necessarily meant that "to change Germany internally was to change Europe, and to change Europe was to change the world."[32]

Broadly stroked, then, the Wilsonian impulse reflects the constant tension between what George Kennan calls the universalistic and particularistic approaches to international politics. The particularistic approach reflects the realist predilection to define foreign policy objectives in terms of narrowly formulated national interests, where security is said to be calculated in terms of threat assessment. The universalistic approach seeks to establish universally applicable rules and procedures to solve international problems, thus inviting the recognition of conventions, collective obligation, and responsibility in inter-state relations.[33] Further,

It assumes that if all countries could be induced to subscribe to certain standard rules of behavior, the ugly realities—the power aspirations, the ugly prejudices . . . would be forced to recede behind the protecting curtain of accepted legal restraint, and that the problems of our foreign policy could thus be reduced to the familiar terms of parliamentary procedure and majority decision.[34]

Similarly, Henry Kissinger, the consummate realist, observes that

America's leaders made exertions and sacrifices unprecedented in peacetime coalitions on behalf of appeals to fundamental values and comprehensive solutions, instead of the calculations of national security and equilibrium that had characterized European diplomacy.[35]

My discussion of the Wilsonian impulse shows that realist interest-based arguments concerning U.S. security fall short of explaining how and why postwar Allied and East-West relations evolved in a particular manner. In short, beliefs helped define interests.[36] The Wilsonian impulse included in its construction of American national interests universalist beliefs advocating the democratic organization of international life characteristic of American politics and under American leadership.

Realist lessons claim to eschew universalism, but in fact many self-defined American realists have promoted a balance of power approach to international politics in which values and interests are merged. In this way, the American version of liberal internationalism claims realists and Wilsonians among its ranks. However, the Wilsonian impulse as a policy prescription goes beyond that theoretical construction in that it contains an operationalized set of beliefs based on historical lessons learned concerning American foreign policy in the World War I and interwar years.[37] It reflected the projection of American beliefs as defined by Woodrow Wilson in the experience of World War I. It was the American version of liberal internationalism, and Wilson's belief that the European balance of power system was corrupt was historically and culturally grounded in American tradition. His influence remained prominent, "not because he was so good or so successful, but because he was so American."[38]

The Results: Versailles vs. Munich

The Wilsonian impulse should therefore be thought of as a set of ideas that were a response to specific historical developments. The real experience of Versailles and the interwar years turned those ideas into historical lessons regarding the conduct of foreign policy, thereby evolving as a set of policy prescriptions that influenced post–World War II American policymakers. Further, a number of central policymakers of the immediate postwar era actually experienced Versailles and the interwar years firsthand. Dulles was present at the creation of the Wilsonian security blueprint and at the Versailles Conference. As will be seen in my discussion of major players like Dulles and McCloy, the experience intensified their commitment to Wilsonian ideas and assumptions. For them, the Versailles lessons were as powerful as those of Munich, if not more so. The interjection of the Cold War rivalry with the Soviets did not diminish the power of the Wilsonian impulse or the Versailles remedial, although the Versailles and Munich lessons often coexisted awkwardly.[39]

The appeasement of Hitler at Munich by the West in 1938 certainly influenced American policymakers in the period after World War II, and it is a phenomenon that has received wide attention. Following from that lesson were the beliefs that democracies must remain ever vigilant in the face of potentially aggressive dictators, and that aggression must be dealt with promptly and convincingly. For self-styled American academic and policy realists in the Cold War era, the Munich lesson served as a critique of the West's failure to balance against German aggression in the period preceding the outbreak of war in 1939.

The set of Wilsonian beliefs that also heavily influenced policymakers after 1945 did not conform to the realist tenets of the Munich lesson. Nor did they adhere to the realist assumptions that inter-state conflict and international anarchy dominate in the world and lead to the demand for balancing behavior, and where the national interest adheres to a narrowly defined set of interests. According to the Wilsonian beliefs, the outbreak of war in 1939 could be understood as the failure of Western policymakers to heed the warnings of Woodrow Wilson that a calamity lay in waiting if they did not proceed to build a community of like-minded democratic nations that would supersede the antiquated European balance of power system.

For an influential group of American policymakers, opinion leaders, academics, and members of the business elite, the real historical lessons of World War I and the interwar years included the conviction that the United States needed to take a leading role in international politics, and that the role should be one of encouraging and building a more open and cooperative international economic system than had heretofore existed. Many excellent works have dealt with these people and the impact of their convictions.[40] For example, in his piece, "Creating Yesterday's New World Order," G. John Ikenberry argues that a group of innovative thinkers on both sides of the Atlantic contributed significantly to the Anglo-American approach to postwar international order. Their prescriptive ideas about international economic and monetary policy emanated largely from the historical lessons of the interwar period.[41]

Similarly, the lessons of the failed Wilsonian experiment in interstate power management led many members of the American elite to adopt a number of prescriptive ideas concerning international security issues.[42] Fromkin observes: "A quarter of a century earlier, the American establishment had not followed Woodrow Wilson. Regretting it, they did so now."[43] Included was the objective of building a transnational security community to replace what was interpreted as the outmoded European balance of power system. Accompanying that objective was the perceived necessity of integrating a democratic Germany into the community. Regarding American policy toward West Germany after World War II, key decisionmakers like Hull, Truman, Dulles, and McCloy selected policy options according to the Versailles remedial that proved pivotal in building the Western Alliance.[44]

The Wilsonian Impulse and Policy Making

Beginning with the New Deal, the State Department advocated an open international trading system that was deemed "central to American economic and security interests."[45] The longtime secretary of state under Roosevelt, Cordell Hull, was a leading voice for this open international system. He was also a champion of the Wilsonian impulse, advocating transnational community-building in place of an international order based on balance of power or spheres of influence. At the series of summits and conferences attended by the wartime allies during the 1940s, Hull consistently advocated the application of Wilsonian principles to the postwar settlement. The Wilsonian influence, receiving a great deal of bipartisan support and backed largely by the American public, often constrained Roosevelt's ability to find agreement with the British and Soviets.[46]

Many at the State Department shared the vision, and the State Department became the center of activity for the Wilsonian impulse. Included was the group called the Europeanists and, especially, those both wary of German history and extremely sensitive to Bonn's demands. The perception was that failure to win West German loyalty after the war would be costly. The historical memory of Germany as a great power thwarted after defeat was pervasive. Frank Costigliola notes that this American view of the Germans tended to be condescending, where the West Germans were treated as the "problem children" in Europe. He argues that State Department officials especially, but other American elites as well, "cared about the Germans while regarding them as dangerously emotional, anxious, and susceptible to extremism."[47] Whether this was the case or not, the West Germans were able to achieve much by standing in the shadow cast by Versailles.

Bonn's appeal to the American historical memory of the failed Wilsonian policy toward Germany and Europe after World War I was an especially important and successful strategy implemented by West German policymakers, starting with Adenauer. He strategically appealed to the impulse to effect U.S. policy on unification and East-West issues. He and his successors thereby helped to reinforce the Wilsonian impulse and Versailles remedial at State and constrain U.S. action. John Foster Dulles revealed the concern of leaders in Washington and elsewhere in stating of the Germans that:

They have demonstrated a very great quality, perhaps even frighteningly so. You cannot neutralize and paralyze a people like that in the center of Europe. If the effort were made there would be a move on their part to build up toward power and try for a balance of power as far as Europe is concerned.[48]

Just as Ikenberry argues in the case of postwar Anglo-American relations, there was no inevitability about the manner in which American–West German–Allied relations evolved after World War II.[49] A widespread realist contention has been that the United States approached questions concerning West Germany and the Western Alliance in light of American-Soviet competition, or according to the demands of bipolarity.[50] However, the crucial point I make is that the Wilsonian impulse led American policymakers to make important judgments about how to treat West Germany and Western security relations that preceded and were separate from the Soviet threat and influenced it in turn.

In fact, the domestic controversy over how to approach the Germans in a general way played out before it was determined that a Soviet threat existed. President Roosevelt at one point in 1944–45 favored the Morgenthau Plan, a scheme named after Secretary of the Treasury Henry Morgenthau, which envisioned an extreme and severely retributive approach toward postwar Germany. The Morgenthau Plan included the deindustrialization of Germany, or its "pastoralization." At the Quebec Conference of September 1944, Roosevelt signed onto the approach and coaxed a reluctant Winston Churchill to accept it.

Roosevelt then backed away from the plan because of the lack of domestic public support it carried, but especially because of the hostile response by key policymakers like Secretary of State Cordell Hull.[51] After it met this opposition, the Morgenthau Plan was quickly dropped. A very different policy was then formulated and carried out under the Truman administration, one more commensurate with American Wilsonian beliefs and directly derived from the perceived Wilsonian historical lessons of Versailles. The United States ended up choosing "rehabilitation over repression" as its approach to postwar Germany, and this approach was intensely supported by President Truman after Roosevelt's death. Interestingly, then, the Wilsonian impulse had implications for how one dealt with adversaries. Reflecting the progressive persuasion, adversaries were to be rehabilitated if possible.[52] More important, Secretary of State Hull held these views out of the conviction that the earlier failed Wilsonian experiment was correct in explaining how international relations ought to work. Calling the Morgenthau Plan "cataclysmic," his State Department's recommendation for the "assimilation" of Germany "on a basis of equality" was adopted by Roosevelt and devotedly pursued thereafter by the Truman and Eisenhower administrations.[53] Reflective of the support such an approach enjoyed were public opinion polls taken in 1944–45 that showed a majority of Americans believing that Germany could be rehabilitated and brought into "a new world league."[54]

THE ORIGINS OF THE ALLIANCE AND THE LIMITATIONS OF REALISM

My argument about the Wilsonian impulse in Allied relations does not prove realism wrong, nor does it attempt to do so. Rather, my claim is that realism traditionally treats alliances too generically.[55] I suggest that American national self-interests can best be understood by looking at the beliefs of the American policymakers who established the Alliance and the ways in which those beliefs constructed their choices.[56] The combination of those beliefs, America's power to realize them once the Soviet threat emerged, and West Germany's ability to use them helped establish the Allied security relationship in a way that deviated from realist expectations. It was also the case that the Wilsonian impulse influenced the expression of West German self-interest.

The basis of realist and neorealist explanations for the successful creation of the Alliance has always been that the United States led the Western effort to balance against the Soviet threat, while middle- and small-sized states in Western Europe mostly followed. Robert E. Osgood presents a narrow and traditional realist reading of the Alliance. He argues that:

To be sure, the North Atlantic Treaty prescribes that an attack on one member shall be regarded as an attack upon all; but its membership is confined to a group of nations sharing a common security interest, who combined to form a military alliance against a particular aggressor; and the obligations it imposes upon its members are narrowly defined so as to serve only that common security interest. . . . No nation is willing to subordinate its special security interests to the general requirements of a system designed to protect a hypothetical international community.[57]

Osgood is correct in claiming that the Western Alliance became a competitive alliance in relation to the Warsaw Pact, and was in that sense "the kind of entangling alliance . . . that President Wilson hoped would be replaced by a universal concert of nations."[58] However, traditional realist contentions such as Osgood's overlook the predominantly political goal of American Western security policy to construct a Western community that was indeed influenced by Wilsonianism. This fact determined that the political goal of Allied cohesion would over time often take precedence over narrowly conceived military considerations and that member states with their own agendas, such as West Germany, could and did influence Allied and American policy in ways unexplained by the realist reading. One must likewise go outside Osgood's account to understand the importance of the Versailles remedial in granting Bonn special privileges in the Alliance.

Likewise, structural realism assumes that the basis for NATO, or any alliance, is that of balancing against threats, where threats are defined in terms of power capabilities. It assumes further that states balance according to narrowly defined self-interests, where each state assesses the threats in the international environment according to the power capabilities of other states. One objective of the Western Alliance was certainly to balance against the Soviet threat. Because it served other purposes as well, however, American self-interest was not defined as narrowly as realist assumptions suggest.

For reasons that realism itself does not articulate well, the realist position is accurate in an important way. As Stephen D. Krasner argues in his explication of the evolution of postwar U.S. commercial and monetary policy, a consensus regarding the pursuit of an open and liberal international economic system was not agreed upon domestically until U.S. policymakers framed such a strategy within the context of a struggle against international communism.[59] The realists are therefore right insofar as the Soviet threat induced American policymakers and then the public to act.

What realism does not adequately explain is that the Soviet threat galvanized into action a set of interrelated American beliefs that preceded the threat, which then influenced the evolution of policies that were separate from the threat. Accompanying the global bipolar dimension of U.S. postwar security policy were the separate political goals of achieving the economic and political reconstruction of a stable Europe from its vulnerable and war-ravaged position in 1945, of creating trans-Atlantic interdependence, and of assuring a peaceful and durable resolution of the German problem as it appeared at the time by democratizing Germany.

Thus, for example, it is clear that from the implementation of the Marshall Plan in 1947 to the inclusion of West Germany in NATO in 1955, one aim of American foreign policy was to counter the Soviet threat on all fronts. It is also clear, however, that those policies served two other preexisting objectives: to create a trans-Atlantic community and to integrate Germany into the community of Western democracies. These goals were made clear earlier through the declaration of the Atlantic Charter in 1941, Hull's optimistic assessments of the "declaration" that was agreed upon at the Moscow Conference in 1943, the creation of open internationalism at the Bretton Woods and Dumbarton Oaks Conferences in 1944, and the rejection of the Morgenthau Plan in 1945.[60]

Realists and Wilsonians superficially found some common ground in what American goals regarding Germany's position in Western Europe should have been. George Kennan expressed the concern of both in 1948:

> If there is no real European federation and if Germany is restored as a strong and independent country, we must expect another attempt at German domination. If there is no real European federation and if Germany is *not* restored as a strong and independent country, we invite Russian domination. . . . This being the case, it is evident that the relationship of Germany to the other countries of western Europe must be so arranged as to provide mechanical and automatic safeguards against any unscrupulous exploitation of Germany's preeminence in population and in military-industrial potential.[61]

What the pronouncement does not reveal is that the Wilsonian impulse accorded West German policymakers an enhanced ability to determine the direction such rehabilitation would take. It also allowed Bonn to constrain American, European, and East-West security policy in ways that neither Kennan nor a generic realist position would explain or advocate. I will examine further this facet of the Wilsonian impulse later by analyzing the multilateral force (MLF) issue of the 1960s. Here was a case of the United States pursuing a policy that made little military sense, but was promoted for intra-Allied political reasons. Specifically, it was advocated in order to placate perceived West German future demands regarding equality of status.

An obvious realist response to any analysis positing West German influence is that Bonn got its way as often as it did with the United States precisely because it was such an important Cold War ally, a rather tautological claim. Of course, part of the problem is that yet another realist interpretation claims that the West Germans got their way only when their interests coincided with those of the United States, particularly in the 1950s.[62] Because both explanations assume U.S.–West German relations to be driven by power calculations, neither can clarify the peculiarities in the relationship that in fact drove the Allied and East-West relationships.

THE WILSONIAN IMPULSE AND THE ALLIANCE

What were the specific operative qualities of the Alliance from its initiation in 1949 that revealed the Wilsonian impulse in the Western security relationship? First of all, the universalistic principles informing the Alliance's institutionalization promoted the expectation that a North Atlantic political community was to be established through the elaboration of an expected code of behavior. Thus, within the broader context of the global anticommunist struggle informing U.S. foreign policy objectives was a Wilsonian vision of the international political order that directly affected America's Western security policy in a distinctive way.

David Calleo's assessment of the Wilsonian influence on the Alliance differs greatly from mine. In discussing the universalism of the Wilsonian impulse versus the particularism of Kennan's approach, he argues that the former was intrinsically anti-European and sought to mask American hegemony. Relating to the American role in the Alliance, for example, he states that the "American military protectorate for Western Europe was packaged in the multilateral hocus-pocus of NATO." Obviously, my analysis focuses on this aspect of the security relationship and assesses it quite differently.[63]

Kissinger employs a realist perspective and renders an insightful critique of Wilsonianism in his book, *Diplomacy*. In examining the historical record of the U.S. approach to the Alliance, he makes note of an influential State Department document from 1951 that surveyed alliances throughout history:

Its conclusion was that the North Atlantic Treaty differed from them all, "both in letter and in spirit." . . .

The Atlantic Alliance upheld principle, it was said, not territory; it did not resist change, only the use of force to bring about change. . . . It seeks not to influence any shifting "balance of power," but to strengthen the "balance of principle."[64]

Kissinger's analysis indeed captures the influence of the Wilsonian impulse. As I argue throughout this study, it infused the State Department and was institutionalized in it. Kissinger correctly observes: "In short, the Atlantic Alliance, not really being an alliance, possessed a claim to moral universality. . . . In a sense, the role of the Atlantic Alliance was to act until such time as the United Nations Security Council 'has taken all the measures necessary to restore peace and security.' "[65] It is not surprising that, once in power, Kissinger often sought to bypass the State Department in key foreign policy matters.

What is striking about U.S. foreign policy in the 1945–1955 era was the persistence of Washington in promoting not only multilateralism but also a series of institutionalized interlocking relationships to achieve its security policy objectives of community-building.[66] Through its policy of linking sets of interests and relationships, such as the United Nations and the Western Alliance, and of advocating the application of universalistic principles for both, Washington largely influenced the future course of Western relations.

The consciously constructed interconnectedness of U.S. postwar foreign policy is frequently overlooked in much of the alliance literature. This multipronged approach achieved operational form through the creation of a number of economic and assistance programs, through the founding of various international and regional economic and military organizations, and through the promotion of international political organizations. A common denominator of American support and sponsorship of varied policies and programs such as, among others, the Marshall Plan, the International Trade Organization, and various organs of the United Nations, was the fundamental commitment to the three goals set out above, and an emphasis of method on institutionalization, collective participation, and voluntary collaboration. The Western Alliance was intimately tied to the principles and guidelines of the more globally conceived United Nations, whose goals of community-building foundered on the shoals of the Cold War.

In fact, the North Atlantic Treaty explicitly adheres to the universal principles of reason and the rule of law set out in the United Nations Charter, another indication of its Wilsonian heritage. The signatories of the treaty are "expected to settle differences by the exercise of reason and adjustment, according to the principles of justice and law. This requires a spirit of tolerance and restraint on the part of all the members."[67] The security interests of NATO members were therefore directly tied to the principles of the United Nations Charter and these principles were to be applied to one and all alike. One of the guiding principles established in the UN Charter and applied to the American conception of the Western security community is that of the "sovereign equality of all its members."[68] Adenauer and all subsequent West German leaders would constantly reinforce this principle.

The pursuit of Western security as agreed upon in the North Atlantic Treaty extends beyond narrow military considerations in other ways, as well. The consensus reached concerning security incorporates the area of economic cooperation, wherein the Allies "agree to eliminate conflicts in their economic life."[69] Here again is the link back to the postwar innovation in ideas and policy that has been examined in the international political economy literature. U.S. policy sought European reconstruction as a response to the Soviet threat, not only as a safeguard against potential internal turmoil in these countries, but also as a means through which to achieve international economic stability and the political basis for a Western community. The process required institutionalization and interdependence, both advocated by Dean Acheson, one of the first postwar secretaries of state, and important European counterparts, like Jean Monnet. Kissinger is insightful in his analysis of Acheson and the influence of Wilsonianism. He observes that the sophisticated Acheson was "sufficiently American in his approach to diplomacy to be convinced that, left to its own devices, Europe had made a mess of the balance of power."[70] For Acheson, the Atlantic Alliance needed to promote international cooperation "and to promote respect for the principle of equal rights and self-determination of peoples."[71] In other words, Acheson believed that NATO "could be justified by the doctrine of collective security, which Wilson had first put forward as the alternative to the alliance system."[72]

This Wilsonian goal of trans-Atlantic community-building was especially important in that it signified early on in the Western security relationship that the Alliance was not convened strictly for defense against the Soviet threat.[73] As John Foster Dulles put it, a great emphasis of the Alliance was "on cooperation *for* something rather than merely *against* something."[74] It also means that the U.S. mission went beyond Steve Weber's interesting premise that NATO was created according to an American predilection for multilateralism.[75] From the beginning, the Alliance was envisioned as the predominant vehicle through which an Atlantic Community would be established, and this goal is clearly prescribed in the Preamble and in Articles 2 and 4 of the North Atlantic Treaty. Also, as interpreted by the North Atlantic Council in 1956, there existed "the insistent feeling that NATO must become more than a military alliance . . . and . . . the very real anxiety that if NATO failed to meet this test, it would disappear with the immediate crisis which produced it." Therefore, the need was great to establish "the habits and traditions and precedents for such cooperation and unity."[76]

The emphasis on consultation, consensus, parliamentary procedure, and cooperation among freely associating partners would heavily inform the future direction of the relationship and the positioning of various states therein. The inclusion of principles like equality of status and opportunity, noncoercion, and nondiscrimination among members infused the relationship with political obligation and diffuse reciprocity and would benefit states other than the United States. They were especially helpful to West Germany. The principles were further reinforced through the explicit rules of timely consultation among Allies, stated in Article 4 of the treaty, and have been frequently invoked during periods of trans-Atlantic discord, along with the regularity of information exchange and assembly. Herein lies quite clearly the embryonic conception of the Alliance as a security community and wherein the agreed-upon elaboration of principles, rules, and procedures becomes central to the life of the Alliance.

These influences determined that the political goal of Allied cohesion would over time often take precedence over narrowly conceived military considerations. It is in this light, for example, that President Eisenhower's sincere efforts to find a nuclear sharing arrangement in the West, having given up on sharing through the United Nations, should be partly understood. Dulles stated to Governor Harold Stassen in 1956:

I doubted very much whether the concept of the United States as a "benevolent dictator" would be good enough in the long run. . . . I felt that President Eisenhower had a unique authority and that it would be a tragedy if it were not used to move the world ahead by climbing up at least one more rung in the ladder that led toward community control of this vast destructive power.[77]

To further highlight this distinction and the influence of the Wilsonian impulse as an operational code, I will examine the two relevant cases of German reunification and the MLF in subsequent chapters. Both show the American concern for assuring equality.of status within the Alliance and clearly led it into a thicket with allies and adversaries alike over essentially political concerns.

THE WEST GERMAN CONNECTION

The code of behavior established for all in the Allied relationship and the immediate access to the policy-making process granted to its members insured each the potential and the right to influence collective policy formulation and direction. The infusion of middle-sized and small states' interests into the Alliance was thereby assured through the principles of equality of status, nondiscrimination, and noncoercion. Under Adenauer's leadership, West Germany would, in fact, persistently seek to reinforce those principles while appealing to the historical experiences of American Wilsonians. Throughout the 1950s, the target of Adenauer's Western policy would be to concretize the security convention of 1954, which was based on the Wilsonian principles already established in the 1949 North Atlantic Treaty, and enforce it as the foundation of West German loyalty to the West. In this, he was extremely successful.

Although the Federal Republic was not formally admitted to NATO until 1955, it was clear by 1949 that Washington had begun a courtship of Bonn with the purpose of securing West German loyalty to the West. Much of the work in political science and history about this period has stressed the near absence of choice and maneuverability on Bonn's part concerning West German allegiance to the West. For example, many analysts and observers view Chancellor Konrad Adenauer's Western integration policy as an *Ersatz*, or substitute, for West Germany's pursuing autonomy and sovereignty.[78] I interpret the situation quite differently. Through its integration policy, Bonn was able to achieve much national sovereignty and gain influence within the West by appealing to the principles of sovereignty, nondiscrimination, noncoercion, reciprocity, and equality of status that informed Washington's Wilsonian impulse.

Much like Harold Nicolson's analysis of French strategy in gaining readmittance as a great power in the immediate post-Napoleonic war period that established the Concert, the examination of post–World War II relations reveals similarly that West German foreign policymakers, particularly Adenauer, were astute in availing themselves of the opportunities presented through the various postwar initiatives of the United States.

Nicolson depicts Tallyrand as able to perceive and exact French benefits from both the "rules of the game" that were established through British sponsorship in the aftermath of the Napoleonic wars and from the disarray of opinion that existed among the victorious powers in 1815. In discussing Tallyrand's ability to play on the existing norms and rules underwriting the international order at the time, such as the sovereign equality of states, Nicolson reveals the following:

In every conference the problem of organization, the actual plan of procedure, acquires a significance which is often underestimated. . . . It was in the fissure which this problem created in the frontage of the Quadruple Alliance that Tallyrand inserted his little wedge.[79]

The strategy pursued by Adenauer regarding West German integration into the Western community during the late 1940s and early 1950s reflects much the same phenomenon. In seeking to maximize West German national sovereignty and international influence through a policy advocating Western integration for the FRG, Adenauer appealed at different junctures to the rules and principles implicitly or explicitly informing the U.S.–led alliance efforts. Adenauer set the terms for winning West German loyalty to the West in terms of the already established principles set out by the Wilsonian impulse. For example, the principle of free association of sovereign states underlying the Alliance particularly by 1949 was invoked constantly by Adenauer in order to capture as much national sovereignty for West Germany as possible. He viewed this as a fair price to be paid by the other Western powers in exchange for West German participation in and loyalty to the Western community.[80]

The signing of the Petersberg Agreement in 1949 by the Allied High Commission furthered the cause of West German sovereignty through its recognition of West Germany as a participant in Western and international organizations and by its acceptance of Bonn's right to formally open international diplomatic channels. In exchange, West Germany agreed to join the Council of Europe, a commitment that was welcomed by Adenauer, and to prevent West German rearmament of any kind, a point that unleashed little controversy domestically in the Federal Republic.[81] Yet, the commitment by Adenauer and some Western policymakers, especially many in Washington, not to allow West German rearmament was tenuous even in 1949.[82]

Adenauer's success in establishing the FRG as a legitimate player in the international system by appealing directly to the Wilsonian impulse was even more clearly reflected in the drawn-out 1950–1952 Allied-West German negotiations that culminated in the Convention on Relations Between the Three Powers and the Federal Republic of Germany, or the Bonn Conventions. This agreement, which would become operative upon the enactment of the European Defense Community (EDC), went much further than the Petersberg Agreement of 1949 in securing West German sovereignty and equality of status within Europe. Bonn was to receive, with some notable exceptions, full authority over its internal and external affairs, and the Occupation Statute was thereby to be abrogated. The Federal Republic was also now entitled to participate in the European Defense Community with equal status, although restrictions on West German rearmament would appear in the EDC treaty, signed May 27, 1952.[83] In the face of continued French resistance to full West German rehabilitation, Adenauer insisted on the implementation of the principles of noncoercion, nondiscrimination, and equal status in relations among freely associated states. On these issues, he had support from Acheson and the State Department. The final report issued by High Commissioner John McCloy is telling:

The final conventions bear little resemblance to those which were initially proposed, and the differences are primarily due to Allied concessions to the German negotiators and to Allied recognition that in the new relationship the Federal Republic was justified in demanding full equality.[84]

The years 1950–1953 thus witnessed the increased ability of Adenauer and West German policymakers to attain successfully national goals by linking Washington's concern with military security during this period of heightened international tension to the norms and principles codified within the 1949 North Atlantic Treaty. With the French remaining almost adamant in refusing to consider a rearmed West Germany, Washington became more committed to such rearmament, despite the restrictions agreed upon in the recently completed Petersberg Accord. While encouraging the U.S. position, and constantly reinforcing Western anxiety about the Communist threat, Adenauer persisted in invoking the principles of equal status and nondiscrimination among freely associating states if a West German military contribution was to be forthcoming.[85] He pressed this point strongly, particularly during the tense days of the Korean War. His persistence in pressing for West German equality of status is indicated by the following passage: "My precondition for German participation in European defence was complete equality between Germany and the other European nations. Equal duties presupposed equal rights."[86]

By promoting the idea that the West German military contribution should be made strictly within a collective European or Atlantic forum, Adenauer appealed to the three-pronged American postwar foreign policy agenda. Such a plan accommodated at once the perceived needs of meeting the Soviet security threat, contributing to the stability and progress of a cohesive Europe, and integrating a stable and democratic Germany into the Western fold. Even more so, Adenauer's approach facilitated the evolution of the political culture for a trans-Atlantic community envisioned by the Wilsonian impulse and necessitated by the Versailles remedial. The events of 1954 leading to West Germany's admittance to NATO reveal the continued American commitment to the Wilsonian collective security concept. The United States pursued ever more adamantly the admittance of West Germany into the Western fold and, encouraged by Adenauer, continued its advocacy of applying the universalist approach to Atlantic relations, which provoked heightened antagonisms among the Allies. For example, a National Security Council memorandum from the period stated:

Underlying the US position was the assumption that it was crucially important to associate Germany in sovereign equality with the West. We agree with Adenauer's own estimate that he cannot go on much longer maintaining his position unless we take positive action.[87]

It is in this context that the more nationalist European approach of France to Western integration presented "a grave dilemma" to American and British policymakers.[88] France's inclination to procrastinate in addressing the West German rearmament question, its persistence in linking cessation of the Occupation Statute to the resolution of the Saar issue as it had done throughout the EDC negotiations in the 1950–1954 period, as well as its continued concern with dismantling the West German armaments industry and its propensity to give higher priority to the Brussels Treaty Organization than to NATO (the former being less supranational in character than NATO), were but some of the issues of contention between Paris and Washington concerning the approach to Western integration and West German participation. (The issue of the Saarland caused much friction between France and West Germany between 1949 and 1955. Both states sought control of the region, but it had been put under French occupation after the war. In 1955, however, the Saarlanders voted to join West Germany. This process was completed in 1957 after continued French-German negotiations.) Washington's persistence in insisting on restored West German sovereignty and integration into the Western defense community on terms that were "without restrictions unacceptable to the Germans as discriminatory or arbitrarily imposed" remains one of the great historic tributes to the Wilsonian legacy.[89] Also, following Acheson's lead, John Foster Dulles was one of the more outspoken supporters of West Germany after the collapse of the EDC. In response to the French Parliament's rejection of its own proposal, Dulles stated:

It would be unconscionable if the failure to realize EDC through no fault of Germany's should now be used as an excuse for penalizing German. . . . It is a tragedy that in one country nationalism, abetted by Communism, has asserted itself so as to endanger the whole of Europe. The tragedy would be compounded if the United States was thereby led to conclude that it must turn to a course of narrow nationalism.[90]

On this issue of bringing France and Germany together, which broadly included binding together two historic enemies and specifically saw the resolution of the long-standing Saar dispute, the collective security requirement of managing potential community conflict peacefully was extremely successful. It, along with the Versailles remedial that drove it, is too often overlooked in the international relations literature. Just as the American postwar response to West Germany cannot be deduced from realist assumptions concerning national interests, the arrival of the Soviet threat in Europe did not automatically relieve the enmity between France and Germany. The history of those immediate postwar years reveals the intensity and tirelessness with which American policymakers pushed to abolish that rivalry, applying pressure to both countries.[91]

CONCLUSIONS

In sum, West Germany's speedy integration into the Western Alliance helped operationalize the Wilsonian impulse. The phenomenon reflects the limits of the U.S. willingness to use coercive power as a hegemon in its socialization of West Germany into the Western fold and reflects Bonn's adeptness at winning concessions as it acquiesced to the American-led order.[92] The political legitimacy of the Alliance as a Wilsonian security community was decisive in maintaining the Western security bond, in enhancing the role of the FRG, and in promoting the peaceful evolution of East-West and West-West relations. Thus, the Alliance would evolve as a hybrid between a collective defense pact that targeted an external threat and a collective security community wherein institutionalization and interdependence were to bind together the countries of the West.

In the following chapters, I will examine the impact of the Wilsonian historical lesson on U.S. foreign and security policy formulation. It was during the Eisenhower administration that the Wilsonian impulse became operationalized in essential Allied areas of concern and helped forge the Washington-Bonn connection. The Wilsonian experiences of key postwar American foreign policy players like Acheson and Dulles influenced directly the policy alternatives they perceived as available to them. The Wilsonian assumptions typically underlying the American approach to foreign policy were thereby reinforced and given concrete form. The intervention of the Versailles remedial had great consequences for the evolution of the Allied relationship and international relations over time, especially as it became institutionalized in the State Department and in the Alliance.

I will examine two issues particularly crucial in activating the Wilsonian impulse. First, I look at the way the Eisenhower administration chose to handle the issue of German unification. Specifically, I examine the relationship of Konrad Adenauer, the first West German chancellor, and the Eisenhower administration regarding the issue. The close relationship of Adenauer and Dulles was especially important in forging the U.S.–West German relationship.[93] The construction of the unification question as part of Allied responsibility and the ability of Adenauer to reap West German advantage based on the principles spawned by the Wilsonian impulse reflect both the vitality of the political culture that was evolving on both sides of the Atlantic and the centrality of the Versailles lesson for Dulles and Eisenhower.

Second, I examine the revealing topic of nuclear sharing, focusing mostly on the multilateral force controversy. I look at the MLF issue as an example of how the Wilsonian impulse heavily colored the Eisenhower administration's perception of Allied policy. Here was an item that had practically no military value, but that was seen as politically important in ensuring the principle of equality of status for West Germany and in creating a community of Western states through shared responsibility.

NOTES

1. See John Gerard Ruggie's discussion of this in "Multilateralism: The Anatomy of an Institution," in *Multilateralism Matters: The Theory and Praxis of an Institutional Form* (New York: Columbia University Press, 1993), pp. 3–47, esp. p. 10.

2. J. David Greenstone, *The Lincoln Persuasion: Remaking American Liberalism* (Princeton, N.J.: Princeton University Press, 1993), p. 5.

3. See Yuen Foong Khong's excellent study, *Analogies at War: Korea, Munich, Dien Bien Phu, and the Vietnam Decisions of 1965* (Princeton, N.J.: Princeton University Press, 1992), pp. 252, 253. Khong breaks new ground in examining the competing historical analogies that influenced American decision making concerning Vietnam in 1965. A classical treatment of beliefs and their impact on foreign policy remains Alexander George, "The 'Operational Code': A Neglected Approach to the Study of Political Leaders and Decision-Making," *International Studies Quarterly* 13 (1969), pp. 190–222. See also Judith Goldstein, *Ideas, Interests, and American Trade Policy* (Ithaca, N.Y.: Cornell University Press, 1993), esp. pp. 250–59. On the significance of images and their effects on policymakers' perceptions of and orientation to international politics, see Richard Ned Lebow, "Generational Learning and Conflict Management," *International Journal* vol XL (40), no. 4 (Autumn 1985), pp. 555–85, esp. pp. 555–59. Finally, see Jerel A. Rosati, *The Carter Administration's Quest for Global Community: Beliefs and Their Impact on Behavior* (Columbia: University of South Carolina Press, 1987). He discusses on pp. 26–27 the importance of historical lessons and the intervention of external events in producing change in an individual or collectivity's set of beliefs.

4. A brief list of Wilsonians from this period includes Presidents Truman and Roosevelt, Secretaries of State Cordell Hull and John Foster Dulles, and John J. McCloy. I would include Dean Acheson, as well.

5. David Fromkin, *In the Time of the Americans: The Generation That Changed America's Role in the World* (New York: Alfred A. Knopf, 1995), p. 542.

6. Frank Ninkovich, *Modernity and Power: A History of the Domino Theory in the Twentieth Century* (Chicago: University of Chicago Press, 1994), p. 46. See his interesting discussion of Wilson's sophisticated understanding of the balance of power, esp. pp. 45–56.

7. Ibid., p. 55.

8. One of the classic discussions of this phenomenon remains that of Arthur S. Link, "Wilson: Idealism and Realism," in his edited work, *Woodrow Wilson: A Profile* (New York: Hill and Wang, 1968), pp. 163–77.

9. Jordan A. Schwarz, *The New Dealers: Power Politics in the Age of Roosevelt* (New York: Alfred A. Knopf, 1993), p. xii and see esp. Part 1.

10. John Milton Cooper, Jr., "Wilsonian Democracy," in *Democrats and the American Idea: A Bicentennial Appraisal*, ed. Peter B. Kovler (Washington, D.C.: Center for National Policy Press, 1992), pp. 203–27; quote on p. 215.

11. See the insightful explication of Wilson's emphasis on world opinion and its connection to building a community of nations in Ninkovich, *Modernity and Power*, pp. 56–65. The idea of developing a shared culture corresponds to Ninkovich's discussion on p. 58 of Wilson's belief that a "new international psychology" could develop out of the ashes of World War I.

12. Ninkovich, *Modernity and Power*, p. 60. On p. 41, the author observes that Wilson promoted "international understandings" and "the need for a cosmopolitan awareness that transcended mere local knowledge."

13. John Mueller, "The Essential Irrelevance of Nuclear Weapons: Stability in the Postwar World," in *The Cold War and After: Prospects for Peace*, ed. Sean Lynn-Jones and Steven Miller (Cambridge, Mass.: MIT Press, 1993), pp. 45–69. Sounding Wilsonian, Mueller concludes by saying on p. 69 that "since preparations for major war are essentially irrelevant, they are profoundly foolish."

14. Michael Doyle's work is particularly relevant, although obviously indebted to Kant more than Wilson. Among others, see his "Liberalism and World Politics," *American Political Science Review* 80, no. 4 (December 1986), pp. 1151–69.

15. Ninkovich, *Modernity and Power*, p. 62.

16. Tony Smith, *America's Mission: The United States and the Worldwide Struggle for Democracy in the Twentieth Century* (Princeton, N.J.: Princeton University Press, 1994), esp. ch. 7.

17. See Anne-Marie Burley on this regarding the American proclivity to project abroad its domestic regulatory practices, in "Regulating the World: Multilateralism, International Law, and the Projection of the New Deal Regulatory State," in *Multilateralism Matters: The Theory and Praxis of an Institutional Form*, ed. John Gerard Ruggie (New York: Columbia University Press, 1993), pp. 125–56. See as well the discussion by Frederick S. Calhoun in *Power and Principle: Armed Intervention in Wilsonian Foreign Policy* (Kent, Ohio: Kent State University Press, 1986), esp. pp. 2–5. See also Robert Dallek, *The American Style of Foreign Policy: Cultural Politics and Foreign Affairs* (New York: Alfred A. Knopf, 1983), esp. ch. 3.

18. Inis L. Claude, Jr., *Power and International Relations* (New York: Random House, 1962), p. 111.

19. Ibid., p. 146.

20. Ibid., esp. pp. 144–49.

21. Karl W. Deutsch, Sidney A. Burrell, Robert A. Kann, Maurice Lee, Jr., Martin Lichterman, Raymond E. Lindgren, Francis L. Lowenheim, and Richard W. Van Wagenen, *Political Community and the North Atlantic Area* (Princeton, N.J.: Princeton University Press, 1968), p. 5.

22. Claude, *Power and International Relations*, esp. pp. 144–49.

23. See discussion of Keohane in Ruggie, "The Anatomy of an Institution," p. 11.

24. Ibid.

25. See Charles Kupchan and Clifford Kupchan, "Concerts, Collective Security, and the Future of Europe," *International Security* 16 (Summer 1991), pp. 114–61.

26. Ibid.

27. Woodrow Wilson, quoted in Ray Stannard Baker, *Woodrow Wilson: Life and Letters* (New York: Doubleday Doran, 1939), p. 507.

28. Woodrow Wilson, quoted in Ninkovich, *Modernity and Power*, p. 65.

29. Ninkovich, *Modernity and Power*, p. 65.

30. Joseph Nye's *Bound to Lead* expounds the legitimacy of American soft power and incorporates many Wilsonian assumptions. The title itself is suggestive of the influence. See *Bound to Lead: The Changing Nature of American Power* (New York: Basic Books, 1990).

31. Thomas Alan Schwartz, *America's Germany: John J. McCloy and the Federal Republic of Germany* (Cambridge, Mass.: Harvard University Press, 1991), p. 296. He calls such lessons the "Weimar analogy."

32. Smith, *America's Mission*, p. 331.

33. Russell Hardin, *Collective Action* (Baltimore, Md.: Johns Hopkins University Press, 1982), p. 155. He states, "self-interest may be somewhat muddled by norms or moral codes which themselves are sustained in part by other conventions, perhaps held by a larger or partially different population." The evolution of conventions in relationships leads to behavior guided by mutual expectation and driven by implicit or explicit norms, principles, rules, and procedures.

34. George F. Kennan, in *Containment: 1945–1950*, pp. 97–98.

35. Henry Kissinger, *Diplomacy* (New York: Simon and Schuster, 1994), p. 461.

36. See G. John Ikenberry's discussion of beliefs and their impact on interests in "Creating Yesterday's New World Order: Keynesian 'New Thinking' and the Anglo-American Postwar Settlement," in *Ideas and Foreign Policy: Beliefs, Institutions, and Political Change*, ed. Judith Goldstein and Robert O. Keohane (Ithaca, N.Y.: Cornell University Press, 1993), pp. 57–86, esp. pp. 60–68.

37. For an excellent study of Wilson's influence on American foreign policy, see Smith, *America's Mission*.

38. Calhoun, *Power and Principle*, p. 4.

39. In *In the Time of the Americans*, Fromkin notes the dual influence of realism and Wilsonianism on Roosevelt, p. 477. Also see Smith's discussion of the tensions of realism and Wilsonianism in his *America's Mission*, pp. 179–91.

40. Among the many works, see John Maynard Keynes, *The Economic Consequences of the Peace* (New York: Harcourt Brace, 1929); David P. Calleo and Benjamin M. Rowland, *America and the World Economy* (Bloomington: Indiana University Press, 1973); Benjamin J. Cohen, *Organizing the World's Money* (New York: Basic Books, 1977); Peter Hall, *Governing the Economy: The Politics of State Intervention in Britain and France* (New York: Oxford University Press, 1986); John G. Ruggie, "International Regimes, Transactions, and Change: Embedded Liberalism

in the Postwar Economic Order," *International Organization* 36 (Spring 1982), pp. 379–416; Ikenberry, "Creating Yesterday's New World Order"; David P. Calleo, *Beyond American Hegemony: The Future of the Western Alliance* (New York: Basis Books, 1987); Fromkin, *In the Time of the Americans*.

41. Ikenberry, "Creating Yesterday's New World Order."

42. In *America's Mission*, Tony Smith makes the interesting argument that Wilson did not fully grasp the importance of economic internationalism and liberalism, and therefore the link between economic and political security.

43. Fromkin, *In the Time of the Americans*, p. 487.

44. See Fromkin's discussion, ibid., p. 516.

45. Ikenberry, "Creating Yesterday's New World Order," p. 66.

46. See Fromkin, *In the Time of the Americans*, p. 487.

47. Frank Costigliola, "LBJ, Germany, and 'the End of the Cold War,' " in *Lyndon Johnson Confronts the World: American Foreign Policy 1963–1968*, ed. Warren I. Cohen and Nancy Bernkopf Tucker (New York: Cambridge University Press, 1994), pp. 173–210, quotation at p. 177.

48. John Foster Dulles, quoted in Andrew H. Berding, *Dulles on Diplomacy* (Princeton, N.J.: D. Van Nostrand, 1965), p. 36.

49. Ikenberry, "Creating Yesterday's New World Order," p. 59.

50. Among many, see John Mearsheimer, "Back to the Future: Instability in Europe After the Cold War," *International Security* 15 (Summer 1990), pp. 5–56.

51. One of the best accounts of the Morgenthau Plan and Cordell Hull's position is found in Hull's memoirs. See his *The Memoirs of Cordell Hull, vol. 2* (New York: Macmillan, 1948), esp. pp. 1602–22. See also Robert Dallek, *Franklin D. Roosevelt and American Foreign Policy, 1932–1945* (New York: Oxford University Press, 1979), esp. pp. 470–78, and his *The American Style of Foreign Policy: Cultural Politics and Foreign Affairs* (New York: Alfred A. Knopf, 1983), esp. pp. 145–48. See also Fromkin, *In the Time of the Americans*, p. 481.

52. See William E. Leuchtenburg, *The Perils of Prosperity, 1914–32.* (Chicago: University of Chicago Press, 1993), esp. pp. 166–67. See also Bruce S. Jansson, *The Reluctant Welfare State* (Belmont, Ca.: Wadsworth, 1988).

53. See Hull, *Memoirs*, vol. 2, p. 1614, and Dallek, *The American Style of Foreign Policy*, p. 147.

54. Robert Dallek, *The American Style of Foreign Policy*, pp. 146–47. On page 146, Dallek notes that about 60 percent of Americans felt that Germany could be rehabilitated. The OPOR poll results cited by Benjamin I. Page and Robert Y. Shapiro are less persuasive, although seemingly not contradictory. See their excellent study, *The Rational Public: Fifty Years of Trends in Americans' Policy Preferences* (Chicago: University of Chicago Press, 1992), esp. pp. 194–96.

55. Arnold Wolfers noted this problem some time ago. See "National Security as an Ambiguous Symbol" in his *Discord and Collaboration: Essays on International Politics* (Baltimore, Md.: Johns Hopkins University Press, 1975), pp. 147–65.

56. See especially Judith Goldstein, *Ideas, Interests, and American Trade Policy* (Ithaca, N.Y.: Cornell University Press, 1993), esp. pp. 250–59.

57. Robert E. Osgood, "Woodrow Wilson, Collective Security, and the Lessons of History," in *The Philosophy and Policies of Woodrow Wilson*, ed. Earl Latham (Chicago: University of Chicago Press, 1958), pp. 190, 193.

58. Ibid, p. 190.

59. Stephen D. Krasner, "United States Commercial and Monetary Policy: Unraveling the Paradox of External Strength and Internal Weakness," in *Between Power and Plenty: Foreign Economic Policies of Advanced Industrial Countries*, ed. Peter J. Katzenstein (Madison: University of Wisconsin Press, 1978), pp. 51–87, esp. pp. 53–56. In this way, the Wilsonian impulse benefited from an external threat to thwart American tendency toward isolationism.

60. For brief discussions of Dumbarton Oaks and Bretton Woods, see Fromkin, *In the Time of the Americans*, esp. p. 475. He states that, "both conferences were held in an attempt to realize the new and largely American vision of a unitary world whose vision would be dealt with by international institutions." See also Walter LaFeber, *The American Age*: *U.S. Foreign Policy at Home and Abroad Since 1896, vol. 2* (New York: Norton, 1989), esp. pp. 423–24 for his discussion of the Moscow Conference.

61. Kennan, in *Containment, 1945–1950*, pp. 118–19.

62. See Wolfram F. Hanrieder, *Germany, America, Europe: Forty Years of German Foreign Policy* (New Haven, Conn.: Yale University Press, 1989).

63. Calleo, *Beyond American Hegemony*, esp. pp. 330–37.

64. Kissinger, *Diplomacy*, p. 458.

65. Ibid., p. 460.

66. See Anne-Marie Burley on this regarding the American proclivity to project abroad its domestic regulatory practices, in "Regulating the World: Multilateralism, International Law, and the Projection of the New Deal Regulatory State," in *Multilateralism Matters: The Theory and Praxis of an Institutional Form*, ed. John Gerard Ruggie (New York: Columbia University Press, 1993), pp. 125–56.

67. Dean Acheson, "Radio Address by the Secretary of State on the North Atlantic Treaty, March 18, 1949," quoted in Raymond Dennett and Robert K. Turner, eds., *Documents on American Foreign Relations, 1949* (Princeton, N.J.: Princeton University Press, 1950), p. 600.

68. United Nations Charter, Chapter 1, Article 2, quoted in Peter R. Baehr and Leon Gordenker, *The United Nations: Reality and Ideal* (New York: Praeger, 1984), p. 177.

69. Acheson, "Radio Address," p. 603.

70. Kissinger, *Diplomacy*, p. 460.

71. Dean Acheson, quoted in Kissinger, *Diplomacy*, p. 460.

72. Ibid.

73. Alfred Grosser defines this two-pronged approach to Western security in Europe as the combination of "a constructive internationalism with timorous anti-Communism." See his discussion in Alfred Grosser, *Germany in Our Time: A Political History of the Postwar Years* (New York: Praeger, 1971), p. 67.

74. John Foster Dulles, quoted in C. Burke Elbrick, "American Policy and the Shifting Scene," *Department of State Bulletin* 35, no. 890 (July 16, 1956), 108–13, at p. 111.

75. Steve Weber, "Shaping the Postwar Balance of Power: Multilateralism in NATO," in *Multilateralism Matters: The Theory and Praxis of an Institutional Form*, ed. John G. Ruggie (New York: Columbia University Press, 1993), pp. 233–92.

76. Final Communiqué, Ministerial Session of the North Atlantic Council, Paris, December 11–14, 1956, quoted in Paul E. Zinner, ed., *Documents on American Foreign Relations, 1956* (New York: Harper and Row, 1957), pp. 116–17.

77. John Foster Dulles, "Memorandum of Conversation with Governor Stassen," Dulles Papers, Box 4, DDE Library, cited in Mary N. Hampton, *The Empowerment of a Middle-Sized State: West Germany, Wilsonianism and the Western Alliance* (Los Angeles: UCLA Press, 1993).

78. This was certainly the position of the SPD under Schumacher. Schumacher insisted that German independence and neutrality be pursued outside of the emerging bipolar bloc system.

79. Harold Nicolson, *The Congress of Vienna: A Study in Allied Unity, 1812–1822* (New York: Viking, 1968), pp. 135–37. Also see discussion in Baeher and Gordenker, *The United Nations*, pp. 2–3.

80. Joffe, "The Foreign Policy of the Federal Republic of Germany." In *Foreign Policy in World Politics*, ed. Roy C. Macridis (Englewood Cliffs: Prentice-Hall, 1985). 6th Ed., pp. 72–113. p. 124.

81. See discussion in Richard J. Barnet, *The Alliance. America-Europe-Japan: Makers of the Postwar World* (New York: Simon and Schuster, 1983), pp. 54–55.

82. George Kennan suggests that some policymakers in Washington were already seriously contemplating West German rearmament in 1949. George F. Kennan, *Memoirs* (New York: Bantam Books, 1969), p. 472. Also see the ambiguity of Truman's response in 1949 to the question, "there have been persistent reports that American policy in Western Germany now contemplates the creation of a small German army. Would you comment on that?" in "The President's News Conference of November 17, 1949," reprinted in Harry S. Truman, *Public Papers of the Presidents of the United States: Harry S. Truman* (Washington, D.C.: U.S. Government Printing Office, 1964), pp. 570–71. Adenauer adeptly encouraged the American position over French resistance. See Konrad Adenauer, *Memoirs, 1945–1953* (Chicago: Henry Regnery, 1966), p. 199.

83. See discussion of Bonn Conventions in ibid., pp. 150–58.

84. John McCloy, quoted in Dean Acheson, *Present at the Creation: My Years in the State Department* (New York: W. W. Norton, 1969), p. 640.

85. Konrad Adenauer, *Briefe Ueber Deutschland: 1945–1951* (Berlin: CORSO bei Siedler, 1985), pp. 102–4.

86. Adenauer, *Memoirs*, p. 270. Given the increased risks to West Germany during the Korean War, Adenauer pushed harder for West German "equal rights in the company of other nations," pp. 280–83.

87. NSC Paper from 1954, "Memorandum of a Conversation, by Russell Fressenden of the Office of European Regional Affairs," in *Foreign Relations, 1952–1954*, (Washington: U.S. Printing Office, 1974), p. 1253.

88. "US Policy Toward Europe—Post EDC," Washington, D.C., September 10, 1954, reprinted in ibid., p. 1175.

89. "Statement of Policy by the National Security Council," Washington, D.C., September 25, 1954, in ibid., p. 1269.

90. Dulles further observed that: "The Western nations now owe it to the Federal Republic of Germany to do quickly all that lies in their power to restore sovereignty to that Republic and to enable it to contribute to international peace and security." John Foster Dulles, "Statement by the Secretary of State, Washington, August 31, 1954", in ibid., pp. 1121–22.

91. For an excellent history of this period, see Schwartz, *America's Germany*.

92. See John Ikenberry and Charles A. Kupchan, "Socialization and Hegemonic Power," *International Organization* 44 (Summer 1990), pp. 283–315, esp. pp. 285–92.

93. On their relationship, see Hans-Juergen Grabbe, "Konrad Adenauer, John Foster Dulles and West German–American Relations," in *John Foster Dulles and the Diplomacy of the Cold War*, ed. Richard Immerman (Princeton, N.J.: Princeton University Press, 1990), pp. 109–32.

Chapter 2 ————————————————

THE EISENHOWER ADMINISTRATION AND THE WILSONIAN IMPULSE

The specific impact of the Wilsonian impulse and the Versailles remedial intensified under Dulles and Eisenhower. Richard A. Melanson points out that Eisenhower chose as his initial group of foreign policy advisors internationalists who had been with Colonel House at Versailles.[1] The most important of these advisors was, of course, John Foster Dulles.[2] A few pitfalls notwithstanding, Dulles maintained a close working relationship with Eisenhower and thereby assured his influence throughout the administration's tenure.[3] The Eisenhower administration was the last one under which a consensus existed between the president, his top foreign policy advisor, and the State Department regarding the Wilsonian impulse and Versailles remedial.[4]

Dulles has been typically presented as the Cold Warrior par excellence. In fact, he was much more consistent and clear in his objectives that followed from the Wilsonian impulse than he was in those meant to respond to the Soviet Union. As one analyst observes of him: "Dulles' policies toward Europe, which reflected his interest and preparation, differed qualitatively from those toward the remainder of globe, about which he was largely ignorant."[5] During the Eisenhower administration, Secretary of State Dulles viewed the U.S. relationships with West Germany and the Western Alliance through the prism of the failed Wilsonian experience at the end of World War I. This point is important in challenging the pervasive assumption that the dominant paradigm guiding early postwar American policymakers was based on the Munich analogy.[6] In a similar way, Richard Challener discusses John Foster Dulles's inclination to encourage admitting the defeated Japan into a Western collective security system and to ensure that Japan "not be humiliated as Germany had been in 1919."[7]

The Wilsonian impulse was very important in the years directly preceding and following West Germany's accession to the Alliance and it increased Adenauer's maneuverability. What I intend to dispel is the common wisdom that interprets the Adenauer-Eisenhower era as one in which the West Germans maintained leverage over the United States only as long as interests in Bonn and Washington coincided. For example, Wolfram F. Hanrieder claims that the American postwar security strategy for Europe was one of "double containment,"[8] of containing the Soviets and the West Germans. Regarding West German foreign policy and the reunification issue during the 1950s, he states: "In light of these forbidding diplomatic circumstances, no one then or now could deny or underestimate the weight of necessity, the burden of acquiescence that was placed on the German government in these early years when the Federal Republic had neither the power nor the authority to conduct its own foreign policy."[9] Hanrieder's observation mirrors that of so many others in that it emphasizes external factors that allegedly severely constrained Bonn's ability to influence international events during the 1950s and later. Hanrieder's depiction of American postwar "double containment" is a traditional realist reading of Allied relations.

My account of America's dual policies is that it included containing the Soviet threat and creating a cohesive Atlantic community. The difference in emphasis is crucial. While pursuing the second goal did include containing a potentially destabilizing German foreign policy, the objective of creating a Western community was laden with the Wilsonian vision of a security community, underwritten by mutually shared principles, rules, and so on. It was not a policy based on balance of power notions so central to America's approach to the Soviet Union. Hanrieder acknowledges the importance of principles such as the issue of equality of status in maintaining West German loyalty, but does not examine the unique context that the maintenance of such principles fostered in the Allied relationship. The active role of the Versailles lesson gave West German leaders much more leverage over American foreign policy than such realist readings acknowledge.

Second, while it is true that the fate of West Germany was tied to the Alliance after 1954, Bonn insisted that continued West German loyalty to the West depended on the Allies meeting their obligations made to the West Germans in the 1954 security convention, and of the Wilsonian principles underwriting the convention. Bonn never surrendered its sovereignty by agreeing to Western integration. Rather, it gained West German sovereignty *through* integration, since one of the Wilsonian principles of the

1954 security convention was that underscoring Allied membership by *freely associating sovereign states*.[10] The West Germans then agreed to constrain that sovereignty only as long as the collectively agreed-upon principles were upheld. Thus, if West Germany was "contained" in Western multilateral structures like the Alliance, it was "self-contained"; that is, it chose to be contained according to principles, rules, and understandings that bound its Allies as well. The fear among many American policymakers was that if the West failed to uphold its side of the bargain, Germany might once again be loosed from its Western moorings.

The influence of the Wilsonian impulse and the Versailles remedial in the American courtship of Adenauer and Bonn therefore aided West German success. In the 1954 Paris Accords that admitted the FRG to the Alliance, a bargain was struck, by which West Germany regained much of its sovereignty upon entering NATO in return for renouncing the right to produce nuclear weapons and agreeing to pursue German reunification in "peace and freedom." There was little controversy in West Germany concerning the renunciation of nuclear weapons, and the Allies now declared as part of formal Allied policy that "the Federal Republic was the sole spokesman for the entire German nation in international affairs and that the achievement of a reunited German nation, without prior determination of its allegiance, was an essential and fundamental goal of their policy."[11] Adenauer was able to exact a price for the latter agreement: The Alliance must assume formal responsibility for peaceful German reunification and recognize Bonn as the only legitimate representative of the German nation. Under Dulles's prodding, the Allies accepted. Adenauer and all subsequent West German leaders would constantly return to this reciprocal agreement in furthering West German interests in Western and East-West security matters. This vow by the Allies, and especially by Washington, would prove crucial in the evolution of German unification policy as it developed in the coming decades, culminating in the peaceful and rapid unification of Germany in 1990.

As will be seen, the Wilsonian impulse also played a major role in constructing American and West German perceptions and choices regarding the crucial issue of nuclear weapons and the Alliance. The debate continued throughout the 1950s and would again be heavily influenced by Wilsonian beliefs such as equality of status. Before turning to these cases directly, I will first discuss Dulles as the quintessential Wilsonian and how that influenced the West German–Western Alliance relationship.

JOHN FOSTER DULLES: IN WILSON'S FOOTSTEPS

A close examination of foreign policy making in the Eisenhower years reveals how influential Secretary of State Dulles was. Taking nothing away from Eisenhower's role, Dulles's energy was boundless in prompting movement toward European and trans-Atlantic integration. For example, his open and behind-the-scenes influence was critical in sustaining the momentum toward German membership in NATO and the EDC in the early 1950s.[12] His objective of reconciling West Germany and Europe remained constant and reflected very clear Wilsonian assumptions concerning integrating Germany as an equal partner into an Atlantic security community.[13] Ronald Preussen observes that Dulles maintained an "intense concern for what he described as 'the suicidal strife' between France and Germany: . . . a 'firetrap' that had engulfed too many," and one that had to be replaced by a supranational approach.[14] As Hans-Juergen Grabbe observes of Dulles's attitude, "Alliances come and go; only supranational, 'organic' cooperation was irreversible."[15] From this position, clearly Wilsonian in its emphasis on institutionalized relations, he vigorously pursued the failed EDC and then the admittance of West Germany into NATO.

This constancy becomes even more significant when measured against the inconsistencies regarding Dulles's thinking and policy toward the Soviet Union and discussed in recent scholarly work.[16] Although Preussen regards Dulles's attitude toward the Soviets as one that was more balanced than those of many contemporaries, he interestingly attributes this fact to Dulles's first objective of integrating Europe.[17] Even without a Soviet threat, Dulles is quoted by Preussen as saying that the most urgent task was addressing "that danger that comes from within" the Western constellation of states.[18] Always sensitive to domestic politics and public opinion, it is quite likely that Dulles allowed his Soviet policy to adapt more to domestic demands with "melodramatic rhetoric" than he was his European policy.[19]

Therefore, whereas common wisdom has regarded Dulles as the consummate Cold Warrior, I believe that his role as the Wilsonian community-builder was more important and certainly more clearly defined. Many have argued that anticommunism was part of the Wilsonian legacy.[20] However, the Cold Warrior Dulles and the Wilsonian Dulles were not necessarily complementary. And where U.S. concern with the Soviet Union competed with Washington's regard for the West Germans and Western integration, the approach was often tempered in favor of the Wilsonian impulse.

It can also be said that Dulles was never quite sure about the nature of the Soviet threat itself, that is, "whether the Soviet Union was to be thought of in national or ideological terms."[21] At times, it appeared that Dulles saw the promise of rehabilitating the Soviet Union through the process of democratization and liberal reform. [22] Here was an expression of the Wilsonian hope about the effects of spreading democracy. He believed that even the Soviet system would gradually but perceptibly follow "a certain movement toward Western ideas of law."[23]

The Versailles remedial was operative as well. Dulles on many occasions allowed Adenauer to intervene with West German demands that had direct consequences for American relations with other states. Bonn's appeal to the American historical memory of the failed Wilsonian policy toward Germany and Europe after World War I was especially important in influencing U.S. policy on reunification and nuclear sharing during the Eisenhower administration. The perception in Washington was that failure to win West German loyalty would be costly, since the active historical memory of Germany as a great power thwarted after war was pervasive. John Foster Dulles revealed the concern of Wilsonians in Washington and elsewhere in stating of the Germans:

They have demonstrated a very great quality, perhaps even frighteningly so. You cannot neutralize and paralyze a people like that in the center of Europe. If the effort were made there would be a move on their part to build up toward power and try for a balance of power as far as Europe is concerned.[24]

Dulles was not just a Wilsonian because of his experience at Versailles as a young legal counselor.[25] His writings and speeches and the archival record reveal that Dulles's assumptions about international relations parallel those of Wilson to a striking degree. For example, regarding the treatment of postwar Germany, he also shared the general Wilsonian predisposition to favor rehabilitation over repression of the defeated, and therefore "campaigned after World War II to treat the vanquished nations with unprecedented leniency."[26]

Not only was he a student of Wilson's at Princeton and considered Wilson "the moral leader par excellence," Dulles shared Wilson's belief that America had a moral mission to play in world affairs.[27] Also, it is interesting to note that Dulles, like Wilson, was the son of a Presbyterian minister and that religion was a prominent influence throughout his life. They therefore shared the "religious and crusading drive" behind America's moral role in the world.[28] Further, like Wilson, his crusading views were underscored by faith in the Western legal tradition and international law.

He also shared most of Wilson's domestic beliefs concerning the roles of public opinion and the democratic organization of international life.[29] For example, it is clear that Dulles held to the Wilsonian notion of community-building among states, that community would be created through the cultivation of an inclusive common political culture and the development of "truly authoritative international institutions. Nations that shared in a well-ordered moral consensus could contribute to the development of such institutions."[30] Dulles was in fact one of the architects of the United Nations Charter and its Commission on Human Rights.[31] In essence, a Western liberal political culture was envisioned, wherein like-minded democracies cooperated across a number of issue areas. Like Wilson, peace and cooperation were the objectives in Dulles's understanding of international relations, and community-building was the operative method of achieving those goals. I quote Brian Klunk on this point:

International cooperation on various issues could be the agent of the psychological and intellectual transformation that Dulles believed was the prerequisite of a world community. The struggle against economic maladjustment, injustice, disease, and other problems that plagued mankind could provide the focus of common action. Common action could lead the nations to perceive themselves as part of the global community.[32]

Dulles went even further than Wilson in promoting the institutionalization of international life; Dulles saw at the end of the process a world government.[33]

As stated in the last chapter, the Wilsonian impulse therefore did not predispose American policymakers like Dulles to embrace realist assumptions concerning the nature and operative features of international life. For him, the system of warring sovereign states could be reformed through habituation and institutionalization and replaced by an international community of like-minded democracies. "What had been accomplished in most domestic societies could be done in the international system,"[34] led, of course, by the United States. Like the Wilsonians in the Roosevelt and Truman administrations, Dulles continued applying the Wilsonian understanding of international politics to the Western area, where chances were best that a security community could evolve.

THE WILSONIAN IMPULSE AND
THE VERSAILLES REMEDIAL

The consistency of Allied policy on German unification was the result of American and West German efforts and reveals strikingly the vitality of the Wilsonian political culture as it evolved in Western security relations. On this absolutely central national security issue, the West German government accepted a political agreement that obligated the West to help achieve German unity over an unspecified period of time. The legitimacy of this political agreement constructed the choices made by Bonn over the next four decades. In return, the formal commitment made by the Allies to the policy of German reunification would tie especially Washington's hands in a number of important instances and would provoke disagreements between the United States, France, and Great Britain, as well as between the United States and the Soviet Union. Adenauer constantly stymied and constrained East-West initiatives by interpreting the Allied guarantee of German reunification as he went along. He won official U.S. and Allied support for his "policy of strength," under which German reunification was to be gradually attained through a united and militarily strong Western posture. Adenauer strongly urged this posture on reunification throughout his tenure of office and thereby quite successfully influenced Western, and particularly American, policy toward East Germany and even the Soviet Union.[35]

Thus, there was from the beginning a symbiosis between the West's ability to "entangle and integrate" the FRG in the multilateral structures of the West and Bonn's ability to entangle the West in its own concerns, such as the unity issue.[36] The "contradictions and paradoxes" that Western integration posed for Bonn were therefore projected onto and shared by the Alliance as well. George Kennan stated this point negatively in the late 1950s:

I recognized that Moscow had recently shown no enthusiasm for German unification, and conceded that perhaps the Soviet leaders did not want it on any terms. But I pointed out that their position had never been realistically tested by negotiation. How much of their lack of enthusiasm was resignation in the face of our own unrealistic position, we could not know.... I urged, therefore, that we drop our insistence that an eventual all-German government should be free to join NATO, and declare ourselves instead the partisans of a neutralized and largely disarmed unified Germany.[37]

The obviously true point Kennan's statement raised, which caused a stir upon its dissemination, was that the perceived American responsibility for the German reunification issue colored the way the United States approached the East-West relationship. His position had little resonance with Dulles and others in the Eisenhower administration.[38] It would have a strong impact on Kennedy, who had little understanding and less tolerance of the Wilsonian bargain in Allied relations.

The Alliance and German Reunification

The issue of German reunification was extremely important and complex throughout this period. In fact, the Allied pledge to German reunification has probably influenced the course of Western security policy, and eventually of East-West security policy, more than most issues. The goal of German unification was inherently revisionist. The problem has always been how to balance that revisionist commitment with the traditional status quo alliance objective of maintaining defense and security against the Soviet threat. Also, from the perspective of international relations theory, the Allied pursuit of a revisionist objective undercuts assertions that the West, and especially the United States, have been status quo supporters of the balance in the international system. The fact remains that the United States, because of its commitment to the 1954 Allied convention and its fear of the consequences that reneging on the commitment might provoke, was persuaded by Bonn time and time again to uphold West German revisionist claims in the system. These often competing interests became readily apparent during the Eisenhower administration. Until the SPD (West German Social Democrats) came to power in the FRG during the mid-1960s, Bonn was extremely successful in thwarting Western efforts at promoting detente with the Soviets. Once the SPD assumed power in the Grand Coalition of 1966, Bonn would achieve great success in defining West German East-West detente as an Allied policy and then in forging ahead with it.[39]

Until the end of the Eisenhower years, amidst the Gaullist challenge to Alliance cohesion, and under pressure from many quarters for an overall change in U.S.–Soviet relations that suggested a possible move toward detente policies, Washington remained sensitive to the possibility that such policies could arouse West German suspicions regarding the West's commitment to reunification. A briefing for President Eisenhower in 1960 noted:

A reliable source has reported views of Chancellor Adenauer on the subject of Summit. Adenauer is apparently suspicious of U.S. inclinations to get along with Kruschev. He appears to be regarding De Gaulle as the only truly reliable force. He says also that reunification is a hopeless cause for the present and should not be allowed to interfere with European integration. He praised this latter goal as a means of independence from [sic] the Anglo-Saxons.[40]

Aware by the latter 1950s and early 1960s that his "policy of strength" posture was quickly becoming unpopular in the West, Adenauer continued linking West German reunification claims to the detente framework and thereby making progress on the latter dependent on movement toward the former. In this way, Adenauer linked the reunification issue to disarmament and any East-West movement in the security area. Disarmament measures would jeopardize West German goals of reunification and its military status in the Alliance by moving toward recognition of the postwar status quo, thereby cementing the division of Germany and the nonnuclear status of the FRG. Helga Haftendorn observes: "To counter these dangers the Bonn government in 1955 and 1956 formulated a flexible linkage between disarmament, European security, and the German question, whereby agreements in one area would be linked to progress in the others."[41]

At the same time, Adenauer and other West German policymakers were unwilling to exclude for the FRG a nuclear option.[42] Not only would that cement the FRG in a position of inequality with other allies, but as Uwe Nerlich stated in a 1965 paper, "It is in the interest of the Federal Republic to hold open for itself a nuclear option as a bargaining point for reunification talks, and also to avoid formalizing Germany's non-nuclear status, in the event that reunification might finally be excluded as a real possibility." Nerlich also observed the link between the reunification and nuclear issues dating back to the 1954 treaties in which the FRG gained entry into the Alliance: "The bases of Alliance policy on this issue are the treaties of 1954, which contain a unilateral German renunciation of the production of nuclear weapons and the commitment by the other Allies to further German reunification."[43] The implicit threat was that Allied failure to uphold their unification responsibility might abrogate West Germany's duty to renounce nuclear weapons.

The problem for the FRG at this time was that as the blocs went increasingly nuclear and yet moved toward detente, the possibility existed that West Germany would be left both nonnuclear, and therefore unequal and vulnerable, and also permanently divided. This worst case scenario would have undercut all that Bonn had tried to accomplish in its postwar Alliance policies and it would have undermined the reciprocal agreements made between the FRG and its Western Allies. In this situation, "the only acceptable arrangement for the Federal Republic would be an agreement which connected steps toward denuclearization with steps to reunification."[44] Through his linkage strategy, Adenauer was subsequently largely successful in impeding Western progress on detente initiatives. The constant threat that Bonn's loyalty to the West could be questioned in the face of too much movement on detente without sufficient movement on the German unity issue was a powerful influence on Eisenhower's administration.

Through the end of the Eisenhower administration, policymakers in Washington were concerned about this dilemma, and there was a continued effort to stress reunification of Germany as an Allied priority. Upon informing Adenauer in 1960 about the upcoming talks between Khrushchev and himself, Eisenhower stated that he would "stand on our rights and . . . will make no agreement of any kind that is not acceptable to the people concerned, to wit, the Germans."[45] It has often been argued that the Eisenhower administration was from the beginning less than sincere in its desire and support for German reunification; if accepting reunification rhetorically, even cynically, as a formal Allied policy won the loyalty of Adenauer in the more important issue of the East-West competition, fine.[46]

Such a convenient trade-off was not possible for the United States. Rhetorical acceptance of reunification did not suffice to maintain West German loyalty to the West on East-West matters. Adenauer's strategy was to use the reunification issue over and over again to influence both his position in the West and the course of East-West relations. He did not promote the idea that West German loyalty to the West was sealed. To the contrary, he and policymakers like Franz Josef Strauss, the late head of the conservative Bavarian-based Christian Social Union (CSU), continued to

stress the fact that loyalty was dependent upon the West meeting its obligations to Bonn and fulfilling its Wilsonian obligations concerning equality
of status and the eventual self-determination of the Germans.

Also, by constantly raising the issue of domestic vulnerability in the face
of Western inaction on policies important to the FRG, Adenauer reminded
the West of the potential international disruptions a dissatisfied FRG
might cause, always appealing to the Versailles remedial. The perception
was strong in Washington that another failed Wilsonian experiment
would result in catastrophes similar to those of the interwar years. Adenauer's personal ties with Dulles and other important American policymakers like General Lauris Norstad were often used to confirm such
perceptions.

Adenauer and the Nonrecognition of East Germany

The Eisenhower administration certainly took the German unity issue
seriously enough to allow Adenauer's concern to influence heavily U.S.
and Western security policy. There has been a great deal of debate, particularly among German analysts, on whether Adenauer himself ever really
sought reunification in earnest. Although there is evidence that leaves his
unification objective in doubt, what is important is not so much whether
he actually wanted reunification, as he adamantly claimed to, but how he
used the issue to affect U. S. and Allied security policy.[47] First, Adenauer
successfully used the unity issue in demanding that the Western powers
deny diplomatic recognition of the German Democratic Republic (GDR).
It had been agreed upon in the 1954 accords granting NATO membership
to the FRG that Bonn represented the only legitimate representative for the
German people. While many in the West argued as early as the 1950s that
recognition of the GDR was a necessary step in the detente process, U.S.
recognition was not granted until 1974.[48]

What Adenauer perceived as a Western tendency to renege on its commitments to German reunification by contemplating recognition of the
GDR was revealed again in the period from 1958 to 1960. With Khrushchev's various threats during the Berlin Crisis and amid the West's
growing desire for detente, many in the West considered compromising
on some issues vital to the Soviets while holding firm on those issues that
the West already claimed as its responsibility, such as its guarantee on
West Berlin. Much to Adenauer's chagrin, one of the items discussed by
Eisenhower and his advisors as a possible area for compromise was that of
recognition of the GDR and Polish borders. In January 1959, Dulles raised
the issue of dealing with the East Germans as "agents" of the Soviet
Union. Adenauer was rankled and the discussion was dropped.[49] The
Eisenhower administration held firm in its policy of nonrecognition of
East Germany, despite an obvious British willingness to pursue "a range

of options" on the issue. In 1959, Eisenhower's position was at one point stated as follows:

The essential problem for the present is to prevent any new accrual of legitimacy or prestige to the Government of the so-called German Democratic Republic while simultaneously encouraging the greatest possible measure of contact between the people of the Federal Republic and the Soviet Zone.[50]

On the issue of not recognizing the GDR, Adenauer had de Gaulle's support in 1959, and that support would be crucial over the next year. Alfred Grosser notes of the two leaders' position concerning Western recognition of the GDR and of the Oder-Neisse line: "Their consent to the summit of May 1960 was . . . contingent on the condition that the Western powers make no concessions, and this demand doomed the conference to failure from the start."[51]

Despite pressures for change, Washington held to nonrecognition throughout the Kennedy and Johnson administrations.[52] In July 1961, just a month before the Berlin Wall was erected, the State Department's Paris Working Group in Washington, whose task was to analyze the situation in Berlin, reported its conclusions to Kennedy. The working group determined that no changes should be made in the U.S. position vis-à-vis Berlin and the German question outlined by the Eisenhower administration in the Western "Peace Plan" of 1958. The group also agreed that there should be discussion of neither the borders, the Oder-Neisse line, nor Western negotiations with East Germany.[53] Although many in the Kennedy administration found the group's conclusions to be a tired repetition of past pronounced policy, the serious limitations set on Washington in redefining the issue underscored the success of Adenauer's efforts.[54] The continued importance of the issue is reflected in a letter sent from William E. Griffith to W. W. Rostow just a few weeks earlier. Returning from a fact-finding trip to the FRG, Griffith wrote to Rostow about the importance of Washington maintaining nonrecognition of the GDR, reiterating the concerns of the Eisenhower administration:

It is in respect to West Germany, it seems to me, that the real danger comes here. Sooner or later, once the U.S. is no longer felt to be completely committed to reunification, the West Germans will become unreliable allies for us. Negotiations with the DDR regime would be considered by them (correctly, I think) to be such a step. . . . The Germans will be watching us to see if we display any signs of weakness, indecision, or compromise; if we do, sooner or later they will begin to look elsewhere.[55]

The issue of recognition was important. If the West, and particularly the United States, had proceeded to recognize the GDR and deal with it as a

legitimate state, a vital area of West German control over the future resolution of the German question would have been lost. It is interesting that
the United States did not recognize the GDR until 1974. By that time,
Bonn, under the leadership of Willy Brandt, had safely assured West Germany the dominant Western role in dealing with the East German state.
Beginning with the Harmel Exercise of 1967, Bonn would seek and receive
Western support for its position that *Deutschlandpolitik,* or German-German relations, should be predominantly the concern of the West Germans.

Under Adenauer, Bonn's policymakers also influenced the course of
Western security policy by insisting upon the linkage between disarmament and reunification. Adenauer opened up a leverage potential over
Western security policy by linking the West German issue of reunification
to the larger East-West issue of disarmament. Thrusting the reunification
question into the disarmament framework also allowed Bonn to raise legitimately its concern for West Germany's nuclear status. In short, Adenauer anticipated future trends in Western security agenda setting and
preempted them by tying them to West German concerns.

Adenauer and East-West Disarmament

Adenauer stated in his *Memoirs* from 1957 that the duty of the FRG was
to ensure that no disarmament agreement be concluded that accepted either the neutralization of Germany or the status quo of the postwar East-
West division. "It was an important task for the FRG to constantly remind
its Western Allies of the responsibility they had assumed for the re-establishment of German unity."[56] Holding steadfast to his position, Adenauer
rebuffed several recommendations made by Western politicians throughout the late 1950s that called for some variation of the Rapacki Plan of
1956; that is, that a reunited Germany be achieved by creating a nuclear
free zone in Central Europe, to include, most importantly, Germany.

At one NATO conference in December 1957, Adenauer persistently
reminded his Western Allies of the pledge they made in 1954 to uphold
German reunification as a Western responsibility, and that German reunification remained the number one point of tension between East and West.
The criticism of the conference raised by Walter Lippmann in a *New York
Herald Tribune* article from December 21 attests to Adenauer's continued
influence on the Western security agenda. In response to Lippmann, who
suggested that American support for the goal of reunification was outdated because it was actually feared by the European allies, "Eisenhower
expressed astonishment."[57] Lippmann observed: "The direct effect is that,
as far as we know, Dulles is sitting off to the side, while the Germans talk
to Moscow."[58] So it would be in 1989 and 1990 as well.

The potential for a repeat of trans-Atlantic grievances similar to those
following the Radford Plan of 1956 occurred in 1957.[59] Eisenhower ap-

peared to support, at least theoretically, some kind of controlled neutral zone in Europe.[60] Eisenhower stated this position at a press conference in May. The State Department then issued a statement within the next week that the United States was against any disarmament plan that called for a neutral zone in Germany. The next day, Dulles held a press conference wherein he stated that there was no American plan for a neutral zone in Germany or anywhere else. But that same year, at the London Disarmament Conference, Harold Stassen rekindled Adenauer's doubts about the American position on this issue. Stassen supported Eisenhower's earlier predilection for a neutral zone. What was worse from Adenauer's and other West European leaders' perspective, Stassen began this important exchange with the Soviets before consulting any of the Western Allies. A row followed in NATO that delayed the conference.[61] Eisenhower and Dulles were both quick to respond to the incident. In a telephone conversation between the two, Dulles anticipated that "Adenauer will feel double-crossed." Eisenhower responded that, "he told Herter he should not be sparing of words to Stassen," and that "before Adenauer complains tell him it was through a mistake and what he learned here is the truth. . . . The President said to tell Stassen he is highly displeased."[62] Stassen lost favor with Eisenhower and Dulles after the episode.

Adenauer pledged the FRG's willingness to pursue controlled disarmament. However, he asserted that such a scheme must be combined with the removal of the political roots of the tensions, meaning, above all, "the removal of the partition of Germany." Concerning this matter, Adenauer obtained from the Western Allies at the conference "a binding promise, especially from France, Great Britain and the United States."[63]

Thus, throughout the 1950s, Adenauer's ability to influence Washington's East-West security policy continued. While Eisenhower had shown interest in some form of demilitarization in Central Europe in the recent past, his reaction to the second offer of the Rapacki Plan by Soviet Foreign Minister Nikolai Bulganin in 1958 revealed a keen awareness of West German sensibilities. Eisenhower made clear his concern for the West German position regarding reunification in a letter to Bulganin. In one section, Eisenhower presented precisely Adenauer's position; "It is therefore unrealistic to ignore the fundamental link between political solutions and security agreements."[64]

Already aware of "disengagement" notions circulating in Great Britain, Adenauer was taken aback in February 1959 when he was informed by the British ambassador in Bonn, Sir Christopher Steel, that Prime Minister Macmillan was on his way to a ten-day meeting in Moscow with Khrushchev.[65] After the meeting, Macmillan met with Eisenhower in Washington to discuss the outcome of the talks. Adenauer learned again of what he perceived as a British willingness to discuss a "disengagement" scheme with Moscow.[66] As a result of Adenauer's strong protestations to Washington, backed by U.S. General Lauris Norstad, the British were pressured to reformulate and water down their suggestions.[67] Even though Eisenhower notes in his diary from 1959 that Adenauer seemed "to have developed an almost psychopathic fear of what he considers 'British weakness,' " the point is that Adenauer nevertheless successfully thwarted any real movement in the West toward detente and disarmament.[68]

In Adenauer's last meeting with Dulles in February 1959, it is clear that Adenauer warned his long-time friend that the proposals for a neutralized Germany espoused by such influential Americans as George Kennan and Senators Humphrey and Fulbright would be "suicide" for the United States and lead the FRG and eventually all of Europe into the hands of the Soviets.[69]

West German Domestic Politics

Encouraging the evolution of the political culture envisioned by the Wilsonian impulse, Adenauer constantly referred to the potentially unstable domestic situation in the Federal Republic, a circumstance that could be easily aggravated by discriminatory Allied policy toward the Bonn government. Adenauer thus reinforced Washington's loyalty to him, particularly that of Dulles. Had Adenauer not willingly steered West Germany along the course toward democratization and membership into the Western institutions? Dulles stated that, "after the Treaty of Versailles there was a liberal government in Germany that wanted to eliminate militarism. If we had taken advantage of that, we could have avoided World War II."[70] The United States must not now lose this chance.

The West German domestic political situation was indeed uncertain, and there was tremendous public resistance to West German compliance with Allied demands.[71] Lest he be too harshly cast domestically as "the Chancellor of the Allies," as the opposition Social Democrat (SPD) leader, Kurt Schumacher, called him during the Petersberg negotiations, Adenauer was quick to remind Washington that the SPD was the only other possible legitimate political alternative.[72]

It should also be recalled that up until its Bad Godesberg Party Program of 1959, the SPD represented strong domestic forces in the FRG that supported German reunification as the top priority in foreign policy, that supported a neutral Germany to that end, and that therefore rejected membership in NATO. Adenauer was adept at constantly reminding Washington of his domestic vulnerability vis-à-vis the opposition. The more openly nationalist course advocated by the SPD, and particularly by Schumacher, and the perceived threat that the SPD would be more open to promoting German neutralism, a unified Germany outside of the bipolar blocs, and/or a *modus-vivendi* with Moscow, helped persuade most Western leaders that Adenauer must be rewarded for his efforts.[73] The phenomenon reveals striking similarities with recent American concerns for Mikhail Gorbachev, Boris Yeltsin, and the current crop of reformers in Russia.

During the course of negotiations for the Bonn Conventions, Adenauer pointed out to the Allies "the dangerous SPD policies that stressed the incompatibility of rearmament with the primary goal, reunification."[74] The SPD continued its opposition to Adenauer's Western policy, and there was fear that the Soviet Peace Note of 1952, which indicated Moscow's presumed willingness to pursue a reunified Germany, might fall on sympathetic ears in the Federal Republic.[75]

Washington was aware of the distrust existing in the FRG regarding the probable negative effect that any form of West German rearmament under Western auspices would have. These apprehensions were constantly expressed by the SPD, and represented one of the most divisive elements in CDU–SPD politics. The Allies were particularly anxious about the negative public reaction in West Germany in the early 1950s to the possibility of German rearmament. The widespread popularity among young people in the Federal Republic of the *"ohne mich"* (without me) sentiment to rearmament was indicative. In a similar vein, a segment of the West German public favoring rearmament was more supportive of a national army rather than an integrated European force.[76]

Western, and particularly American, support of Adenauer appeared all the more crucial after attempts failed to bring Schumacher around to the Allied way of thinking. Alongside this dead-end, the Allies found the 1951 West German state elections somewhat alarming due to the dwindling domestic support for Adenauer and the gains made by the neo-Nazi Socialist Reich Party in the May 6 elections in Lower Saxony.[77] This was more evidence that the legitimacy of Adenauer's government, and maybe even that of the new democracy itself, were still suspect.

Nuclear Weapons and the Wilsonian Impulse

Like reunification, the issue of nuclear weapons illuminates the importance of Wilsonian beliefs that motivated American and West German policymakers and that helped form the political culture of the Alliance.[78] At the end of the 1950s, Eisenhower first broached the subject of nuclear sharing in the Alliance. His administration's concern about West German sensitivities regarding equality of status increased as nuclear weapons became the military centerpiece of the Alliance.[79] Political considerations, not strategic assessment, led him to contemplate seriously advocating the joint ownership of a nuclear-capable multilateral naval force.

As early as 1953, the Eisenhower administration had been seeking a way to get a "bigger bang for the buck," or to reduce military spending, with-

out harming the West's military credibility.[80] Before the Soviet launch of
Sputnik in 1957, the main Soviet military threat was perceived in Washington as being superiority in conventional forces. With its edge in strategic nuclear weapons, the Eisenhower administration developed the
doctrine of massive retaliation and thereby reoriented American doctrinal
thinking. Eisenhower's so-called "new look" envisioned a U.S. military
policy of extended nuclear deterrence, which would be a cheaper guarantee for Western European security than the high costs of large conventional forces. At the 1952 Lisbon convention, the United States had agreed
with its West European Allies on the primacy of conventional forces,
through local and forward defense, as the main security guarantee for the
West. If the "new look" were to be implemented, the centerpiece of Western defense would be the American strategic nuclear arsenal, with the
West European conventional forces contributing to needed tactical defense.[81] Dulles revealed the shift in American thinking in a 1954 speech:

Local defenses must be reinforced by the further deterrent of massive retaliatory
power. . . . But before military planning could be changed, the President and his
advisors, as represented by the National Security Council, had to make some basic
policy decisions. This has been done. The basic decision was to depend primarily
upon a great capacity to retaliate, instantly, by means and at places of our choosing. . . . As a result, it is now possible to get, and share, more basic security at less
cost.[82]

The rationale behind U.S. rethinking reflected the kind of national defense planning one would expect of a superpower from the neorealist perspective. Clearly, the "new look" was directed at the postwar security goal
of meeting and containing the Soviet military threat.

The American scheme would become hostage to the Wilsonian impulse
and the Versailles remedial, thanks to Adenauer's persuasion. For example, in the mid-1950s, Allen Dulles was sent to Bonn not long after disclo-
sure of the Radford Plan, a plan that was leaked to the press and called for
the modernization of NATO forces and the reduction of American conventional forces worldwide by some 800,000, many of them to come from
Western Europe. The plan proposed, in keeping with Eisenhower's "new
look," a major reorientation in NATO away from conventional defense
and toward the deterrent use of nuclear weapons. The proposal completely contradicted and undercut Adenauer's conception of Alliance
strategy, which he considered best served by "the strengthening of conventional NATO forces," in order to "repel any potential attack without
resort to nuclear weapons."[83]

Dulles was warned by Adenauer that the operationalization of a plan
calling for the withdrawal of American troops "would jeopardize everything." One could read this statement in several ways. One way it could

have been read, and no doubt was by many in Washington, was that West German loyalty to the West would be thrown into jeopardy upon operationalization of such a plan. Without the presence of American troops, which symbolized America's commitment to Europe, Adenauer was announcing to Washington that "the incorporation of the western half of Germany into an Atlantic community could never be secure."[84] Adenauer thus reminded Washington in rather stark terms of the potentially disruptive domestic repercussions such a policy could have in the FRG and thereby of the negative consequences for West German foreign policy. He also alluded to the importance of Washington maintaining its side of the reciprocal agreement reached the previous year, thus reinforcing the power of the Allied security convention.

Adenauer actually began a campaign in Washington to ensure that the Radford Plan never become official U.S. policy. He enlisted the support of powerful congressional Democrats and made certain that prominent individuals in Washington perceived his displeasure. As Richard Barnet puts it, "his goal was ambitious, nothing less than to exercise a veto on American policy in Europe. In this he was remarkably successful." Barnet offers a fascinating discussion of Adenauer's campaign against the Radford Plan. Not only did he enlist the support of prominent Democrats such as Averell Harriman, Adlai Stevenson, and Lyndon B. Johnson, he let his displeasure be known to such people as John McCloy and Dean Acheson. He also quotes the somewhat euphoric statement of West German Foreign Minister Heinrich von Brentano, who told Adenauer, "I believe that it is . . . largely within our power to determine the policy of the United States during the next few years."[85] Dulles himself stated at a meeting with Eisenhower in October of 1956 that "it was one thing for us [the United States] to rely on the new look, not being subject to insurrectionary or conventional attack as the Europeans are, and it is something else to propose it for the Europeans."[86]

Dulles's closing remarks at the meeting reflected his desire to discuss necessary military streamlining to cut the budget, but also the clear impediments to doing so. He concluded "that reduction in number of divisions does not look practicable at this time."[87] In fact, troops were not removed from Europe, and Eisenhower would later reminisce that "every time he had tried to do something about bringing our troops back, Secretaries Dulles and Herter had pled with him with tears in their eyes not to talk about any withdrawal of American forces from Europe."[88]

The "new look," then, never was operationalized in the manner envisaged by policymakers in Washington. After the fallout of the Radford Plan, in fact, Dulles publicly backed away from a heavy reliance on massive retaliation. Obviously, other factors were at play besides the furor the episode created in trans-Atlantic relations. The successful launching of Sputnik in 1957 and the perception thereafter that the United States had lost its advantage in strategic nuclear matters led policymakers away from the massive retaliation doctrine and toward a more flexible military policy. Clearly, however, the challenge by Adenauer and other West European leaders affected Washington's position. The fact that Dulles voiced misgivings about the "new look" in 1956, the year before Sputnik, and cited specifically his concern about the effect of the "new look" on the West Europeans, is indicative. The desire for Allied cohesion and West German loyalty to the Alliance played a prominent role in Washington's decision to back away from the "new look."

As I will discuss below and in the next chapter, once Adenauer perceived the importance of nuclear weapons in Western defense strategy, his government would pursue a policy, along with Great Britain and France, of obtaining access to American nuclear weapons through NATO. Fear that the issue of nuclear weapons would leave Bonn in an unequal status vis-à-vis its Allies largely influenced Adenauer's behavior. David N. Schwartz persuasively argues that a significant consideration in Adenauer's pursuit of this strategy, given his previous strong stand against nuclear weapons, was the goal of maintaining West Germany as an equal partner within the alliance. Denying the German army access to powerful weapons available under various control arrangements to other NATO armies would place Germany in an inferior position. This argument was used repeatedly to justify new German interest in nuclear weapons.[89]

The MLF: Nuclear Status and the Alliance

Over the following years, American sensitivity to the West German demand for equality on the nuclear weapons issue would inspire a number of trans-Atlantic episodes, such as the multilateral force issue, that make little sense from a realist position. Toward the end of the Eisenhower administration, the U.S. balance of payments problem became keen. As had been previously raised during his tenure, the issue of reducing American forces in Western Europe was again broached as a way to bring the balance of payments "into more reasonable equilibrium."[90] The issue of reducing troops was raised constantly in top-level meetings in the latter 1950s, but was always met by resistance from the State and Defense Departments. As a testimony to Adenauer's access through the Wilsonian impulse and the Versailles remedial, the fear of negative repercussions in West Germany was often cited as the reason for discouraging plans concerning troop reductions. In a phone conversation in 1957 between Dulles and Secretary Quayles, Dulles assumes that Quayles is, "not thinking of any significant change in those five and a third divisions at the present time." because, "what he did not want was to have a scare get out through NATO which would hit Germany during the last days of the election."[91] The continuous inability to get any action on the troop reduction issue despite the worsening balance of payments problem led Eisenhower to reflect in October 1960 that he was aware of the problem, but that

he had been trying, over the years, to secure a reduction in forces in Europe and a reduction in independents and had been confronted each time with what was believed by the Departments of State and Defense to be adverse political circumstances in European countries.[92]

Thus, while Western security policy was obviously motivated by concern for the Soviet threat, it was also motivated by the related but separate consideration of internal Alliance politics, interpreted through the Wilsonian lens. The positive Alliance goal of securing a politically peaceful and cohesive Western community that included an equal Germany remained central to American and other Western policymakers. Documents from the period attest to the pervasive concern with attaining that goal.

In 1958, Adenauer won an important reelection in the FRG. One of the issues on the CDU–CSU agenda was the nuclear modernization of NATO, which included the stationing of nuclear weapons on West German soil. The SPD vehemently opposed this policy.[93] While Adenauer had earlier been known to be against the stationing of the Thor and Jupiter missile systems in the FRG, he and the CSU, led by Franz Josef Strauss, fought a volatile battle with the SPD, justifying why the FRG should in fact be receptive to acquiring NATO's "most modern weapons."[94] As before, he also sought to influence the West, particularly Washington, by alluding to his domestic opposition. Until 1960, he could subtly warn Washington that the domestic alternative, the SPD, if elected, would pursue a security policy advocating the neutralization of Germany and the withdrawal of the FRG from NATO.[95]

According to Adenauer's strategy, until such time that disarmament coupled with reunification appeared likely, the FRG was not going to become increasingly stigmatized by its nonnuclear status in an ever more nuclear world, especially after the "new look" opened Pandora's Box regarding nuclear proliferation in the Alliance. As he had done earlier, Adenauer would again make his case for the principle of equality of status, this time with the nuclear issue. In his memoirs, Adenauer recounted his responses to West German domestic opposition over the issue of arming the FRG with tactical nuclear weapons. He claimed that denying such a development would mean

the dissolution of NATO. How was it thinkable that the German troops in NATO should be worse armed than the Americans, the Belgians, the French, the Dutch, or the Italians, without thereby being inferior? Discrimination against the German soldiers meant in practical terms the dissolution of the entire Western security alliance.[96]

Adenauer and the CDU made clear their determination that the FRG was not to accept an unequal, second-class position during the nuclearization of the East-West military competition.[97] The ascendancy of nuclear weapons as the centerpiece of the East-West military competition had become fact. David N. Schwartz observes that the publication in Great Britain of the Sandys 1957 *White Paper on Defense*, wherein plans for a British nuclear deterrent force were operationalized, "gave Adenauer the opportunity to advance the argument for arming the Bundeswehr with nuclear weapons."[98] One can speculate that he became increasingly receptive to the idea of some sort of nuclear role for the FRG as a countermeasure to the various proposals being raised in the East and West calling for a nuclear free zone in Central Europe.

The Eisenhower administration's concern for this issue was great, especially as Washington became increasingly worried about nuclear proliferation generally. Adenauer's concern with West German nuclear status pushed Dulles and Eisenhower in a direction regarding nuclear policy that they wished not to go.[99] Adenauer's sensitivity on the subject of nuclear weapons convinced many in Washington that some form of multilateral NATO force was necessary. Ninkovich observes that Eisenhower went so far in desperately wanting to keep NATO alive that he "proposed greater participation in nuclear policy among the NATO powers as 'one way of keeping alive the morale and spirit of NATO.' "[100] What is interesting about Eisenhower's position is that it advocated multilateral control of an MLF force, and even seriously contemplated multinational ownership. Dulles was himself interested in pursuing nuclear sharing arrangements, and was willing to contemplate it at the level of the UN as well.[101] Eisenhower's concern about the nuclear sharing issue and some form of multilateral NATO force that would address the situation is reflected in a high-level conversation held during 1960:

The President said he had been mulling this question over at-length. It was clear that the establishment of such a NATO force on the basis of national contributions in ships, men, and material would not be satisfactory. In fact he thought the best way would be through the establishment of a kind of a "Foreign Legion" under exclusive NATO control and financed by contributions of the member states. This was the only manner to do away with nationalism and to prevent the possibility of the withdrawal by any nation of its units. Only a force loyal exclusively to NATO would be safe from such a danger.[102]

Further, when Mr. Merchant asked about multinational ownership of the submarines, Eisenhower "said he saw much advantage in our keeping ownership of the ships, but allowing the Europeans to put in their own missiles." The president said further "that if the group came to the conclusion that it is necessary to have genuine NATO ownership for the vessels, he would give his approval to trying to work this out."[103]

Eisenhower's and Dulles's attitudes of advocating nuclear sharing, and even abolition in Dulles's case, both reflect the Wilsonian concern with collective security, where security is indivisible, and foreshadowed the future abolitionist and sharing schemes of Carter and Reagan. The nuclear sharing issue reflected the belief that joint management and even ownership would help build a community of shared interests and responsibilities among the Allies, and would answer the demand for equality of status from states like West Germany.

The MLF was formally introduced by the United States in 1962 under the Kennedy administration. Once it was formally put on the Allied agenda by Kennedy and then maintained by Johnson, the MLF turned out to be a issue that was rife with controversy. While it gradually petered out as an Alliance issue by 1966, it was never formally abandoned. The American ambassador to Great Britain at that time, David Bruce, stated in an interview for the Johnson Library, "The possibility of the MLF force was always there. . . . It seemed to me it had gone on like the Old Man and the Sea, for years."[104]

Kennedy would drop the coownership aspect and redefine the issue around American ownership and control. Emphasizing strategic calculation and eschewing past deference to the Wilsonian impulse, Kennedy created a storm. By the end of his administration, however, the Wilsonian impulse would be reasserted, thanks to domestic pressure from American Wilsonians and the persistence of Adenauer.

CONCLUSIONS

In sum, the evolution of the Alliance in the 1950s reflects the limits of U.S. willingness to use coercive power as a hegemon in its socialization of West Germany into the Western fold and reflects Bonn's adeptness at winning concessions as it acquiesced to the American-led Wilsonian order.[105] The willingness of the FRG to seek its own goals within the established context of the Western security relationship was pivotal in securing NATO's evolution as a regional Wilsonian security community. Unlike Great Britain and France, the FRG would concentrate most of its efforts on keeping the Western security relationship Wilsonian, as it was in that context that Bonn had so much access to influence and legitimacy in the face of lingering fears about Germany.

On the nuclear issue, the leverage Bonn held over the Alliance, and especially over Washington, was that West German loyalty to the West again depended on the Allies upholding the principles of reciprocity and equality of status that were established in 1954. At that time, Bonn had agreed not to produce nuclear weapons on West German soil and not to pursue reunification on its own provided that the Allies take collective responsibility for achieving eventual German reunification. Therefore, movement by any of the Allies toward detente with the Soviet Union before positive action on the German unity issue was achieved was interpreted by Adenauer as a challenge to the reciprocity of the Allied relationship. It would also mean that West Germany's loyalty to the West could no longer be assumed, and that Bonn might seek alternative routes in securing its foreign policy interests.

It is also clear that the Wilsonian impulse and especially the Versailles remedial became institutionalized in the State Department. The lessons of Versailles and the failure of the League of Nations to manage European power relations led to the determination to build a Western community and to ensure the peaceful integration of a democratic Germany. Even when faced with continuing a less than credible departmental policy that supported German unification, Dulles did not adopt a contrary position.[106] Over the following decades, attempts to move away from the impulse would often be thwarted by the State Department.

Interestingly, whereas the American Wilsonian impulse encouraged diffuse reciprocity based on historical experience and a set of beliefs and assumptions concerning international relations, Bonn's policymakers strategically pursued outcomes based on those beliefs but grounded in the specific political agreements reached during the 1954 Paris Accords that admitted West Germany into the Alliance. In this way, the Western Alliance reflected both the American Wilsonian stamp applied at the close of World War II and the West German ability to use that influence to its own advantage and further cement shared expectations.

On the other hand, by accepting the diffuse reciprocal agreement made by the Allies wherein they assumed responsibility over the long run for achieving peaceful German unification, Bonn's policy was a major sign that the Wilsonian political culture was being accepted by West Germans. It revealed that long-term expectations based on Western cooperation constructed fundamental national security concerns in distinct ways. Therefore, the fact that the Allied relationship was conceived from the outset as a means to institutionalize Western interstate security relations through the application of norms, principles, rules, and procedures to which all members were beholden, colored the way West German actors determined their own security policies.

I look next at how these same issues were approached and interpreted during the Kennedy era. The contrast in how assumptions were made regarding American interest in West Germany and Western security issues is great. Kennedy, himself a realist, had very different generational and personal experiences and was not predisposed to honor the Wilsonian impulse to the same extent as his predecessors. He was more inclined to follow the lessons of Munich and balance of power thinking than the lessons of Versailles and community-building. The Eisenhower administration would be the last in which near consensus existed between the president, his secretary of state and the State Department. Yet, by the end of Kennedy's short tenure, he was captured to a large extent by the process already established through previous policy.

NOTES

1. Richard A. Melanson, "The Foundations of Eisenhower's Foreign Policy," in *Reevaluating Eisenhower: American Foreign Policy in the 1950s*, ed. Richard A. Melanson and David Mayers (Urbana: University of Illinois Press, 1987), p. 331. Melanson states that this small group of advisors was dubbed "The Inquiry." See discussion of the Wilsonian internationalists, the "informal brain trust," in Walter Isaacson and Evan Thomas, *The Wise Men: Six Friends and the World They Made* (New York: Simon and Schuster, 1986), pp. 28–29.

2. For a brief discussion of Dulles at Versailles, see Rolf Steininger, "John Foster Dulles, the European Defense Community, and the German Question," in *John Foster Dulles and the Diplomacy of the Cold War*, ed. Richard H. Immerman (Princeton, N.J.: Princeton University Press, 1990), pp. 79–108, esp. p. 79.

3. See Ronald Preussen, "The Predicaments of Power," in *John Foster Dulles and the Diplomacy of the Cold War*, ed. Richard H. Immerman (Princeton, N.J.: Princeton University Press, 1990), pp. 21–45, esp. pp. 25–27.

4. See David Fromkin, *In the Time of the Americans: The Generation That Changed America's Role in the World* (New York: Alfred A. Knopf, 1995), esp. chs. 58, 59, epilogue.

5. Richard H. Immerman, "Introduction," in *John Foster Dulles and the Diplomacy of the Cold War*, ed. Richard H. Immerman (Princeton, N.J.: Princeton University Press, 1990), p. 19. Immerman is commenting on Ronald Preussen's observation of Dulles.

6. See, for example, Michael Mandelbaum, *The Fate of Nations: The Search for National Security in the Nineteenth and Twentieth Centuries* (Cambridge: Cambridge University Press, 1988), pp. 145–49.

7. Richard D. Challener, "Dulles: Moralist as Pragmatist," *The Diplomats, 1939–1979*, ed. Gordon A. Craig and Francis L. Lowenheim (Princeton, N.J.: Princeton University Press, 1994), p. 140.

8. Wolfram Hanrieder, *Germany, America, Europe: Forty Years of German Foreign Policy* (New Haven, Conn.: Yale University Press, 1989), p. 144.

9. Ibid., p. 144.

10. I thank Ron Rogowski for helping me develop this point.

11. Catherine McArdle Kelleher, *Germany and the Politics of Nuclear Weapons* (New York: Columbia University Press, 1975), p. 23.

12. See Frederick W. Marks III, *Power and Peace: The Diplomacy of John Foster Dulles* (Westport, Conn.: Praeger, 1993), esp. pp. 60–61. See also Steininger, "John Foster Dulles," p. 97–103.

13. See the excellent discussion by Thomas Alan Schwartz, in his *America's Germany: John J. McCloy and the Federal Republic of Germany* (Cambridge, Mass.: Harvard University Press, 1991), esp. ch. 10.

14. Preussen, "The Predicaments of Power," p. 34.

15. Hans-Juergen Grabbe, "Konrad Adenauer, John Foster Dulles, and West German–American Relations," in *John Foster Dulles and the Diplomacy of the Cold*

War, ed. Richard H. Immerman (Princeton, N.J.: Princeton University Press, 1990), pp. 109–32, quote on p. 121.

16. See especially Brian Klunk, *Consensus and the American Mission: The Credibility of Institutions, Policies and Leadership, vol. 14.* (Lanham, Md.: University Press of America, 1986), esp. ch. 2. See also Marks, *Power and Peace*, esp. chs. 4–5 and his discussion of Dulles's subtle grasp of communism and Soviet statecraft. Also see Fromkin, *In the Time of the Americans*, esp. p. 547.

17. Preussen, "The Predicaments of Power," p. 35.

18. Ibid.

19. On p. 28 of "The Predicaments of Power," Preussen discusses Dulles's keen and lifelong interest in domestic affairs and public opinion. The quotation, cited by Gaddis (below), comes from Ronald Preussen's biography, *John Foster Dulles: The Road to Power* (New York: Free Press, 1982). See also John Lewis Gaddis's excellent revisionist treatment of Dulles's views on the Soviets and communism, in his "The Unexpected John Foster Dulles: Nuclear Weapons, Communism, and the Russians," in *John Foster Dulles and the Diplomacy of the Cold War*, ed. Richard H. Immerman (Princeton, N.J.: Princeton University Press, 1990), pp. 48–77.

20. Among others, see Frank Ninkovich, *Modernity and Power: A History of the Domino Theory in the Twentieth Century* (Chicago: University of Chicago Press, 1992).

21. Fromkin, *In the Time of the Americans*, p. 547.

22. See Challener's discussion, "Dulles: Moralist as Pragmatist," p. 140.

23. Klunk, *Consensus and the American Mission*, p. 79.

24. John Foster Dulles, quoted in Andrew H. Berding, *Dulles on Diplomacy* (Princeton, N.J.: D. Van Nostrand, 1965), p. 36.

25. For a discussion of Dulles's experience at Versailles, see Deane Heller and David Heller, *John Foster Dulles: Soldier for Peace* (New York: Holt, Rinehart and Winston, 1960), esp. ch. 5.

26. Marks, *Power and Peace*, p. 122.

27. Ibid., pp. 46, 119.

28. I quote Thomas A. Schwartz, whose depiction of Dulles's crusade concerns the Cold War. See Schwartz's "Eisenhower and the Germans," in *Eisenhower: A Centenary Assessment*, ed. Guenter Bischof and Stephen E. Ambrose (Baton Rouge: Louisiana State University, 1995), pp. 206–21, quote on p. 226. See also Tony Smith, *America's Mission: The United States and the Worldwide Struggle for Democracy in the Twentieth Century* (Princeton, N.J.: Princeton University Press, 1994), p. 189.

29. See discussion by Klunk, *Consensus and the American Mission*, esp. ch. 2.

30. Ibid., p. 60.

31. Marks, *Power and Peace*, p. 124.

32. Klunk, *Consensus and the American Mission*, p. 52.

33. Marks, *Power and Peace*, p. 129.

34. Klunk, *Consensus and the American Mission*, p. 36.

35. Konrad Adenauer, quoted in his *"Es musste alles neu gemacht werden." Die Protokolle des CDU-Bundesvorstandes 1950–1953* (Stuttgart: Ernst Klett Verlage, 1986), p. 648.

36. Hanrieder, *Germany, America, Europe*, p. 144. He quotes Dean Acheson as saying that the American objective for West Germany was that Bonn become "entangled and integrated" into the West.

37. George F. Kennan, *Memoirs 1950–1963* (New York: Pantheon, 1972), p. 243.

38. See Ninkovich, *Modernity and Power*, p. 233.

39. See Mary N. Hampton, *The Empowerment of a Middle-Sized State: West Germany, Wilsonianism and the Western Alliance* (Los Angeles: UCLA Press, 1993), esp. chs. 4–5. For an excellent discussion of this, see Timothy Garton Ash, *In Europe's Name: Germany and the Divided Continent* (New York: Random House, 1993), esp. chs. 2, 4.

40. "Synopsis of Material Presented to the President, May 16/60," Dwight D. Eisenhower (hereafter, DDE) Library, Whitman File, DDE Diary Series, Box 49, Folder: Briefing May 1960, p. 2.

41. Helga Haftendorn, *Security and Detente: Conflicting Priorities in German Foreign Policy* (New York: Praeger, 1985), p. 58.

42. Konrad Adenauer, *Erinnerungen 1955–1959* (Stuttgart: Deutsche Verlags-Anstalt, 1967), pp. 296–97.

43. Uwe Nerlich, "Die Nuklearen Dilemmas der Bundesrepublik," 17.6.1965, Lyndon B. Johnson (hereafter, LBJ) Library, National Security File; Country File; Europe and USSR; Germany, Container 182, 183, 186, 190, 191; Folder: Germany Memos Volume 9. 7/65–1/66, p. 14.

44. Ibid.

45. See conversation between Eisenhower and Adenauer held in Washington during 1960 in "Memorandum of Conversation; March 15, 1960, 10:30 A.M., The White House," DDE Library, Eisenhower Papers; Ann Whitman File; International Series, Box 13. Folder: Adenauer Visit to Washington, March 1960. On page 4, Adenauer stated during the conversation that, "if no effective controlled disarmament program went into effect, Germany would be forced to increase its military effort—with NATO concurrence, of course."

46. See Anne-Marie Burley, "Restoration and Reunification: Eisenhower's German Policy," in *Reevaluating Eisenhower: American Foreign Policy in the 1950s*, ed. Richard A. Melanson and David Mayers (Urbana: University of Illinois Press, 1987), pp. 220–38. See also, "Memorandum for Mr. McGeorge Bundy, June 1, 1961," from Marc Raskin, John F. Kennedy (hereafter, JFK) Library, National Security File, Box 75-81, Folder: Countries—Germany-General-Berlin; 6/1/61–6/15/61. In the paper, Raskin asserts that during the years of the Eisenhower administration, both the United States and the Soviet Union approached the German reunification issue with insincerity: "Thus each side has made non-negotiable demands on each other. Each side pretended to seek the reunification of Germany on its own terms, while actually caring very little about ending the partition. What each side really wanted was the preservation of the status-quo, although neither was willing to admit it for fear of alienating the German." (pp. 1–2); finally, see Hans-Juergen Grabbe's discussion of Dulles and the trade off between German reunification and European integration in "Konrad Adenauer, John Foster Dulles, and West German–American Relations," pp. 109–32, esp. pp. 115–16.

47. For one example of an analyst who questions Adenauer's reunification aims, see Paul Frank, *Entschluesselte Botschaft: Ein Diplomat macht Inventur* (Munich: Deutscher Taschenbuch Verlag, 1985), esp. pp. 86–88.

48. Hans W. Gatzke, *Germany and the United States: A Special Relationship?* (Cambridge, Mass.: Harvard University Press, 1980), p. 258. Gatzke states that before 1974, "Washington strictly adhered to the policy of nonrecognition adopted by West Germany under Adenauer."

49. James L. Richardson, *Germany and the Atlantic Alliance: The Interaction of Strategy and Politics* (Cambridge, Mass.: Harvard University Press, 1966), pp. 266–67. Richardson does state that although the "agents" concept was dropped from public discussion, it did become part of American policy.

50. "President's Trip To Europe: August–September 1959, General Scope Paper," DDE Library, Eisenhower Papers; Ann Whitman File; International Meetings Series, Box 3. Folder: European Trip—General, August–September/59. The paper further states: "Realistically considered, it seems unlikely that any progress can be made with the Soviets at this time on the subject of German reunification. However, nothing must be done which would have the effect of closing the door to such eventual reunification and we must maintain our position that reunification is an essential ingredient of any long range peaceful settlement in Europe," p. 4.

51. Alfred Grosser, *The Western Alliance: European-American Relations Since 1945*. (New York: Vintage Books, 1985), p. 192.

52. "Memorandum for Mr. McGeorge Bundy, August 7, 1961," from W. W. Rostow, JFK Library, Box 82; Collection: NSF Countries; Folder: Germany; Berlin; General 8/6/61–8/8/61. Rostow states: "At a time when maximum pressure is on us to recognize the GDR—and we wish to deflect that pressure—it is wholly proper for us to dramatize the kind of regime that exists sixteen years after the war in East Germany. . . . We are prepared to encourage the West Germans to engage in a widening range of contact and discourse with the East Germans," p. 1.

53. "Memorandum for the Secretary, July 27, 1961," JFK Library, Box 52, Collection: NSF-Countries, Folder: Germany-Berlin-General 7/27/61, p. 2.

54. Arthur M. Schlesinger, Jr., *A Thousand Days: John F. Kennedy in the White House* (Boston: Houghton Mifflin, 1965), p. 384. He states that the report "was a tired and turgid rehash of documents left over from the Berlin crisis of 1958–59. . . . By this time it was too late to do anything but put the paper out, which the White House did, though after attaching a more cogent summary of its own."

55. William E. Griffith in a letter to W. W. Rostow, June 21, 1961, JFK Library, National Security Files, Boxes 75–81, Folder: Countries—Germany-Berlin-General; 6/17/61–6/22/61, p. 1.

56. Adenauer, *Erinnerungen*, p. 283.

57. Ninkovich, *Modernity and Power*, p. 233.

58. Quoted in Schlesinger, *A Thousand Days*, p. 346.

59. See discussion in Hampton, *The Empowerment of a Middle-Sized State*, esp. ch. 2.

60. Adenauer was already beginning to have doubts about Eisenhower. In an interview from October of 1957 with James Reston, the *New York Times* reporter, he observed that the State Department and the White House appeared sometimes to work at cross purposes. Adenauer feared that Eisenhower might be too eager to do something dramatic for the world peace before he left office. (Adenauer, *Erinnerungen*, p. 321.) Further, see Lincoln P. Bloomfield, Walter C. Clemens, Jr., and Franklyn Griffiths, *Khrushchev and the Arms Race: Soviet Interests in Arms Control and Disarmament, 1954–1964* (Cambridge, Mass.: MIT Press, 1966), p. 134. Adenauer's fears about Eisenhower were not illusory. The authors state in a footnote that, "In 1955 and later the Eisenhower administration showed interest in demilitarization of Central Europe, but could not obtain Adenauer's support."

61. Adenauer, *Erinnerungen*, pp. 306–7. See also "Telephone Call to the Vice President; Saturday, June 8, 1957, 7:17 P.M.," DDE Library, Papers of John Foster Dulles; Telephone Calls Series, Box 6; Folder: Memoranda of Telephone Conversations—General, May 7/57–June 27/57 (2), p. 1. Dulles complains to Nixon about Stassen's behavior. He says of Stassen: "He gave the Russians a written memo the first thing. . . . There was violent reaction by our allies. . . . We told our allies we disavowed it. He is discredited with our allies and we don't know what we will do. The President is aware of it and says for the first time his confidence has been shaken."

62. "Telephone Call from the President; Tuesday, June 4, 1957, 12:14 P.M.," DDE Library, Papers of John Foster Dulles, Telephone Call Series, Box 12, Folder: Memoranda of Telephone Conversations—White House, March/57–August 30/57 (2), p. 1.

63. Adenauer, *Erinnerungen*, p. 307. Adenauer also recounts a conversation he and von Brentano, the West German ambassador in Washington, had with Dulles in May before the conference in Washington. The two West Germans insisted to Dulles that talk of disarmament and detente between the bloc could not be separated from the underlying political questions concerning the division of East and West. Such a separation of issues "would lead, at least in West Germany, to a loss of faith. If that would then make it possible for the opposition, with their well known position, to win the election, I don't know" (pp. 308–9). My translation. Not surprisingly, a translated speech given by Adenauer in 1957 stressing this position is on file in the Eisenhower Papers. In the speech, Adenauer discusses the SPD's policy of seeking a neutralized Germany, which Adenauer again claims can only lead to Soviet domination in Western Europe. He also states again, in connection with Bonn's support of disarmament negotiations, that "the question of Germany's reunification must also be settled during these negotiations." Speech by Adenauer, undated, July, 1957, DDE Library, Eisenhower Papers, Ann Whitman File, International Series, Box 14, Folder: Adenauer, 1957–58 (1), pp. 7–8.

64. Hans-Gert Poettering, *Adenauer's Sicherheitspolitik 1955–1963* (Duesseldorf: Droste Verlag, 1975), p. 173. Poettering quotes the letter. My translation.

65. Adenauer, *Erinnerungen*, pp. 468–69.

66. Ibid., pp. 480–81.

67. See discussion by Robinson in *Germany and the Atlantic Alliance: The Interaction of Strategy and Politics* (Cambridge, Mass.: Harvard University Press, 1966), p. 268.

68. Quoted in Burley, "Restoration and Reunification: Eisenhower's German Policy." In *Reevaluation, Eisenhower: American Foreign Policy in the 1950s*, ed. Richard A. Melanson and David Mayers (Urbana: University of Illinois Press, 1987), 220–40.

69. Adenauer, *Erinnerungen*, pp. 474–75. Further, on pp. 284–92, in a discussion with Basil Kingsley-Martin, an English journalist, Adenauer held firm in his conviction that reunification must be approached only through general nuclear disarmament. A neutralized reunified Germany would simply be bait for the nearby Soviets and such a Germany would be more vulnerable than ever in the event of a nuclear confrontation between East and West.

70. Dulles, quoted in Berding, *Dulles on Diplomacy*, p. 37.

71. See "Summary Record of a Meeting of United States Ambassadors at Paris" (Paris, October 22, 1949), and "The United States High Commissioner for Germany

(McCloy) to the Secretary of State" (Frankfurt, October 28, 1949), both reproduced in *Foreign Relations, 1949, vol. 3*, pp. 287–93.

72. See discussion in ibid., p. 351. Also see Adenauer, *Briefe Ueber Deutschland,* pp. 81, 87–89, and Hans-Peter Schwarz, ed., *Konrad Adenauer: Reden, 1917–1967* (Stuttgart: Deutsche Verlags-Anstalt, 1975), p. 240.

73. See discussion in Richard J. Barnet, *The Alliance, America-Europe-Japan: Makers of the Postwar World* (New York: Simon and Schuster, 1983), p. 57.

74. Kelleher, *Germany and the Politics of Nuclear Weapons*, p. 18.

75. Ibid., p. 143.

76. Richardson, *Germany and the Atlantic Alliance.*

77. Richard P. Stebbins, ed., *The United States in World Affairs, 1951*, p. 67–68.

78. On the MLF, see Hampton, *The Empowerment of a Middle-Sized State,* esp. chs. 2–4. See also the classic study by John D. Steinbrunner, *The Cybernetic Theory of Decision: New Dimensions of Political Analysis* (Princeton, N.J.: Princeton University Press, 1974). More recently, see Steve Weber, "Shaping the Postwar Balance of Power: Multilateralism in NATO," in *Multilateralism Matters: The Theory and Praxis of an Institutional Form,* ed. John G. Ruggie (New York: Columbia University Press, 1993), esp. pp. 265–67.

79. See the excellent discussion of this in Robert A. Wampler, "Eisenhower, NATO, and Nuclear Weapons: The Strategy and Political Economy of Alliance Security," in *Eisenhower: A Centenary Assessment,* ed. Guenter Bischof and Stephen B. Ambrose (Baton Rouge: Louisiana State University Press, 1995), pp. 162–90.

80. Kelleher, *Germany and the Politics of Nuclear Weapons.,* p. 16. Also see the excellent discussion in Gaddis, "The Unexpected Dulles."

81. Kelleher, *Germany and the Politics of Nuclear Weapons,* pp. 15–16.

82. John Foster Dulles, "Outlines of Strategy: Address by the Secretary of State Before the Council on Foreign Relations, New York, January 12, 1954," reprinted in Peter V. Curl, ed., *Documents on American Foreign Relations, 1954* (New York: Harper and Brothers, 1955), pp. 9–10.

83. Grosser, *The Western Alliance,* p. 167.

84. Barnet, *The Alliance,* p. 174.

85. Ibid., p. 175.

86. "Memorandum of Conference with the President; October 2, 1956," DDE Library, Eisenhower Papers as President, Ann Whitman File, DDE Diary Series, Box 19, Folder: October '56 Diary—Staff Memos, p. 3.

87. Ibid.

88. Allen W. Dulles, "Memorandum for the President, August 22, 1961," JFK Library, pp. 97–98.

89. David N. Schwartz, *NATO's Nuclear Dilemmas* (Washington, D.C.: The Brookings Institute, 1983), p. 44.

90. "Memorandum for the Record, Meeting with the President, Tuesday, October 4, 1960, 10:30 A.M.," DDE Library, Papers as President; Ann Whitman File, DDE Diary Series, Box 53, Folder: Staff Notes—October 1960 (2), p. 3.

91. "Telephone Call from Secretary Quayles, August 28, 1957, 1:05 P.M.," DDE Library, Papers of John Foster Dulles, Box 7, Folder: Memoranda of Telephone Conversations—General, July 1/57–August 31/57 (1), p. 1.

92. "Memorandum for the Record, Meeting with the President, Tuesday, October 4, 1960, 10:30 A.M.," DDE Library, Papers as President; Ann Whitman File, Box 53, Folder: Staff Notes—October 1960 (2), p. 3.

93. For a detailed account of the CDU/CSU position versus that of the SPD, see the Bundestag debates from 20 March (3. Legislaturperiode, 18. Sitzung) and 2 July, 1958 (3. Wahlperiode, 38. Sitzung).

94. Schwartz, *NATO's Nuclear Dilemmas*, pp. 70–72.

95. Speech by Adenauer, circa July 1957, DDE Library, Eisenhower Papers; Ann Whitman File; International Series, Box 14; Folder: Adenauer, 1957–58 (1), pp. 7–9.

96. Adenauer, *Erinnerungen,* p. 298. My translation.

97. See West German parliamentary debate, "3. Wahlperiode—38, Sitzung, Bonn, Mittwoch, den 2. Juli 1958," Strauss, in responding to SPD accusations that the Adenauer government's nuclear policy ran counter to the FRG's pledge in 1954 not to produce, own, or use nuclear weapons, reaffirmed Bonn's commitment not to produce nuclear weapons. However, he goes on the argue that in light of technological developments, with the Soviet bloc armed with nuclear weapons, the FRG, like its other allies, must be willing to expand in the nuclear armaments field.

98. Schwartz, *NATO's Nuclear Dilemmas,* p. 48. See also "Memorandum of Conversation: NATO Atomic Force, October 4, 1960, 8:00–9:15 A.M.," DDE Library, Papers as President, Ann Whitman File, DDE Diary Series, Box 53, Folder: Staff Notes—October 1960 (2), p. 1.

99. See Wampler, "Eisenhower, NATO, and Nuclear Weapons," p. 189.

100. Ninkovich, *Modernity and Power,* p. 233.

101. See Gaddis, "The Unexpected John Foster Dulles," esp. pp. 55–58. See also Wampler, "Eisenhower, NATO, and Nuclear Weapons."

102. "Memorandum of Conference with the President, October 13, 1960," DDE Library, Papers as President, Ann Whitman File, DDE Diary Series, Box 53, Folder: Staff Notes—October 1960 (2), p. 6.

103. Ibid.

104. Interview with David Bruce by Thomas H. Baker, December 9, 1971. LBJ Library, Container AC 73–39, Collection: Oral History: David K. Bruce, Folder: David Bruce, OH, p. 5.

105. See G. John Ikenberry and Charles A. Kupchan, "Socialization and Hegemonic Power," *International Organization* 44 (Summer 1990), esp. pp. 285–92.

106. Ninkovich, *Modernity and Power,* p. 234. The author states: "The State Department realized full well that the end of movement on reunification would have a demoralizing effect on the Germans, yet it was nevertheless at a loss for new policies. In response to a presidential directive, Dulles admitted that his department 'had not come up with anything new and brilliant.' "

Chapter 3 —————————————————————————————

THE KENNEDY ADMINISTRATION AND THE LONG WILSONIAN SHADOW

In the preceding chapter, I analyzed the pivotal influence of the Wilsonian impulse on American decisionmakers such as John Foster Dulles. Postwar international relations throughout the Eisenhower administration were more complex than the international relations theory literature has allowed. My study acts as a corrective for the field's overemphasis on the impact of bipolarity for international politics generally and on American foreign policy specifically. In defining the American approach to postwar Western security relations through the Eisenhower administration, the impact of Wilsonianism and the Versailles remedial was particularly strong. Generally, much consensus existed between President Eisenhower, Secretary of State John Foster Dulles, and the State Department regarding what to do about Europe and West Germany. The active Wilsonianism determined that Allied relations would evolve in a unique way and become a hybrid between a traditional security pact and a security community. The role of the Versailles remedial was critical in rehabilitating Germany and specifically in imprinting Washington-Bonn relations.

Despite the fact that John F. Kennedy entered office in 1961 set on inaugurating the "Grand Design," the essence of which was to be "creative harmony between the United States and Europe for economic, military and political purposes,"[1] the erosion of cooperation, multilateralism, and community-building in the Western Alliance increased in the 1961–1963 period. Kennedy's Grand Design, his "lofty Declaration of Interdependence," was intended to continue, or actually improve, the chances for European integration in an Atlantic partnership.[2] The necessity of maintaining West German loyalty to the West, or of "engrossing Germany in the full majesty of the Atlantic vision," was clearly recognized as central to that goal.[3] Yet, the Kennedy administration was much more inclined to impose unilaterally its vision of the Grand Design on European leaders, especially on Adenauer, than the Eisenhower administration had been, and was therefore itself responsible for much of the erosion in Allied cohesion.

One of the reasons for this, I suggest, is that the Kennedy administration was not as influenced by the Wilsonian notions of collective security and community-building that so heavily colored the Eisenhower administration's approach to the Western security relationship. Despite Kennedy's aims of promoting liberal democratic internationalism, his outlook on and approach to international relations in the trans-Atlantic context, and strategic matters generally, accommodated more easily the particularistic approach assumed by realism.[4]

The absence of the Versailles remedial in John F. Kennedy's approach to West Germany and the very passive influence of the Wilsonian impulse in his orientation to Western security relations had immediate and strong consequences for U.S.–West German and U.S.–European relations. Many arguments have been offered as to why the American–West German and U.S.–Soviet relationships changed during the 1960s, which they did. Central in the realist and neorealist interpretations is the view that, as American power declined relative to others, the tight bipolarity of the Alliance relaxed and allowed more influence to be wielded by West European states like the FRG. Thus, we saw a more assertive Bonn emerge during the 1970s and onward.

While it is obvious that West Germany's influence was enhanced as its economy grew during the 1960s and onward, I have shown that West German influence over American foreign policy was especially high during the peak of U.S. hegemony in the early and mid-1950s. Thus, power capability explanations are simply not plausible in explaining how and why policymakers like Dulles were so beholden to Wilsonian ideas about West European security and West Germany in particular. Nor can such interpretations accurately depict the shift in America's foreign policy that accompanied the change in administration from Eisenhower to Kennedy.

Another perspective that attempts to explain theses changes focuses on the alteration in thinking on strategic matters that occurred under Kennedy. For example, Steve Weber holds that Kennedy maintained a different set of beliefs about deterrence and nuclear weapons than did policymakers in the Eisenhower administration. Because of that differing perspective, the Kennedy administration brought an abrupt change to NATO's nuclear policy and thereby undermined the multilateralism that defined Eisenhower's approach.[5] This is an interesting approach but one that begs the question of why Kennedy and Eisenhower had different ideas about Allied politics and nuclear policy to begin with. For example, Weber states that "Eisenhower had hoped that nuclear weapons could be used to promote European integration and to advance and channel the transition to a multipolar world," but that they "became victims to nuclear strategy" under Kennedy.[6] His explanation is that for "second image" reasons, changes in nuclear and security policy are "explained by the movements of sets of ideas that were disconnected from any objective exigencies of security."[7]

For authors like Weber or Yuen Foon Khong in his insightful *Analogies at War*, Kennedy's policies deviated from those of other presidents because he held a different set of beliefs about international relations.[8] I argue that the influence or lack thereof of the Wilsonian impulse as an effective operational code is in fact most instructive in explaining the shift in policy from the Eisenhower administration to Kennedy's regarding the Alliance, West Germany, and U.S.–Soviet relations.

The difference is in part generational and the result of specific historical experiences. In fact, it is illuminating to compare the differing historical experiences that influenced Dulles and Kennedy as young men.[9] Dulles, as I discussed above, was at the Versailles Conference in 1919 and that experience left him and other "brain trusters" particularly receptive to demands that the Alliance evolve along the lines of a Wilsonian collective security community and that Germany be treated with particular sensitivity. The learned lesson applied in a nonpartisan way, since Republicans and Democrats alike who were "present at the creation" shared similar views.

Kennedy, on the other hand, had a completely different awakening to international affairs. He was a young man during the immediate pre–World War II years when his father, Joseph Kennedy, was the American ambassador to Great Britain. Joseph Kennedy was a staunch supporter of British Prime Minister Chamberlain's appeasement policy toward Nazi Germany. It is instructive that JFK's senior thesis at Harvard in 1940 was critical of that policy and was titled "Appeasement at Munich."[10] Along similar lines, of course, was the publication of his book, *Why England Slept*. His early negative impression of the Germans, garnered during personal travel through that country in the late 1930s, was thereafter reinforced by the English-American failed appeasement policy, and witnessed firsthand by young Kennedy because of his father's pivotal role.[11] His attitude toward Germany did not leave him particularly receptive to the Versailles remedial.

More persuasive than a simple generational argument, however, is the probability that because of Kennedy's predispositions, he did not find the Wilsonian impulse and Versailles remedial convincing as policy prescriptions. There are few references to be found of a direct Wilsonian influence on Kennedy's security thinking.[12] The notion that national interests may be best served through the creation of a security community—one bound by reciprocal understandings, commonly respected principles, rules, and procedures, and dedicated to forging a shared culture among nations— was therefore more alien to Kennedy than it had been for pivotal policy-makers of the previous administrations. Hitler's aggression in the face of persistent peace overtures from the United States and Great Britain had proven to the young Kennedy that national vigilance regarding dictators and revisionist states was essential and of the highest priority. During the San Francisco Conference in 1945 that established the United Nations, Kennedy, then a journalist, expressed fear that the West might appease the increasingly assertive Soviet Union, much as they had done Hitler and his aggressive Germany.[13] Unlike the Wilsonians, then, Kennedy experienced Munich, but not Versailles.

The Munich lesson, often regarded in the international relations theory literature as critical to informing and underwriting U.S. foreign policy throughout the Cold War, became most influential when Kennedy became president. My argument concerning Kennedy and Munich diverges significantly from Khong's position in *Analogies at War*. During the early days of decision regarding Vietnam, Khong claims that Munich "was hardly mentioned in public or private. The administration of fine-tuners fine-tuned their analogies as well." While my study does not presume to cover Kennedy's posture or policy on Vietnam, I believe I have convincingly shown that Munich indeed weighed heavy in JFK's thinking concerning international relations and American foreign policy. To my way of thinking, Khong's argument that Kennedy was fine-tuned in his use of analogies and therefore predisposed to support a flexible response doctrine can be subsumed quite nicely by the Munich lesson. One of the lessons Kennedy learned from Munich was that American foreign policy must be vigilant. That meant it must be sensitized to every potential threat that exists and fine-tuned to meet that threat. Therein lies the flexible response logic.[14]

That Kennedy applied the Munich paradigm but not that of Versailles was crucial. John Lewis Gaddis observes of Kennedy's orientation to Wilsonianism that "the American interest was not to remake the world, but to balance power within it. . . . As George Kennan had insisted in 1948, the goal was particularism, not universalism."[15] Equally instructive is Douglas Brinkley's comparison of President Kennedy's position regarding trans-Atlantic relations with that of former Secretary of State Dean Acheson, who advised Kennedy. Acheson, a pragmatic Keynesian who harbored Wilsonian assumptions about interdependence and community-building in the trans-Atlantic context, believed with Jean Monnet that an institutionally concrete Atlantic Partnership could and should develop. Kennedy "found it difficult to believe that trans-national economic and military ties would in the long run prevail over narrow nationalism."[16] He did not believe that Europeans would "do anything for us even though we have done a lot for them. We must be sure our economic house is in order and use our military, political power to protect our interests."[17] Kennedy's understanding of East/West relations thus was typical of traditional realpolitik, wherein alliances are collective defense or military pacts, and that included the Western Alliance. His view indeed shared most of the assumptions of realism concerning interstate relations.

Through what he considered a realistic assessment of changes in the international political environment, such as increased Soviet military power, Kennedy was determined to redefine and reinvigorate American foreign policy. JFK was very concerned that the balance of power was tilting in favor of Soviet and Chinese communism, especially after Sputnik and the Soviet announcement that it would support wars of liberation throughout the developing world.[18] His policy goals that followed from this perception included reevaluating the Western policy of strength toward the Soviets and refocusing NATO's policy to accommodate changes in the East-West relationship. Such objectives appear perfectly plausible from the realist perspective, where national security interests should be measured and articulated in a particularistic fashion, with an eye to objective changes in the international system. However, from the perspective presented in this analysis, where American security policy toward NATO, and sometimes even the Soviet Union, had been largely defined by the Wilsonian impulse and the Versailles remedial, Kennedy's security policy would potentially undermine the Allied cohesion he sought to maintain. Despite protestations to the contrary,[19] his approach was especially troublesome to the West German leadership. As Catherine Kelleher states of Kennedy's position, "if certain 'legalities' or unrealistic priorities had to be sacrificed in the interest of substance, the trade-off was just."[20]

The Kennedy administration's approach to West German reunification and security concerns was therefore based specifically on strategic calculation of American particularistic security interests, and the sensitivities of the Wilsonian lessons would not materialize.[21] Consequently, the American concern for West Germany was now more likely to be interpreted according to a focus on the bipolar U.S.–Soviet strategic relationship than it was on deference to the security community convention articulated and respected under Eisenhower. Because of his own past, Kennedy was also less susceptible than previous American policymakers to fears of Versailles being rekindled in his dealings with the West Germans. He summarily claimed that the "age of Adenauer is over."[22]

During the first year of his administration, Kennedy was warned by McGeorge Bundy of the potential pitfalls in meeting with Adenauer. Bundy stated that "critics of Adenauer will recall the old Dulles-Adenauer meet-

ings in which 'the U.S. always did what Bonn wanted.' "[23] Even more
telling is a remark made by Arthur M. Schlesinger, Jr. in *A Thousand Days*:

As time passed and Adenauer looked back with growing nostalgia to the days
when John Foster Dulles allowed him a virtual veto over American policy, Bonn's
laments and obstructions mounted. Kennedy, though he preserved polite relations, came to feel that the old Chancellor was hanging on too hard.[24]

For a number of reasons, perhaps including his earlier experience,
Kennedy also did not share Dulles's good relationship with Adenauer.
Quite the contrary. Robert F. Kennedy stated bluntly that JFK did not like
Adenauer, and tired of hearing *Der Alte* reminisce about the good old days
with Dulles.[25] As will be shown, Kennedy's breach with prior policy
would ignite anger among West German policymakers and encourage
them to find innovative ways of recapturing the Wilsonian impulse that
aided their cause. American security policy under Kennedy would in the
end be forced to accommodate the previously accepted intrusion of West
German demands, as Adenauer and other West German policymakers
continued asserting their claims according to the collectively agreed upon
principles of 1954 that were implemented during Eisenhower's tenure.
    Kennedy's choices would end up hostage to the Wilsonian impulse,
given its institutionalization at the State Department, the large number of
Wilsonians still in pivotal positions, the increasingly powerful West German influence in American and Allied politics, and the strong precedents
already set in the trans-Atlantic relationship. For example, writing to Un-
dersecretary of State Chester Bowles in 1961, Eugene V. Rostow, the dean
of Yale Law School and brother of W. W. Rostow, illustrated Bonn's continued ability to fixate American policymakers' attention on West German
concerns as done in previous administrations:

At this stage especially, it is vital that West Germany be treated punctiliously as
equal in every way to Britain and France. We cannot afford to seem to treat Germany as a second-class citizen in any way now. It would threaten all that has been
accomplished since the war and revive the shadow of Rappallo.[26]

By the end of Kennedy's short-lived administration, the Versailles remedial would hamper the Kennedy administration's desire to search for
some sort of new understanding with the Soviets in Central Europe as
Adenauer continued to link West German claims regarding unification to
progress in East-West relations. The continued salience of the Wilsonian
impulse also materialized on the controversial issue of the MLF. While
Kennedy would try to assert American control and leadership in Allied
matters concerning nuclear weapons, Wilsonians in Washington and their
supporters in West Germany insisted on promoting nuclear sharing and

equality of status issues that undermined the president's preferences. More so than with Eisenhower, since a consensual collective image did not exist for the Kennedy administration, what emerged was dissonance. While American policy vis-á-vis German reunification and toward nuclear sharing had become problematical, thereby demanding change according to Kennedy and others, too many voices rebelled against shifting the policies to actually effect change. The hesitance to change was particularly strong at State.

WEST GERMAN PERSISTENCE: EAST-WEST RELATIONS AND UNIFICATION

In this section, I will examine West Germany's continued influence on American and Western security policy during the Kennedy administration. What was striking about this period of Allied history was Bonn's determination to enforce the Wilsonian principles of the 1954 Allied convention regarding issues such as equality of status among members, but especially that of Allied responsibility for German unification, where American preferential treatment of the goal had been based on the Versailles remedial. Adenauer was steeled in this endeavor during the Kennedy years, since Kennedy would unwittingly embark on a course that directly undermined the Wilsonian impulse that had greatly aided Adenauer during the Eisenhower administration.

While few formal changes in policy occurred at the official level, Kennedy's "realistic" approach to East-West relations would lead many in his administration, including himself, to question former American policy regarding German reunification. Kennedy's national security advisor, McGeorge Bundy, openly stated his weariness with past American rhetoric concerning Washington's commitment to German reunification. Responding to a State Department white paper regarding U.S. obligations in Berlin and Germany written just before the Berlin Wall episode, Bundy rejected the paper's tone, which suggested that the United States believed German "unity is possible in the reasonable future. We do not believe that, and other nations know we don't."[27] An aide to Bundy "even ventured to suggest that no one cared very seriously about ending the partition."[28]

An important insight into the issue of the Kennedy administration's orientation to German unification was reflected in a memorandum written three days after the Berlin Wall was erected in August 1961. It was addressed to Bundy from W. W. Rostow, his advisor on the National Security Council. In the piece, Rostow perceived a desire by the Kennedy administration to downplay the German reunification issue. Continuing the sentiments of the Eisenhower administration, Rostow cautioned strongly against such a change in American policy. Insisting that reunification was still an extremely important issue even though most West Germans were realistic enough not to expect any success in the near future, Rostow reiterated the responsibility of Washington in maintaining non-recognition of the GDR and support of reunification. He warned: "We shall disassociate ourselves from that sentiment to our peril," and continued that any lessening of American support for reunification

may trigger in the West Germans a conviction that the West has accepted a split Germany for the long pull, and that they must look to reunification by their own actions. . . . It could mean that the West Germans would look increasingly to a deal with Moscow designed to give them some kind of unity at the expense of the Western connections.[29]

There was widespread discussion at top levels in Washington advocating more flexibility in the Western position on German reunification and recognition of the GDR and the Oder Neisse Line. Ninkovich observes:

More so than the Eisenhower administration, Kennedy's people realized that the hard American interest in Berlin was less than compelling by any objective standard. . . . State Department hard-liners could continue to trot out the legalistic fiction that "there is in actuality no such country" as East Germany, but administration influentials realized that the Soviet investment in the GDR was too vital to allow a continuation of the civic status quo. . . . Beyond that, high officials also recognized that the [unification] of Germany largely on Western terms, was unrealistic.[30]

Kennedy himself questioned in a high-level meeting with Cabinet members in 1961, "whether really it was to our advantage to press the argument for unification, feeling that our position lacks appeal." Interestingly, Acheson, arguing for the importance of continued support for German unification, was not convincing to the president. Kennedy was not persuaded until Dean Rusk, secretary of state, "reminded him that self-determination is a better ground than unification."[31]

The incident revealed again the tendency of the Kennedy administration to recast the U.S.–West German understanding that was reached in 1954. Kennedy called it "silly" to discuss the possibility of risking nuclear war over Berlin, the presumed "future capital of a reunited Germany when all of us know that Germany will probably never be reunited."[32]

Sentiments for seeking changes in the East-West relationship were stronger still in London. Suggestions were presented for reopening talks with the Soviets on the matter of a denuclearized zone in Central Europe (read, Germany). There also existed interest in reaching an agreement with the Soviets for freezing the nuclear status quo in Europe. For example, Averell Harriman suggested in a letter to JFK in September of 1961 that

our long-term interest can be advanced if we use the present occasion to come to an agreement with the Soviet Union for a denuclearized control zone of West

Germany and East Germany to as far East as can be negotiated or perhaps an agreement that no additional European country, either East or West, should obtain independent nuclear capability. This is one step towards arms limitation, but more than that, protects us against the possibility of Germany's getting independent nuclear capability with which she could blackmail both West and East.[33]

Another example was a paper written just a week after the Berlin Wall went up on August 22. Carl Kaysen, the principle national security deputy to McGeorge Bundy, recommended:

It may even be worth considering the value of an announcement by the United States, the United Kingdom, and France, made before the German elections, that we recognize the permanence of the present eastern border of Germany. This, while undoubtedly leading to temporary anger and agitation in Germany, would have the value of starting at once the process of re-thinking old positions, which must go on there as well as here and in Paris and London.[34]

Arguing that the FRG was now firmly in the Western camp, Kaysen stated that "it is no longer the case that we run a great risk of undercutting German participation in NATO by changing our views on the German question." Kaysen went on to urge turning away from the Cold War confrontational posture of Washington vis-à-vis the Soviet Union. Instead, the United States should seek positive political acts that would lessen the confrontation. In assessing past U.S. policy toward the FRG, Kaysen concluded that the only policy that needed to be retained was the guarantee for Berlin. In exchange for that guarantee, the United States should be willing to accept the Oder-Neisse Line "as the final boundary of Germany" and pursue "some form of recognition of the GDR as the government now in control of East Germany." Kaysen further argued that the West German attitude toward the German question was changing: "The Germans have gone along in tacit acceptance of the fact of two Germanys. Indeed, they have gone further than we."[35]

That Kaysen overstated the West German acceptance of division and of the status of East Germany was obvious from Bonn's continued insistence on linking reunification to East-West disarmament and detente initiatives, a position supported by many West German SPD members. Talk among influentials in Washington concerning compromise on the German question and other East-West issues in fact raised fears in the FRG that Washington was willing to entertain seriously active change on issues such as recognition of the GDR and the Oder Neisse line, as well as on the concept of creating a denuclearized Germany. In June 1961, two months before the Berlin Wall episode, the *New York Times* ran a West German article that was highly critical of what certain "diplomats and officials in Bonn" interpreted as the willingness of the Kennedy administration to move unilaterally toward negotiations with Moscow concerning the German question.[36]

The erection of the Berlin Wall and Western inaction only fueled Bonn's growing distrust of Washington's intentions. Kennedy's perceived tepid response to the building of the wall was seen by many West Germans as reflective of Washington's lack of interest in upholding its obligations to Bonn. His inaction appeared particularly egregious in light of his apparent willingness to downplay postwar American and Allied obligations to the FRG in favor of better East-West relations.

Adenauer and other policymakers in Bonn perceived an ill wind in Washington and reacted strongly to it. Adenauer had support on the issue of linkage from Wilsonians in the State Department and advisors around Kennedy referred to as "the theologians."[37] Adenauer also won backing from the opposition Republicans in America, from France's Charles de Gaulle, and from important members of the West German opposition SPD. For example, Willy Brandt, the SPD's governing mayor of Berlin at the time, "stressed that FedRep's foreign policy course initiated under Adenauer cannot be abandoned," even though he acknowledged that "new vigor and emphasis must be given to implementation."[38] Brandt "repeatedly emphasized there must be no isolated solution of Berlin question, but that this matter can in the final analysis only be solved within context of solution of German problem."[39] In a background interview conducted with the former chancellor in 1985, Brandt told me that the Berlin Wall episode and the American reaction to it was a central influence on his future foreign policy thinking. Central to understanding future SPD initiatives was the influence that the Berlin Wall had on such prominent party members. In an interview during the summer of 1986, Karsten Voigt, a prominent parliamentary member of the SPD and one of its major strategic thinkers, cited the building of the Berlin Wall as the first major "Wende," or turning point, in the postwar era.[40] The wall, he held, clearly revealed to leading SPD members that "the rhetoric of military strength led to nothing" and that "military power leads to support of the status quo."[41] Brandt and other members of the SPD would later invigorate and further institutionalize the Wilsonian aspects of the Alliance during the Harmel Exercise of 1967 and thereby concretize West German equality of status in East-West relations.

In the end, the Wilsonian and Versailles lessons won out over arguments for accommodation at the official level. Senator William Fulbright, an accommodationist, conceded that while reunification was impossible at that time, there were reasons why that position couldn't be adopted. Bundy, another potential accommodationist, agreed. Ninkovich posits: "The all too familiar arguments were as persuasive as ever."[42]

When Adenauer met with Kennedy in November 1961, Adenauer apparently succeeded in rerallying the United States around a "hard line" approach to the Soviet bloc.[43] Although now compelled to delink the issues of German reunification, border recognition, and arms limitation in Central Europe from the Berlin question, Adenauer nevertheless again regained the American pledge to link the issues of disarmament, German reunification, and recognition of borders.[44] He thereby hampered the Kennedy administration's desire to search for some sort of accommodation with the Soviets in Central Europe. During a high-level talk between former West German Foreign Minister von Brentano and members of the U.S. State Department in 1963, von Brentano was assured that there was no "note of flirtation" between the United States and the Soviets.[45]

But cracks were evident in the U.S. position. Therefore, recommendations such as Kaysen's, echoed by others including Kennedy, never materialized as official policy. But it became rapidly clear to Bonn that the Kennedy administration lacked the sensitivities accorded to the FRG by the Eisenhower administration. The danger of America's "new thinking" was of course that it downplayed and misunderstood the political basis of West German loyalty to the Alliance. If the United States and the Allies reneged on their obligation to support German unity as articulated since 1954, if they trampled West German claims to equality of status through reassessing their own national interests, they also thereby undermined the basis of West German loyalty to the West.

The crack in the relationship led to a number of West German retaliatory responses in the early 1960s, followed by a number of American reconciliation efforts throughout the 1960s. First, de Gaulle's Franco-German–centered European scheme, one espousing more independence from the United States, would find an increasingly warm audience among the CDU/CSU governing coalition during the Kennedy years. Then, Adenauer and other high-ranking West German policymakers, such as the CSU's conservative defense minister, Strauss, would implicitly and explicitly threaten the possibility of Bonn reassessing its security interests in the face of the West (United States) reneging on its commitments. As will be shown in the section on the MLF, open and public contemplation of a West Germany armed with nuclear weapons was one tactic employed by Strauss to emphasize the direct connection between American policy and future West German policy. Thereafter, the United States would be forced to seek accommodations with Bonn to ensure West German loyalty. For example, Washington under Johnson and then Nixon would scurry to accommodate the FRG's demand for equality of status on the nuclear weapons issue first by promoting the multilateral force idea in NATO, then by supporting a reorganization of the nuclear decision-making process in NATO, and finally by allowing Bonn to hamper American interest in reaching accommodation with the Soviets on a number of issues, such as nonproliferation. These will each be dealt with below. To reiterate: In 1954, the West Germans had agreed not to produce nuclear weapons and not to pursue reunification unilaterally *as long as* the Alliance assumed collective responsibility for reunification and acknowledged West Germany as an equal Alliance partner. These were the conditions of diffuse reciprocity that underwrote the Wilsonian impulse and the Versailles remedial and that members of the Kennedy administration threatened to undermine.

Kennedy vs. de Gaulle

While distrust grew between Washington and Bonn, de Gaulle continued his affront against the supranationalism of the Alliance, and against what he perceived as the predominance of American influence in Western Europe. De Gaulle thought Europe should take care of its own security, but JFK was convinced that the Americans had to lead. Reflecting Kennedy's realist inclinations, Ninkovich observes of him: "If there was to be a balance of power, JFK believed it would have to be based on NATO, the only institution that could assure security, and that in turn depended on the American commitment, without which Europe would be helpless."[46]

Trans-Atlantic, but especially U.S.–West German grievances both encouraged and were fueled by de Gaulle's challenge to the Alliance, his own "grand design," and led to closer Franco-German cooperation. Thus, two "grand designs" competed with one another for the heart of Western Europe. Indeed, the appeal of Gaullism increased among important circles in Bonn during the Kennedy administration, and de Gaulle's support for Adenauer in resisting Washington's overtures for detente with the Soviets was crucial. In a meeting between de Gaulle and Adenauer in February 1962, Adenauer's dissatisfaction with U.S. policy, particularly after the Berlin Wall episode, was clearly voiced.[47] Many in Washington and elsewhere in the West feared the outcome of closer West German–French cooperation. The conclusion on January 23, 1963, of a Treaty of Friendship between Paris and Bonn intensified those fears, even though a West German preamble added to the treaty revealed the reluctance of Bonn to sever itself from the multilateralism and Atlanticism of the Western security relationship.[48]

In his excellent study of Dean Acheson, Douglas Brinkley discusses Acheson's negative reaction to the Franco-German treaty. Acheson was taken aback by Adenauer's submissiveness "in signing a treaty of Franco-German rapprochement and unity" that was "in effect . . . an acceptance of de Gaulle's anti-American, anti-Atlantic policy."[49] He was brought on board by Kennedy to advise Washington and intervene in the matter on the administration's behalf. Acheson then proceeded to direct criticism at de Gaulle's obstructionism. For Acheson, the goal was European unity and integration, and he thought any success had been because of previous American policy. In the Wilsonian tradition, he chastized France for living in the past, for maintaining conceptions of narrow national interests "based on an irrelevant past." For him, France's notion of a "Europe of fatherlands was a historically backward step that would reintroduce the disease of nationalism whose symptoms had been suppressed at such great cost and effort."[50] Similarly, McCloy, a central Wilsonian player, shared the critique of de Gaulle that he was an outdated nineteenth-century thinker, beholden to the anachronistic European balance of power system. Further, Gaullism threatened American multilateralism and McCloy warned that "nationalism, provoked to some extent by French attitudes, is again emerging in Europe."[51]

To counteract Gaullism, Acheson recommended bolstering the American–West German relationship by getting Washington to stress anew its commitment to German reunification, a proposition for which Kennedy held little enthusiasm. By the end of the Kennedy administration, Acheson was disenchanted. His agitation with American policymakers grew as he subsequently realized the Kennedy administration's "complete lack of perception of the intensity of German concentration on reunification and our silly dallying with Moscow over Berlin."[52] With JFK's overemphasis on U.S.–Soviet relations, reflected in intense interest for the Test Ban Treaty, which for Acheson was of limited value, Kennedy appeared ignorant of the fact "that the more the United States negotiated with the Soviets, the more NATO was impaired, the more Bonn worried about a Moscow-Washington deal on Berlin." He worried "that the one sure way to lose Germany is to convince Germans that we are prepared to sacrifice German interests for an accord . . . with Russia."[53]

Acheson's role aside, distrust in Washington concerning the Franco–West German treaty was not completely erased. In fact, a few days after the signing of the treaty, the CDU's Kai Uwe von Hassell was sent by Bonn to Washington to convince Kennedy of the treaty's "harmlessness."[54] This was followed by some high-level meetings in March between Heinrich von Brentano and members of the U.S. State Department. At one point, von Brentano was told that although the United States welcomed Franco-German rapprochement, there was considerable concern over the signing of the treaty, given de Gaulle's recent behavior. "These doubts still remained." Secretary Rusk went so far at one point in the conversation as to warn von Brentano that de Gaulle's remarks just prior to the signing of the treaty might give Americans "the feeling that the American connection was not wanted in Europe." Rusk claimed that such a position would make it impossible for any American president to keep U.S. troops there. The secretary then "expressed the hope that the Bundestag and the Federal Government would be able to make it clear that the Franco-German Treaty would not mean a change in German policies." Von Brentano remained very reassuring throughout, offering advice on how best to deal with and understand de Gaulle.[55]

Unlike many in Washington, de Gaulle perceived the West German position in the treaty correctly as a rejection of his European grand design. Alfred Grosser quotes General de Gaulle's reaction to the preamble that was added unilaterally and at the last minute by Bonn: "It is not our fault if the preferred and permanent ties Bonn has contracted with Washington have deprived this Franco-German treaty of its spirit and substance."[56] From this point onward, de Gaulle began forging an independent French detente policy with the Soviet Union, to the consternation of policymakers in both Washington and Bonn.

De Gaulle's courtship of Bonn was therefore not entirely successful, and de Gaulle apparently learned the limits of Bonn's cooperation earlier than did Washington. Washington's misgiving in this area was, however, actually an asset for West German foreign policymakers, who continued to promote closer Franco-German relations as a point of leverage over the United States. When it occurred, Franco-German collusion was indeed extremely effective in thwarting Washington's desire for greater U.S.–Soviet cooperation. Members of Adenauer's government also used U.S. fears of Franco-German collusion as a means of enhancing their importance in Washington, offering at various times to interpret de Gaulle's behavior and policies to the Americans and thereby increasing their own role. This strategy would be repeated in the future, as when Chancellor Helmut Schmidt offered his services to the Carter administration by offering to play the role of mediator between Washington and Moscow during the stalled SALT talks.

In sum, Kennedy's grand design for the West was defined by inherently narrow American particularism as much as De Gaulle's grand design reflected narrow French particularism. Both challenged the Wilsonian impulse that informed U.S. policy toward Western Europe during the Eisenhower administration.[57] While de Gaulle consciously challenged notions of community-building through multilateralism and collectivism, Kennedy perhaps unwittingly undermined them. The result was nevertheless threatening to Western cohesion and especially to U.S.–West German relations.

While Washington thus fueled Adenauer's growing suspicions of the United States and his inclination to seek closer Franco-German relations, Bonn doggedly pursued its claims to legitimacy in the trans-Atlantic security relationship. Adenauer played upon the already existing American–West German understandings to thwart the tentative attempts of the Kennedy administration to reach an accommodation with the Soviets over West German objections. One way Bonn did this was by appealing directly to the American people through astute use of the American press, as it had in 1948, for example, with Adenauer's "trial balloon" on rearmament. Conservative American journals were particularly helpful to Adenauer's cause in leading the public attack on the "soft" British position regarding negotiations with Moscow, including the British willingness to contemplate seriously recognition of East Berlin and the Oder Neisse line.[58] The support of the conservative press and prominent journalists such as Joseph Alsop for Adenauer and de Gaulle's hardline approach highly offended the British government and undercut the ability of the then indecisive Kennedy administration to take new initiatives on the matter. There was a willingness on the part of a number of journalists with connections in the White House, such as Marguerite Higgins, to gain an audience with the president and his advisors in efforts to support Adenauer.[59] Walter Lippmann was one of the few prominent American journalists to speak out in favor of the British position and of negotiations with Moscow concerning recognition of the borders. Adenauer also was once again greatly aided in his efforts by the "Europeanists" in Washington, including many in the State Department and the Republican Party. For example, after Democratic Senator Mike Mansfield gave an "inopportune" speech on June 14, 1961, in which he "proposed that the West negotiate to make Berlin, both East and West, into a free city, a proposal that would have involved renegotiating the postwar agreements," many Republicans aided Bonn by leading an attack on the inexperience and political adventurism of the Kennedy administration.[60]

As will be shown in my discussion of the MLF, the Kennedy administration soon ended up trapped by the Wilsonian impulse that originated the Western security relationship, and by the "hardline" West German position, just as the Eisenhower administration had been earlier and had done more willingly. The issue of the MLF illuminated the potential disintegration of that Western understanding. On the other hand, it also reflected the gradual recognition by Washington that something must be done to reaffirm the principles of the convention. I will deal in some detail with this short but important chapter in Allied relations.

KENNEDY AND THE MLF

Part of Kennedy's reappraisal of American foreign policy centered on NATO policy. Once in office, he immediately assumed the task of trying to update the American and NATO military strategies, as massive retaliation had already lost much of its credibility and because the Kennedy administration perceived American security policy toward NATO as being overburdened by its conventional troop commitments. In short, because Kennedy's focus was more particularistic than had been true earlier under Eisenhower, he sought to rationalize what appeared to be dysfunctional Allied policy that had little strategic value to the United States.[61] The lessons learned from Munich were central for Kennedy. As British inaction during Hitler's rise had shown, defense readiness and the political willingness to face off against external threats to national interests went hand in hand.[62] To Kennedy, NATO policy was shabby on both counts and therefore did not meet the strictly defined requirements of American security needs. Clearly, he was interested in solidifying the security pact aspect of the Alliance, but less keen on the community-building elements.

His partisan loyalties notwithstanding, General Lauris Norstad, in a 1976 interview, offered a revealing account of the differences between Eisenhower's and Kennedy's approaches to Western Europe. In responding to questions concerning his interpretation of those differences, Norstad said of the Kennedy administration:

They didn't have the same understanding of NATO as those of us who had grown up with it over the years. . . . I would simply say that too often they expected me to be the one who would carry out an American decision independently of the NATO countries. And I couldn't or wouldn't do that.[63]

Norstad further stated that his loyalty was challenged at one point by a member of the Kennedy cabinet: "That's the question we have: just to whom do you have an obligation?"[64] At various points in 1962, the general cautioned Kennedy against undermining Western European trust in the United States. He warned against considering the "various force reduction, disengagement and denuclearization schemes, most of which have already been studied and have failed to stand up to searching analysis."[65] Norstad retired as head of SACEUR in late 1962, in the middle of the trans-Atlantic embroilment over Washington's unilateral introduction of the flexible response doctrine.[66]

In the meantime, Dean Acheson submitted to President Kennedy in March 1961 a report entitled "A Review of North Atlantic Problems for the Future." The report basically outlined the features and rationale behind flexible response. Since it coincided with Kennedy's thinking, it was adopted by him immediately as official U.S. policy toward NATO.[67] Supported wholeheartedly by Kennedy and especially by Secretary of Defense McNamara, it became National Security Action Memorandum 40 (NSAM40) and signaled important changes in America's NATO policy. Notably, the flexible response doctrine was introduced as the Kennedy administration's replacement for the technologically and politically outdated massive retaliation doctrine. NATO's conventional forces would be vastly improved in order to reduce the chances for escalation to nuclear war in any East-West conflict.[68]

At the center of the American doctrine was the notion that Western Europe would concentrate on building up its conventional forces while the nuclear role of the Alliance would be firmly left under U.S. control. While Kennedy and the advocates of flexible response were highly supportive of the idea that the United States should increasingly disseminate nuclear knowledge and information to its Western European Allies in order for them to share in Allied nuclear policy, in reality Washington's position in flexible response was that centralized command and control was necessary for NATO nuclear forces, and its center was Washington.[69] NSAM40 even advocated U.S. control over French and British nuclear forces.[70] This was a tremendous break with Eisenhower's sincere efforts to work toward an MLF nuclear sharing scheme in the Alliance that would cultivate community-building and embrace West Germany as an equal. Further, a specific plan introduced earlier by Eisenhower whereby a fleet of five American Polaris missile submarines would be put under NATO control and act as a first step toward greater nuclear sharing in the Alliance was postponed by Kennedy.[71] The submarines were delivered to NATO only in 1963, but for different reasons and under different conditions than Eisenhower had envisioned: to correct the misgivings in the Alliance that ensued after the American-British meeting at Nassau.[72]

The Kennedy administration was aware of but not very sympathetic to the political dimensions of the independent nuclear force status issue in the Alliance. Reflective of Kennedy's position was an observation he had made in 1959:

We should face the fact that the fundamental purpose of the French atomic bomb is not to increase French capabilities but to increase its stature in the Alliance. The French bomb is aimed at Washington rather than Moscow. This is an odd way to run an alliance.[73]

Kennedy and others in his administration began promoting publicly the ideas behind flexible response at NATO meetings and elsewhere. In promoting flexible response, they were also condemning European independent nuclear forces, and reducing the MLF concept to one where Washington owned and controlled the proposed forces.

The reaction of the French and the West Germans to this idea, which was unilaterally introduced by Washington without prior consultation with the Allies, was swift and negative.[74] America's reneging on the equality of status issue and lack of consultation in the process were central to their resistance. Washington's espousal of flexible response only solidified de Gaulle's charge that the United States never desired to share power with its Western European Allies. His position hardened after the Nassau meeting between the United States and Great Britain, where the United States excepted the British nuclear force from its nonproliferation strictures.[75] In fact, having been taken "to the brink" by American security policy during the Cuban Missile Crisis, de Gaulle increased his efforts in promoting Western European independence from the United States after the episode, believing like many Europeans did that there should be no "annihilation without representation." Although de Gaulle supported Kennedy during the Cuban Missile Crisis, his initial reaction to Washington's unilateral action was, "are you informing me or consulting me?"[76] The importance of the independent French nuclear force also increased after this point.

The West German reaction was equally negative and voiced with particular vengeance by Defense Minister Strauss. West German resistance to Kennedy was reflected on many occasions. The West German demand for more nuclear sharing in NATO became pronounced after the erection of the Berlin Wall, when the Kennedy administration made clear that it was less than adamant in its support for German reunification. In 1961, Strauss unnerved many when he promoted at a NATO council meeting a NATO nuclear deterrent that would include participation of the FRG. Following de Gaulle's lead, Strauss had announced a month earlier in Georgetown that "possession of nuclear weapons, and control over these weapons, is becoming the symbol, and even the characteristic aspect, of the decisive criterion of sovereignty."[77]

In 1962, the reaction of the CDU/CSU, and again particularly that of Franz Josef Strauss, to flexible response was dual-edged. While maintaining Bonn's adherence to NATO and the U.S. guarantee, Strauss alluded to other security alternatives for West Germany, such as closer ties to France.[78] These pronouncements by Strauss coincided with and directly challenged the efforts of Kennedy and Robert McNamara in promoting flexible response and contained the implicit message that Bonn would not tolerate the erosion of West Germany's equality of status in the Alliance.

Thus, Kennedy's pragmatism and flexible response approach undermined the Wilsonian understanding of the Alliance. In attempting to move the Alliance in a more realistic direction regarding the important issues of nuclear weapons and their control, he threatened both the underlying influence of the Wilsonian impulse and the policy implications of the Versailles remedial. Ninkovich avers that Kennedy "threatened to throw Europe into nationalist nuclear-armed chaos."[79]

Particularly at a time when nuclear proliferation was growing, witnessed by France's and Great Britain's independent nuclear forces, and when movement in Franco-German relations challenged the trans-Atlantic link, fears of a resurgent Germany became more intense.[80] As Katherine Kelleher puts it,

Given the model of nuclear proliferation then in highest vogue—that proliferation was inevitable and Germany's insistent interventions through NATO and especially through bilateral channels, the expectation of imminent German claims for a direct share in nuclear weapons control was omnipresent.[81]

The concern over the future of West Germany might well have been stronger had it not been for the fact that the FRG was more protected by, and thus more eager to defend, the Wilsonian traits of the Alliance than were its allies. It became clear to the Kennedy administration that to halt the continued unraveling of Allied relations, some corrective was necessary. Again, Acheson's position is instructive. He reversed his earlier recommendations of 1961 and began promoting the MLF.[82] He was now in the company of those Wilsonians working to restore U.S.–West German relations.

The Wilsonians Strike Back

Increased agitation in Western Europe over Washington's demand for centralized control over Allied nuclear policy gave ascendancy to another group in Washington whose views on nuclear sharing were very different from those expressed in the McNamara version of flexible response. This other group consisted of State Department–based "Europeanists," or "theologians," and its concern was to create a truly multilateral NATO nuclear force. The group moved away from the notion that Washington should retain centralized control over nuclear weapons, and their position returned to the Eisenhower administration's earnest concern for collective sharing in the Alliance. As Thomas Schwartz notes, this group "hoped to use the offer to share control of nuclear weapons as a way to encourage the Europeans to create a single unified political executive that could share authority with an American President."[83]

West German Defense Minister Strauss was particularly prominent in waging the campaign for greater multilateralism on the nuclear control issue and thus reinforcing the State Department position. Harking on the principle of equality of status among allies as one of the central tenets of the Western security relationship, Strauss projected that "if NATO could not unite on the Norstad fourth-atomic-power plan or some acceptable substitute, not only would the future of the Western security system be uncertain, but the examples of Britain and France could easily find followers."[84] Strauss continued these barely concealed threats even after the State Department's MLF concept was formally introduced by the United States to the North Atlantic Council in June 1962.[85]

In his excellent study, *The Cybernetic Theory of Decision*, John D. Steinbruner discusses the historical ascendancy of the multilateral force issue in Washington decision-making circles. The victory of the MLF concept over other notions circulated at the time as remedies to the nuclear sharing problem in the Alliance set a precedent in postwar Allied military history.[86] Whereas previous changes in NATO military doctrine and force structure were advocated and implemented through regular military channels both in Washington and at NATO headquarters, as with the flexible response doctrine, the MLF was first raised and then pursued at the behest of the State Department, whose normal area of influence was obviously the political/diplomatic arena.

Thus, while the Kennedy administration continued espousing its version of flexible response out of one side of its mouth, it began seeking Allied support for a multilateral nuclear force out of the other. For a brief period, as the Kennedy administration worried about the possible repercussions of the Franco-German Friendship Treaty that was signed in 1962, the MLF was actively promoted.[87] However, once the fears of French-German collusion subsided with subsequent West German clarifications, Kennedy's tepid response to the nuclear sharing issue reemerged, and he insisted on including the changes he had made the previous year regarding American nuclear control. The core of Eisenhower's MLF scheme, to lay the foundations of a process through which real nuclear sharing would evolve in the Alliance, was thereby gutted. The lack of support for the project by Kennedy and many of his advisors is noted by Glen Seaborg in his study, *Stemming the Tide: Arms Control in the Johnson Years*. Kennedy was more ambivalent than Johnson in pushing the MLF concept domestically and abroad. In reference to Kennedy's domestic efforts at promoting MLF in contrast to more U.S.–Soviet detente-oriented policies, Seaborg states, "I believe Kennedy's attitude reflected his own continued ambivalence toward the MLF and a desire to husband all the senatorial goodwill possible for what he considered more important measures, such as a test ban."[88]

However, MLF did in fact reveal that Kennedy's obvious interest in breaking new ground in U.S.–Soviet relations and in reaching some sort of nonproliferation agreement with Moscow, and his administration's potential interest in creating in conjunction with the Soviets a denuclearized zone in Central Europe, were hampered by Bonn's interventions and counter-campaigns, aided by Wilsonians in Washington and in the State Department.[89] Bonn's insistence that demands of equality regarding the FRG's nuclear status be accommodated influenced the ascendancy of the State Department–sponsored MLF project on the Washington agenda. While Kennedy had stripped it of much of its original value, it still acted as an impediment to his relations with the Soviets. Richard Reeves, in his study, *President Kennedy: Profile of Power*, discusses an interesting example from 1963. In requesting from Kennedy a "sweetener" with which to move U.S.–Soviet cooperation forward, Ambassador Averell Harriman suggested that the president "throw in the MLF." Kennedy's response was; "Of course. . . . It would be great to get rid of that." He did not get rid of that.[90]

The episode of the MLF revealed the continued salience of the Wilsonian impulse and the Versailles remedial. Washington's support of the force was once again based primarily on political considerations. West German demands for nuclear sharing based on equality of status had again directly influenced the evolution of U.S. security policy. Dean Rusk stated that the force was envisioned "to prevent the strains and stresses that would arise if major nations like Germany and Italy would remain permanently in a second-class status in the nuclear age."[91] David Bruce stated of the MLF that one of the principle motives behind those in Washington who pushed the concept was the hope that it would allay any tendency or desire by Germany to have nuclear weapons of its own, but probably more importantly, that it would give the Germans a greater sense of participation in the operations of the NATO Alliance and would tie them even more firmly to the West rather than subject them to any temptations from the East.[92]

Once Johnson became president, his administration would push harder than its predecessor for the MLF cause among the Allies. The issue would cause serious strains in the U.S.–Soviet relationship, thereby undercutting the chances for real gains in detente even more.

CONCLUSIONS

In sum, shifts in perceptions and policy from one administration to the next did not simply accompany clear changes in the international system. Those shifts did indicate that Kennedy had different ideas from those of earlier administrations about U.S.–West German relations, nuclear policy, East-West relations, and so on. His different set of experiences led to different assumptions about international relations. In his operational code, Munich was more of a paradigm than was Versailles. For U.S. policy toward Western Europe and the Soviet Union, this phenomenon had tremendous consequences. Kennedy would pursue objectives that were often at variance with those of previous policymakers.

For Wilsonians, solving the German question peacefully and building a Western security community in the ashes of World War II was as vital an objective as meeting the Soviet threat, and at times even colored the way the threat was interpreted. The duality of goals formed the hybrid quality of the Alliance. For Kennedy, the focus was on the bipolar world where the Soviet superpower and nuclear weapons threatened stability. The objective was therefore to do what was necessary to stabilize that reality. To accomplish that, he approached the Alliance in a more traditionally realist way: that is, as a balance of power defense pact, with the United States as the undisputed leader. The Wilsonian impulse, or the objective of community-building to create a trans-Atlantic security community and shared culture, was very passive. The Kennedy administration would foreshadow the outright realist approach of the Nixon-Kissinger years.

Kennedy did end up often beholden to the old practices, however, since the Wilsonian impulse and Versailles remedial had in many ways become institutionalized into the standard operating procedures of the State Department. During the Kennedy administration, the consistent Wilsonian advocates came from State. Goldstein persuasively argues that ideas can become institutionalized over time and may continue to influence policy even after those ideas have been superseded by new ones.[93] Thus, as the Wilsonian impulse faded as a direct generational experience on presidents and some of their advisors, and the consensus thereby waned, its influence remained with select advisors at State and, as I shall argue, in the Alliance itself.

It is truly illuminating that JFK once said of the eighty-five-year-old Adenauer to Theodore Sorensen, Kennedy's longtime advisor and biographer, "I sense I'm talking not only to a different generation, but to a different era, a different world."[94] He was.

NOTES

1. Joseph Kraft, *The Grand Design* (New York: Harper and Brothers, 1962), p. 22.

2. Henry Kissinger, *Diplomacy* (New York: Simon and Schuster, 1994), p. 613.

3. Kraft, *The Grand Design*, p. 64.

4. Tony Smith, in chapter 8 of *America's Mission: The United States and the Worldwide Struggle for Democracy in the Twentieth Century* (Princeton, N.J.: Princeton University Press, 1994) has an interesting discussion of Kennedy's "neo-Wilsonian" approach in Latin America through the Alliance for Progress program.

5. Steve Weber, "Shaping the Postwar Balance of Power: Multilateralism in NATO," in *Multilateralism Matters: The Theory and Praxis of an Institutional Form*, ed. John G. Ruggie (New York: Columbia University Press, 1993), pp. 233–92.

6. Ibid., p. 266.

7. Ibid., p. 269.

8. See Yuen Foong Khong, *Analogies at War: Korea, Munich, Dien Bien Phu, and the Vietnam Decisions of 1965* (Princeton, N.J.: Princeton University Press, 1992), esp. chs. 4, 7.

9. On the significance of images and their effects on policymakers' perceptions of and orientation to international politics, see Richard Ned Lebow, "Generational Learning and Conflict Management," *International Journal* 40 (Autumn 1985), esp. pp. 555–59.

10. John F. Kennedy, "Appeasement at Munich: The Inevitable Result of the Slowness of Conversion of the British Democracy from a Disarmament to a Rearmament Policy," JFK Library, March 15, 1940.

11. It did take some time for JFK to reject his father's position regarding Germany and appeasement. See discussion in Nigel Hamilton, *JFK: Reckless Youth* (New York: Random House, 1992), esp. Part 6.

12. He did write a League of Nations paper during his senior year at Harvard, but it was another vehicle through which to criticize British inaction in the interwar years. See Hamilton, *JFK: Reckless Youth*, pp. 301–2.

13. Hamilton, *JFK: Reckless Youth*, esp. pp. 695–701.

14. Khong, *Analogies at War*, esp. chs. 4, 7. For example, on p. 177, he argues that Vice-President Johnson and Secretary of State Dean Rusk were the two actors in the Kennedy administration most beholden to the Munich analogy, and that they were not the central players.

15. John Lewis Gaddis, *Strategies of Containment: A Critical Appraisal of Postwar American National Security Policy* (New York: Oxford University Press, 1982), p. 201.

While Gaddis links Kennedy's position to those held earlier by Dulles and Eisenhower, I have argued that the Eisenhower administration was in fact much more influenced by Wilsonianism than traditional analyses suggest.

16. Douglas Brinkley, *Dean Acheson: The Cold War Years, 1953–71* (New Haven, Conn.: Yale University Press, 1992), p. 187.

17. Richard Reeves, *President Kennedy: Profile of Power* (New York: Simon and Schuster, 1993), p. 455.

18. Ninkovich, *Modernity and Power*, pp. 245–247.

19. See "Memorandum for the President," April 6, 1961, JFK Library, Box 117, Collection: POF Countries-Germany-Genera 9/62–12/62, Folder: Germany-Security-Adenauer Meeting-General 4/61. In the memorandum, Kennedy was briefed about the psychological and political dispositions of Adenauer specifically and West Germans generally. On p. 1, he is warned that: "Many Germans, including Adenauer, fear that we will make unwarranted (from the German point of view) concessions on the Oder-Neisse line and on Berlin. There has been a profound misunderstanding about the nature and motives of the reassessment of our strategy." Kennedy is then advised to use an upcoming meeting with Adenauer to dispel such misapprehensions.

20. Kelleher, *Germany and the Politics of Nuclear Weapons*, p. 192.

21. See Frank Ninkovich, *Modernity and Power: A History of the Domino Theory in the Twentieth Century* (Chicago: University of Chicago Press, 1994), p. 254. He states that Kennedy came closest of any administration since World War II to recognizing spheres of influence.

22. John F. Kennedy, quoted in Thomas Alan Schwartz, "Victories and Defeats in the Long Twilight Struggle: The United States and Western Europe in the 1960s," in *The Diplomacy of the Crucial Decade: American Foreign Relations During the 1960s*, ed. Diane B. Kunz (New York: Columbia University Press, 1994), pp. 114–48, quotation on p. 119.

23. McGeorge Bundy, "Memorandum for the President," October 18, 1961, JFK Library, Box 117; Collection: POF Countries—Germany-General 9/62–12/62; Folder: Germany; Security 8/61–12/61, p. 1.

24. Arthur M. Schlesinger, Jr., *A Thousand Days: John F. Kennedy in the White House* (Boston: Houghton Mifflin, 1965), p. 404.

25. See Ninkovich, *Modernity and Power*, p. 264. He cites an RFK oral interview.

26. E. V. Rostow, in letter to Chester Bowles, June 16, 1961, JFK Library, Box #75-81, Collection Title: NSF; Folder: Countries—Germany; Berlin; General, 6/16/61; Correspondence: E. V. Rostow to Chester Bowles, p. 2.

27. McGeorge Bundy, quoted in Schwartz, "Victories and Defeats," p. 122.

28. Ninkovich, *Modernity and Power*, p. 249.

29. See John F. Kennedy, in "Memorandum for Record; Discussion at NSC meeting June 29, 1961," JFK Library, Box: 313, Collection: NSC Meeting and Memoranda; NSC Meetings 475–507, Folder: NSC Meetings 1961, No. 486; 6/29/61, p. 2.

30. Ninkovich, *Modernity and Power*, p. 249.

31. "Memorandum for Record; Discussion at NSC meeting June 29, 1961," p. 2.

32. John F. Kennedy, quoted in Schwartz, "Victories and Defeats," p. 122.

33. Draft Letter from Averell Harriman to JFK from September 1, 1961, JFK Library, Box: 82, Collection: NSF Countries, Folder: Germany Berlin General

8/29/61, pp. 1–5. Quotation on p. 5. Also see Kelleher, *Germany and the Politics of Nuclear Weapons*, p. 200.

34. Carl Kaysen, "Thoughts on Berlin, 8/22/61," JFK Library, Box 82, Collection: NSF Countries, Folder: Berlin General Kaysen Memo 8/22/61, pp. 1–12. Kaysen continues by saying that we should pursue "agreement on the proposition that unification can come about only by discussion between the two German governments, and, accordingly, initiation of such discussions; and . . . discussion of mutual security guarantees for both Germanys by the Warsaw and NATO nations, including the creation of a nuclear-free zone in Germany." (pp. 9–10) On p. 10, Kaysen clearly advocates recognition of the GDR as being both in U.S. and West German interests.

35. Ibid., p. 6.

36. *Times* article from June 1961, cited in Kern Montague, Patricia W. Levering, and Ralph B. Levering, *The Kennedy Crisis: The Press, the Presidency, and Foreign Policy* (Chapel Hill: University of North Carolina Press, 1983), p. 67. Also see Schwartz, "Victories and Defeats," p. 125.

37. Schwartz, "Victories and Defeats," p. 128.

38. "Willy Brandt's Views on Berlin and Related Subjects," Incoming Airgram to Secretary of State, March 4, 1961, JFK Library, Box 117, Collection: POF Countries-Germany-General, 9/62–12/62, Folder: German Security 1/61–6/61, p. 2. Brandt actually backed Adenauer's insistence that the Berlin question not be delinked from the more general East-West agenda, a position that failed.

39. "Willy Brandt's Views," p. 1.

40. Karsten Voigt, background interview, July 7, 1986, Bonn, West Germany. Although not a member of the Brandt generation that experienced the Wall in a direct fashion, Voigt was quite emphatic on the point.

41. Ibid., my translation. See also discussion in Ninkovich, *Modernity and Power*, p. 253.

42. Ninkovich, *Modernity and Power*, p. 250.

43. James L. Robinson, *Germany and the Atlantic Alliance: The Interaction of Strategy and Politics* (Cambridge: Harvard University Press, 1966), p. 292.

44. In *Germany and the Atlantic Alliance*, Robinson observes that this delinking was a concession on the part of Bonn in the sense that during the Eisenhower administration, Adenauer had succeeded in linking the two agendas as an offensive tactic in the East-West dialogue, as "a reassertion of the Western policy for German unity as a prerequisite for a settlement."

45. "Memorandum of Conversation, March 21, 1963," JFK Library, p. 6.

46. Ninkovich, *Modernity and Power*, quote on p. 257. See his interesting discussion of the United States versus de Gaulle and their competing visions for Europe on pp. 257–58.

47. Adenauer, *Erinnerungen*, pp. 136–52.

48. See discussion by Alfred Grosser in *The Western Alliance: European-American Relations Since 1945* (New York: Vintage Books, 1984), pp. 207–8. Adenauer is also criticized by some in the FRG for forfeiting this opportunity to forge much closer bilateral relations between France and the FRG. In a background interview with Dr. Paul Frank, conducted in Hinterzarten, FRG in 1986, this position was made clear. Also see Frank's criticisms of both Adenauer and De Gaulle in *Entschluesselte*

Botschaft: Ein Diplomat macht Inventur (Munich: Deutscher Taschenbuch Verlag, 1985), pp. 89–98.

49. Dean Acheson, quoted in Brinkley, *Dean Acheson*, p. 192.

50. Ninkovich, *Modernity and Power*, p. 258.

51. Ninkovich, *Modernity and Power*, p. 281.

52. Dean Acheson, quoted in Brinkley, *Dean Acheson*, p. 193.

53. Ibid., p. 197; the second half of the quote is from Acheson. It is very interesting to note that Brinkley quotes Acheson on page 198 as saying that Germany was "the most important country in the world to us."

54. Frank, *Enschluesselte Botschaft*, p. 94.

55. "Memorandum of Conversation, March 22, 1963," JFK Library, Box 75-81, Collection: NSF, Folder: Countries-Germany Subjects von Brentano Visit 3/63 (2), pp. 1, 2. The Kennedy administration remained obviously uneasy with the Franco-German treaty. Also see "Memorandum of Conversation, March 21, 1963," JFK Library, Box 75-81, Collection: NDF, Folder: Countries-Germany Subjects von Brentano Visit 3/63 (1), p. 2. Thus, although von Brentano suggested that the FRG was in a good position to try to influence de Gaulle away from his present disruptive course, Washington's worry lay with the FRG. On page 4 it was stated that "the real test lay in the policies which the German Government would be pursuing."

56. Charles de Gaulle, quoted in Grosser, *The Western Alliance*, p. 208.

57. See Ninkovich's similar conclusion in *Modernity and Power*, p. 255. He says that because of Kennedy's actions, trans-Atlantic bonds faltered, and that the administration, "which had ambitions at first of implementing a 'Grand Design' that would tie an increasingly united and self-confident Europe into a greater Atlantic community, found itself hard-pressed merely to preserve the alliance, much less to improve upon it."

58. Montague, Levering, and Levering, *The Kennedy Crisis*, pp. 69, 70.

59. Ibid., pp. 70–71. On p. 71, it is stated: "Higgins, who had no qualms about marching in and talking with Robert Kennedy or his brother, the president, experienced no trouble obtaining a hearing in an administration that was as sensitive about press coverage as Kennedy's was."

60. Ibid., pp. 75–78. Also, on page 394, Schlesinger states in *A Thousand Days* that Dean Rusk met with the three Western allies in Paris during early August 1961. When Rusk suggested the possibility of calling for negotiations with the Soviets, deGaulle flatly refused, arguing that "the opening of negotiations would be considered immediately as a prelude to the abandonment, at least gradually, of Berlin and as a sort of notice of our surrender." The meeting broke up with no positive results, but left Schlesinger to wonder whether "if it had produced an invitation to Moscow to discuss the crisis, the Russians would have dared carry through the drastic action they were preparing for the next weekend."

61. See Ninkovich's discussion in *Modernity and Power*, pp. 262–63.

62. I want to reiterate that Kennedy's concern in both his thesis and book was for the slow and haphazard manner in which Western democracies, especially Great Britain, rearmed to fight Hitler.

63. General Lauris Norstad, in "Oral History Interview with General Lauris Norstad," DDE Library, Folder: OH 385, Nov. 11, 1976, pp. 50, 51.

64. Ibid., p. 52.

65. General Lauris Norstad, quoted in a letter from Norstad to the president, November 1, 1962, JFK Library, Box 103, Collection: POF Subjects Part B-NATO-Norstad Meetings, Folder: NATO-General 1/61–4/61, p. 2.

66. Helga Haftendorn, *Security and Detente: Conflicting Priorities in German Foreign Policy* (New York: Praeger, 1985), p. 107.

67. David N. Schwartz, *NATO's Nuclear Dilemmas* (Washington, D.C.: The Brookings Institute, 1983), p. 152.

68. For more detailed discussions of flexible response, see, among others, ibid., pp. 136–92, and Kelleher, *Germany and the Politics of Nuclear Weapons*, pp. 156–202.

69. Kelleher, *Germany and the Politics of Nuclear Weapons*, p. 182.

70. Weber, "Shaping the Postwar Balance of Power," p. 263.

71. See ibid., pp. 261, 263. See also Brinkley, *Dean Acheson*, p. 129. On a mission for Kennedy in April 1961, Acheson visited Adenauer and informed him of this change in American policy. Adenauer was not happy.

72. See discussion in Theodore C. Sorensen, *Kennedy* (New York: Harper and Row, 1965), pp. 564–76.

73. John F. Kennedy, in Alan Nevins, ed., *The Strategy of Peace* (New York: Harper and Brothers, 1960), p. 100.

74. Schwartz, *NATO's Nuclear Dilemmas*, pp. 165–73.

75. Ibid., pp. 165–67.

76. James A. Nathan and James K. Oliver, *United States Foreign Policy and World Order* (Glenview, Ill.: Scott, Foresman, 1989). De Gaulle, quoted on p. 247.

77. Franz Josef Strauss, quoted in Kraft, *The Grand Design*, p. 53.

78. Haftendorn, *Security and Detente*, p. 107.

79. The Wilsonian understanding was what Ninkovich calls the "international-ist resolve," which was needed for "maintaining the alliance and a cohesive world opinion resistant to Communist expansion." Ninkovich, *Modernity and Power*, p. 273.

80. Adenauer, *Erinnerungen*, pp. 105–8.

81. Kelleher, *Germany and the Politics of Nuclear Weapons*, p. 180.

82. Brinkley, *Dean Acheson*, p. 199.

83. Schwartz, "Victories and Defeats," p. 129.

84. Kelleher, *Germany and the Politics of Nuclear Weapons*, p. 186.

85. Ibid., p. 190. Kelleher cites Strauss's campaign to speed acceptance of the MLF. In one instance, "he reportedly told American officials that an MLF with participation scaled to national achievements was the last chance to meet German strategic requirements and prevent future 'destabilizing developments.' "

86. John D. Steinbruner, *The Cybernetic Theory of Decision: New Dimensions of Political Analysis* (Princeton, N.J.: Princeton University Press, 1974), pp. 194–97.

87. Schwartz, "Victories and Defeats," p. 131.

88. Glenn T. Seaborg with Benjamin S. Loeb, *Stemming the Tide: Arms Control in the Johnson Years* (Lexington, Mass.: Lexington Books, 1987), p. 89.

89. Kelleher, *Germany and the Politics of Nuclear Weapons*, p. 187. She discusses Bonn's leaking verbatim information to the press concerning Washington's plans for a proliferation treaty, in an effort to frustrate interest both in America and the Soviet Union.

90. Reeves, *President Kennedy*, p. 546.

91. "Memorandum for the Record; October 20, 1964," LBJ Library, NSF; Files of McGeorge Bundy, Container: 18, 19, Folder: Misc. Meetings Volume 1, p. 2.

92. Bruce, "Interview with David Bruce," pp. 5–6.

93. Judith Goldstein, *Ideas, Interests, and American Trade Policy* (Ithaca, N.Y.: Cornell University Press, 1993), esp. chs. 3, 6.

94. John F. Kennedy, quoted in Sorensen, *Kennedy*, p. 559.

Chapter 4 _____

RESTORING THE ATLANTIC COMMUNITY UNDER JOHNSON

After the shocks suffered in the Western security relationship by de Gaulle's and the Kennedy administration's assaults on its community-building culture, attempts were made in both Washington and Bonn to recapture the Allied understanding that had been established earlier. The Johnson administration was keen to recapture the Allied consensus on which West German loyalty had been predicated and to undo the damage to the Western security relationship that had been accumulating since the early 1960s. As noted in the last chapter, the problem reflected the Kennedy administration's neglect of the Wilsonian impulse and its legacy by emphasizing the U.S. postwar security objective of thwarting the Soviet threat at the expense of creating an Atlantic community.

My argument in this chapter contrasts a great deal with many made elsewhere. For example, Ninkovich argues that Johnson was even more willing than Kennedy to move "further away from Germany by jettisoning some of the basics of its former German policy."[1] He goes further in claiming that Johnson, like Kennedy, wanted to abandon the pretense of supporting German unification, but was officially constrained, even though the West Germans were themselves aware of the sham policy.[2]

Frank Costigliola interprets Johnson's policies toward the West Germans, especially regarding MLF, as driven by fear of the Germans and his desire to manipulate them. It was his fear of a nationalist, aggressive Germany that explained his attempts to contain Bonn through MLF and other tactics. Costigliola criticizes Johnson and his advisors, particularly those at State, for patronizing the constantly worried West Germans.[3]

Whatever LBJ's beliefs concerning the West Germans, he allowed himself to be heavily influenced by the Wilsonian impulse through key advisors and the State Department. Whether or not those "Europeanists" at State, the "theologian" Wilsonians, patronized the West Germans did not detract from the fact that they remained beholden to the ordering principles of the Wilsonian impulse and Versailles remedial, which guaranteed Bonn continued influence on the American security agenda.[4] By the end of his term, LBJ had allowed the West Germans to influence significantly movement on the Nonproliferation Treaty (NPT). Further, growing concern about his administration's lack of attention to the needs of West Germany and the Alliance led him to give the green light to U.S. acceptance of the Allied Harmel Report of 1967. As will be shown, due to the attention Johnson and his top advisors were devoting to the Vietnam crisis, it was left mainly to representatives from the State Department to negotiate the Harmel Report. Harmel would enhance West German influence in East-West relations and continue to institutionalize the Wilsonian impulse in NATO.

Supporting the claim that Johnson was "sympathetic as always to the German point of view,"[5] pro–West German and Western European State Department representatives maintained a high profile in the Johnson administration on Allied security matters. They in fact captured Johnson's attention immediately after Kennedy's assassination, convincing him of the importance of nuclear sharing and of the U.S. commitment to the MLF.[6]

Their positions often conflicted with other cabinet positions such as those of the Defense Department, thus causing an ongoing rift in the Johnson administration.[7] For example, the continued influence of John J. McCloy, an important Wilsonian braintruster who had been the American high commissioner in Germany, often competed with the preferences of Secretary of Defense Robert McNamara.[8] In a 1968 interview, Eugene Rostow recalled that

McCloy favored the State Department's position against cutting troops in West Europe, while MacNamara and the Defense Department were inclined to favor such cuts. McCloy was a man of great prestige, especially in Germany—a man of great ability.... You see McNamara was trying to get rid of him, trying to fire him. McCloy was very strong, had very powerful ideas.... So it was a very deep and well-conceived thing to try to fortify his own position within the government, because McNamara was pushing hard for a massive cut. And McCloy had prestige in certain circles in Congress, too, you see.[9]

The powerful position of people like McCloy revealed a renewed sensitivity to Bonn and its interests, as highlighted in a memo written by McCloy in 1967, during the important Trilateral Negotiations:

Today, what with the non-proliferation treaty, the strong emphasis upon detente with the Soviet Union and the threatened withdrawals of United States troops, make the Germans feel isolated and a prey to a new form of nationalism based on Gaullism. NATO was not set up for the purpose of surrounding the Germans or encompassing them. But the validity of NATO was that even though it was primarily designed for the defense of Europe, it did furnish a solid position for Germany to occupy in Western Europe without the feeling of separation and isolation which followed World War I.[10]

President Lyndon Johnson, under the influence of Wilsonians like McCloy, returned largely to the approach of the Eisenhower administration. Thus, while there was not a consensus among all major players in the Johnson administration, there were enough Wilsonians in prominent and influential roles to move LBJ toward the positions of the Eisenhower administration. The operational code defined by the Versailles remedial was back in evidence, as was the Wilsonian impulse focus on community-building and the adherence to such principles as equality of status.

McCloy constantly reminded Johnson of the dangers that loomed in abandoning West German demands for equality in favor of progress in the U.S.–Soviet relationship. In one memorandum to the president, and much as Dulles had done ten years earlier, McCloy actively combined the Wilsonian impulse and Versailles remedial by emphasizing the important principle of equality of status for West Germany in considering the MLF versus nonproliferation (U.S.–Soviet relations) debate:

We made a mistake after World War I in our treatment of Germany and we shall be making much the same mistake in respect of Germany now if we take the attitude that we owe nothing to the Germans and "to hell with them anyway." Poincare was wrong in 1919 and so is de Gaulle in 1965. The Germans must be given a position of equality with the other Western powers if they are not, in due course, to go off on another nationalist adventure.[11]

McCloy remained steadfast and clear on his grand design for Europe. He said at one point to Acheson during the debate on German rearmament in the 1950s that he wanted to assure Germany's place in a "collective security system adequate to cope with the Soviet challenge."[12] Later, during the Johnson administration, he remained true to that conviction. He relayed in the memorandum cited above the following:

In talking about the risks of proliferation and the dangers of offending the Soviets or the Gaullists, I think we have lost sight of the deep significance of the Alliance and of the concept of collective security for the Atlantic World, which has been the keystone of our post-war policy. Under present circumstances, if we allow matters to drift along for an indefinite period, say till after the German elections in 1965, we shall see an ever-accelerating deterioration of the Alliance and the Collective security concept we took such pains to build after the close of the war.[13]

As I have been arguing, Wilsonians like McCloy combined into one hybrid framework the traditional defense pact and the Wilsonian security community—NATO. Thus, the Johnson administration would work toward rebuilding the community aspects of the Western Alliance harmed during the Kennedy administration, without undermining defense. However, the problem of reestablishing a balance was exacerbated by the Soviets' increase in military capabilities during the 1960s. The situation led to a search for political compensation in order to assure the principle of equality of status. The result was the Harmel Report of 1967, a Western European–, West German–inspired Alliance finding that was incorporated as policy and would open the door to immense changes in international relations. Its stipulation was simple: Detente and defense were co-equal aspects of NATO policy. While the United States obviously had the monopoly in the latter category, the inclusion of the detente component invited a diversity of political and economic approaches to East-West tensions and assured equal opportunity in that regard among the Allies. When the SPD assumed power in 1969, it would take full advantage of those new opportunities.

HOLDING THE LINE OPEN ON THE MLF

The final withering away of the MLF concept and the eventual success of the Nonproliferation Treaty coincided with the changing of the guard in Bonn. This coincidence of developments does not appear to have been accidental. While most analysts and observers claim that Johnson's speech of December 1964 was the actual death date of the MLF concept in Washington,[14] when he gave his speech withdrawing the active U.S. role of leading Europe on the issue, the American unwillingness to reject the project outright served to keep the issue alive and contentious until late in 1966. It is inaccurate to assume that Johnson's decision not to push MLF on a lukewarm audience in Europe meant an outright rejection of the policy.

In fact, Washington sent extremely mixed messages on the MLF after December 1964, reflecting the divergences within the Johnson administration concerning the matter. It was true enough that many high officials wanted more progress in U.S.–Soviet relations, especially on the NPT, and were thus ready to see the MLF "sink out of sight."[15] By 1964, the Soviets were pressing the United States to drop the provocative MLF and opt for negotiations on a nuclear nonproliferation treaty, in which Johnson was very interested.[16] The MLF was also causing tremendous problems with the British and French by the end of 1964, and domestic opposition in the United States had mounted.

Once again, however, State Department representatives such as George Ball and Dean Rusk were unwilling to back completely away from the issue.[17] While authors like Costigliola interpret U.S. policy from the end of 1964 through the death of the MLF in 1966 as a cynical manipulation of "Germany's desires for security," Costigliola's analysis reflects in fact what I interpret to be a continuing division in the Johnson administration between the so-called "theologians" and the anti-MLF advisors, or the realists.[18] The lack of consensus largely explains the skewed MLF approach through 1966.

In a telegram to the secretary of state dated December 19, 1964, General Douglas MacArthur weighed in with the Versailles lesson:

I observed that it seemed to me deGaulle wished to keep Germany in permanent state of second class citizenship re nuclear defense matters and if this were true it could create major problems and would probably not be more successful than Treaty of Versailles. I thought it would be great error for other European states to join with French in trying [to] impose any diktat on Germany. What was needed were constructive steps that would tie Germany in to Western Europe on basis of equality and its vital interests which included defense.[19]

Voices like these convinced the president that while the MLF project had become increasingly problematic and probably infeasible, the United States should not abandon it completely. Contrary to common wisdom, Johnson did not finally drop the MLF until 1966, and then only after it became clear that it had lost its appeal in the West German domestic context.[20] McGeorge Bundy wrote to Johnson in December that "the Germans are watching us like hawks to see whether we are letting them down on this."[21] The result of Washington's so-called cooling on the MLF was that some MLF enthusiasts resigned, but the State Department instructed U.S. embassies in Europe not to treat the MLF as a dead issue.

Throughout 1965 influential members of the State Department remained sympathetic to, and in some cases insistent on, keeping the collective nuclear force concept alive. McCloy's State connections reinforced the department's influence. Many in the State Department, especially in Bonn and in the European Bureau, continued the argument that equality of status for West Germany included the issue of nuclear status. As Ninkovich observes, these officials believed "that German opinion would not tolerate exclusion from the nuclear club."[22]

In October of that year, John Leddy of the State Department stated that continuation of the perceived uncertainty of the U.S. stand on MLF would weaken the alliance, and further that

The controversy which has surrounded the issue of non-proliferation would intensify and pressures would mount for concessions to the USSR at the expense of

Germany. In order to arrive at a decision in concert with the Germans and the British the U.S. should be prepared to accept some form of a collective weapons system. I believe that this would not only be the safest approach to the German problem in the longer run but also that this will turn out to be the alternative which the Germans themselves would prefer.[23]

McCloy was even more emphatic. He argued that the decision to "go easy" on the MLF, "to put the ball in the court of the Europeans," was already a "great triumph for de Gaulle and for his opposition to the collective security of a Europe united and in partnership with the United States." As McCloy perceived it, such a pattern of behavior invited the rebirth of nationalism in Europe, "caused an increasing fragmentation of the once steadfast German position," and "increased the threat of eventual German possession of a national nuclear weapon."[24] Arguments like those made by McCloy assured that the MLF would not be rejected out of hand.

The result was to hold the line open on the issue. Reflective of this American posture toward MLF, despite intense domestic and foreign pressure to drop it, was a conversation held in November 1965 between Dr. Kurt Birrenbach, CDU member of the Bundestag and advisor to Chancellor Erhard, and high-ranking members of the Johnson administration, such as Rusk, McNamara, Ball, Bundy, and Assistant Secretary Leddy. It is clear from the discussion that members of the U.S. team were trying to feel out the West German position regarding MLF and alternative options to the nuclear sharing problem, and that in return Birrenbach pushed strongly for recognition in any option of Allied responsibility for the German question and West German equality of status on the nuclear issue. For example, Dr. Birrenbach stated that "the Federal Republic should be an integral part of a common nuclear weapons system," one that would, among other things, "provide for equality among the European members; and it should have a European clause in the event of European union and a reunification clause in the event of reunification of Germany."[25] Linking the MLF to the nonproliferation treaty, Birrenbach further advised the United States to continue holding "all nuclear options open, that it should not go beyond the present wording of the US draft treaty."[26]

Although it flies in the face of common wisdom concerning the MLF, it is clear from this conversation that U.S. officials were still in the process of determining how to approach it. Reflecting my earlier point that the Johnson administration's surrender of its activist role regarding MLF did not mean its outright rejection of the policy, Rusk stated to Birrenbach that "The United States had sought to lead before, but Europe was unable to follow and we had gotten nowhere. . . . If the United States is to come forward with proposals, we must be sure that they will be accepted."[27]

Upon stating this, Rusk went on to question Birrenbach about the problems Bonn faced with Great Britain and France regarding MLF and the equality of status issue. Obviously, American policymakers were sensitive to the fact that Great Britain's and now France's independent nuclear status contributed to the FRG's anxiety about retaining equality of status. Rusk "asked what problems de Gaulle might cause for Germany if we were to proceed with a common nuclear weapons system."[28]

During the remainder of the conversation the American representatives, led by McNamara, tried to dissuade Birrenbach from viewing MLF, or hardware solutions in general, as the only alternative in Bonn's quest for equality of status on the nuclear issue, especially in the face of outright French and British opposition to the project.[29] Birrenbach did not back down. Rusk concluded that West Germany "should not be discriminated against," and that the United States "must explore the equality concept." While less than optimistic regarding convincing France, Rusk advocated "intimate" talks between the FRG, Great Britain, and Italy.

Finally, Rusk stated that the United States is "not prepared to give the Soviets a veto over NATO questions."[30] Indeed, alongside the strident objections of important allies, Soviet remonstrations against the MLF mounted through 1964 and 1965. Much as with some of Bonn's West European allies, the Soviets' biggest fear was the possibility of a West German finger on the nuclear trigger. As Seaborg observes, "there was no fear more deeply rooted in the Russian psyche at this time than that of a revanchist Germany with nuclear weapons."[31]

Despite reassurances from Birrenbach, it is clear that the MLF issue was at this time causing tremendous problems in Bonn regarding West German–French relations. By the end of 1964, the French attitude toward the MLF had turned "from scornful indifference to vigorous opposition."[32] Great Britain also went from ambivalence to open hostility to the idea by early 1965, and voiced political objections. First among these, and one that was common in Europe and the Soviet Union, was the fear of a nuclear Germany.[33] The British also duly noted that the force was "both expensive and strategically unnecessary."[34]

By October 1965, West German domestic opinion was itself split on MLF, with the West German Gaullists, led by Franz Josef Strauss and Adenauer among others, in clear opposition.[35] Adenauer by 1965 was complaining about the bankruptcy of the MLF.[36] In State Department memos from the time, key members of the CDU, such as Rainer Barzel, were reported as considering the MLF "dead," although they still advocated "a solution to the nuclear problem which would give the FedRep a greater role in the nuclear deterrent."[37] Costigliola interprets U.S. policy at this time to be highly manipulative by actually encouraging French and British resistance to the MLF, while appearing still sympathetic to the West Germans.[38] If the Americans' plan was to be manipulative, however, they appear to have been trapped in their own web of intrigue, since the MLF was still being discussed seriously.

As interest grew in the USSR and the West, particularly in Great Britain, for a nonproliferation treaty, Soviet willingness to proceed hinged specifically on Washington dropping the MLF, and any clause allowing Bonn access to nuclear weapons.[39] In fact, propaganda value notwithstanding,[40] it is clear that Soviet interest in a nonproliferation treaty was largely inspired by its fear of a nuclear Germany. The Soviets further threatened that West German participation in something like an MLF would hinder any movement toward German reunification.[41] The U.S. refusal to concede, supported and prompted by Bonn, stymied progress on the nonproliferation treaty and negatively affected Washington's relations with Moscow, Paris, and London.[42] The American refusal to drop the issue thus retarded movement for the West in reaching a nonproliferation agreement with the Soviets until the end of 1966.

Keenly interested in a nonproliferation treaty, the British presented a draft of a treaty in June 1965. The British version recommended that existing nuclear states retain veto power over the use of nuclear weapons by any future collective nuclear force. In presenting this concept, the British ran head-on into the Germans, who were not yet prepared to give up completely on the MLF and its promise of a measure of multilateral control. The United States then made an alternative suggestion that tended to support the Germans more than the British, and the latter did not take kindly to that. Secretary of State Dean Rusk observed that "NATO had never before been confronted with so sharp a disagreement between the U.S. and the U.K."[43]

What is remarkable, then, is that Washington was still discussing the MLF at all seriously at this date, given the immense pressures to drop the project. These pressures came from domestic sources as well. Many members of the U.S. military establishment were against the MLF, for the oft-cited and by now obvious reason that the project had little military value.[44] Further pressures emanated from the U.S. Congress, and particularly from members of the Joint Committee on Atomic Energy (JCAE) and from liberal senators. The main concern in the JCAE was that MLF threatened to strike a blow at U.S. security and had the potential of surrendering the American veto over the use of nuclear weapons, a position echoing that of the Kennedy administration and reflecting a clear particularistic concern.

For the liberal senators, including such prominent people as Eugene McCarthy, George McGovern, and Gaylord Nelson, the MLF could potentially "further imperil the prospects of arms control and divide the NATO alliance, all without adding to the defensive security of the United States."[45] Pressure to drop the MLF existed in the cabinet as well, especially among members of the Defense Department, McNamara in particular. During the October 1965 discussion with Birrenbach, McNamara reiterated the most common objection to MLF: that there "was no military requirement for such a system."[46] Finally, again the fear of a nuclear West Germany contributed to domestic opposition to the MLF.[47]

Noteworthy about the final demise of MLF, which faded into oblivion during 1966, is the fact that it disappeared completely from the U.S. agenda only after it became clear that Bonn was not willing to pursue the project actively in the absence of American leadership.[48] For example, reacting to Western interest in a nonproliferation treaty, the Erhard government in the summer of 1965 expressed "renewed German interest in a MLF."[49] Yet, Bonn then actually requested of Washington that MLF discussions be halted until the results of the West German national election in September 1965 were in. In a communiqué issued by State following a visit by the West German ambassador to the secretary of state, it was stated that "we must be very clear that US shift on MLF was based solely on expressed FRG desire to keep matter quiet before elections and was strictly responsive to Bonn wishes."[50] Kelleher quotes a West German during this period as saying of the public discussion in the FRG concerning MLF, "the silence was deafening."[51] After the elections, the State Department portrayed the West German position on MLF as still uncertain:

The situation in regard to the ANF//MLF has not basically changed following the German election. The Germans, who are most interested in the matter, remain divided and unsure about just what they want, although their general concern for an augmented "nuclear" role in the Alliance is clear.[52]

Hanrieder and others interpret the evolution of the MLF as showing Washington's lack of interest in the issue as the Johnson administration turned increasingly to its relations with the Soviet Union. In fact, he posits that America's "about face" on the issue in 1965 helped bring down the Erhard government in 1966, and proved that the United States was easily willing to sacrifice the MLF for such "vital" national interests as "a detente with the Soviet Union, an arms control agreement, and the need to nurture Soviet-American relations."[53]

I have made the case that the MLF was *not* a dead issue in Washington in 1965. Before discussing the West German domestic context, I want to counter again the claim that the United States was not interested in the MLF and so it died. Kelleher emphasizes that the change in Washington's position was one that shifted the center of leadership on MLF away from Washington and onto interested West European states, notably West Germany. Bonn's commitment was now "a necessary rather than a sufficient condition."[54] As I have argued, this was neither a fundamental shift in policy nor an outright rejection of the MLF concept.

Schwartz argues that Johnson's turning away from a Euro-centered foreign policy accompanied his rejection of the MLF, while Costigliola characterizes LBJ's MLF policy by 1965 as extremely manipulative, which would have required a concentrated effort on the part of Johnson.[55] I argue instead that Johnson's increasing preoccupation with his Vietnam policy meant a benign neglect of Europe and granted to the MLF and other Bonn-friendly policies extended life through State's continued focus on the trans-Atlantic community via the ordering principles of the Wilsonian impulse. Thus, LBJ held the door open on the MLF straight through 1966. It is not at all clear what Washington's policy might have been had Bonn decided to pursue actively the MLF option.[56]

In fact, the MLF was actually not yet dead in the spring of 1966 when McGeorge Bundy resigned as national security advisor and was replaced by Walt Rostow, a known MLF supporter.[57] It was because of West German domestic factionalization on the issue and external pressures from Paris, Moscow, and London, that West German policymakers were not willing to push the project. It was also at this time that a break in the West German domestic position became evident. As noted above, both members of the SPD and the CDU were by now expressing interest in alternative solutions to the nuclear sharing problem. After the election of the Grand Coalition in November 1966, the MLF disappeared almost completely in the FRG as an issue.

The timing of this phenomenon is indeed significant. The SPD, now a partner in the coalition government, had been consistently against a so-called "hardware solution" to Bonn's nuclear role.[58] After this date, Bonn placed more emphasis on the importance of the Nuclear Planning Group, created in February 1966, for allowing West German participation in Allied nuclear planning and strategy. Only after this leadership change did Washington drop MLF completely as an issue and pursue in earnest the nonproliferation treaty with Moscow.[59] Even then, as I will discuss below, the treaty remained vague on the multilateral "European nuclear option" that could include West Germany. Bonn under SPD leadership would shift the emphasis of its equality of status and reciprocity arguments from the nuclear, therefore military, realm of Allied relations to the political/economic arenas, and would demand more equality of status in influencing Western relations with the Eastern bloc through Ostpolitik.

Thus, despite real interest in Washington during the Johnson administration for seeking increased detente in East-West relations, American concern about West Germany stalled progress.[60] The power of the Versailles remedial at the State Department largely kept the Johnson administration from pursuing faster progress in East-West arms control. Johnson surrounded himself with Wilsonians and came to be persuaded by them, because as one of his advisors, Bill Moyers, saw it, these advisors were effective in promoting their position and "the old German cause they serve ahead of realistic considerations."[61]

The NPT: Waiting for Bonn

Progress on a nonproliferation treaty had been stalled since the early 1960s because of Soviet objections to MLF and West German objections that such a treaty would permanently leave the FRG in second-class nuclear status. During the Johnson administration, the issue of an NPT was raised already at the end of 1963. The Gomulka Plan, first presented in December 1963 and then again in February 1964, promoted a nuclear freeze in the Germanys, Poland, and Czechoslovakia. It stipulated that governments in that zone "would have promised not to manufacture nuclear weapons and not to import new weapons." There was support for this plan in the West, especially with the newly elected Labor Party in Great Britain, who were openly in favor. The plan was rejected by Bonn and consequently by the West.[62]

Johnson became serious about actively seeking a nonproliferation treaty in January 1966. This he revealed in a message to the European Nuclear Disarmament Committee (ENDC). However, even at this late date, Johnson worded his message in such a manner as to lead the Soviets once again to object on the grounds that the wording would still "permit West Germany to gain 'access' to nuclear weapons within the framework of a NATO collective force such as the MLF."[63] The two governments communicated back and forth for the next several months on what wording would be acceptable for a nonproliferation treaty. The desire in the Johnson administration to divert public attention away from the Vietnam War led to a serious push during these months for progress on the treaty. Still, however, presidential advisor Jack Valenti asked of UN Ambassador Arthur Goldberg, "How would we be able to get an NPT without serious reactions in Germany?"[64] U.S. refusal to agree to wording too prejudicial to the FRG and the idea of a European collective nuclear force continued to impede progress through late spring.[65]

Real progress between Moscow and Washington was made by October 1966. It should be remembered that, by this time, West German interest in MLF had faded. Further, as soon as it was announced by the Soviets that the major obstacles barring a nonproliferation treaty had been overcome, the State Department was approached by the West German ambassador, Heinrich Knappstein. Knappstein asked about the U.S.–Soviet negotiations and made it clear that Bonn "could not consider participation in an NPT until the nuclear problems of the alliance had found a satisfactory solution."[66] Knappstein was reassured that the interests of the FRG and NATO would not be sacrificed. The American and Soviet negotiators reached tentative agreement on wording of the treaty in December 1966. After complaints were lodged by the Allies that this tentative agreement had been reached without consultation with them, more than a year of intense negotiation and consultation ensued, including much bilateral interchange with the West Germans.[67]

For the next year and a half, the West German government did indeed stall final acceptance of the NPT, and thereafter hedged for another year on signing the treaty. The center and right of the West German political spectrum were particularly vocal in their objections to the NPT. Kiesinger, CDU chancellor of the Grand Coalition, got great publicity by publicly stating that he saw the treaty as evidence of U.S.–Soviet complicity, although he assured Washington that he basically supported it.[68] As usual, Strauss, other members of the CSU, Adenauer, and the Gaullist faction were openly hostile. Once again playing to their American audience as well as to the domestic arena, Strauss likened NPT to the Versailles Treaty, while Adenauer insisted it was even worse than the Morgenthau Plan.[69]

Brandt and the SPD were also surprisingly hostile to the NPT. Brandt's argument was that the NPT would negatively affect West German domestic industry by unfairly discriminating against West German nuclear power policy. The SPD did not, however, emphasize the issue of nuclear status. Since the SPD's basic policy on nuclear weapons was not opposed to an NPT, one can conclude with Kelleher that "Although always committed to early signature, Brandt and his colleagues felt constrained to demonstrate their defense of German national interests and of the national groups most concerned, especially the business community so long identified with the CDU."[70]

By emphasizing domestic constraints and the sacrifice that would be entailed by West German acceptance of NPT, Brandt and the SPD could and did use compliance with NPT to bolster their political leverage in other areas of foreign policy. Having joined the CDU/CSU in playing the NPT issue politically during the 1967–68 period, the SPD could and did now use signature of the treaty as a send-off for their Ostpolitik policies beginning in 1969,[71] and as a convenient example of their loyalty to the West. Interestingly, just as Adenauer and the CDU in the past had linked the nuclear status question to disarmament and thereby to the German question, so too did Brandt with the NPT. In discussing the reservations the SPD had during NPT negotiations, Brandt set out four clusters of questions that were presented to the United States, and whose resolution he found satisfactory. Two of those clusters are central: In accepting the NPT there should be "A clear connection with general disarmament," and, "no diminution of regional—and in our case European—efforts for unification."[72]

Thus, with little political cost to its own stance vis-à-vis nuclear weapons for West Germany, and after the great deal of international attention the FRG drew to itself during the 1966–67 period, the SPD/FDP coalition government gained much political credit in both East and West by signing the treaty.[73] Further, Brandt used the issue of domestic constraints to gain further concessions from Washington regarding the final NPT. Signing the NPT therefore really did little or nothing to compromise the SPD's position concerning the nuclear status issue. As noted above, Brandt and the SPD solidified their position on the equality of status issue on another Allied front through the Harmel Report.

West German sensibilities found a ready and timid audience in Washington. In 1967, as West German and Japanese objections to inspection and safeguard aspects of the nonproliferation treaty continued, Walt Rostow warned that Washington "was moving too far, too fast on the NPT and was not giving adequate consideration to the political problems it might create for our allies." Glen Seaborg states that he interpreted the objections as being raised "deliberately to obstruct forward movement on the NPT. I pressed various State Department officials to lean on the Germans, but to no avail."[74] Seaborg recalls: "As we have seen, there was a great reluctance in the administration, from President Johnson on down, to treat the Germans other than with kid gloves."[75] That year, McCloy sent a memorandum to Johnson in which he stated:

The non-proliferation treaty, the rough treatment of Erhard, the increased emphasis on a detente with the Soviet Union, have all created fears that a Soviet-U.S. arrangement is emerging in substitution for the original NATO concept of an equal partnership Alliance. The stability of Germany and its firm adherence to NATO is a vital element of the security of the Alliance.[76]

For all the controversy surrounding the NPT and what the FRG sacrificed in signing it,[77] the treaty did not foreclose the possibility of a future European or Atlantic collective nuclear force, as is generally thought.[78] In a 1968 interview, Eugene Rostow illuminated this fact. When asked about the so-called Atlantic solution to the nuclear sharing problem, which to date had not materialized, Rostow responded:

In the NPT negotiations, we've been very careful to keep the European option open. That is, if a Europe is formed, then that Europe could become a nuclear power by virtue of the doctrine of succession—that is, by succession to the French and the British nuclear potentialities.[79]

Responding further to the question of whether "the NPT did not doom forever and all time any MLF-type solution at some future time," Rostow stated, "No, or a more fundamental one. But it didn't and it couldn't and it won't. This the President made very, very clear—either a European plan or an Atlantic one."[80]

The treaty was finally formally presented to Johnson on July 2, 1968. By this time, the Harmel Exercise had been accepted by NATO, and the way was opened for Bonn to pursue its own Ostpolitik with the East bloc.

During Nixon's first year in office and before Senate ratification of the treaty, Bonn was able to intercede as it had in the past in the American political arena and gain further concessions on the treaty. On the question of termination of the treaty, the Senate verbally recognized the dissolution of NATO as an example of the "extraordinary events" noted in the NPT for which Bonn could give its three months notice of treaty termination.[81] This is not trivial when viewed in combination with the above-noted opening left in the treaty for a collective Western nuclear force. Seen in this light, the West Germans retained the possibility of future national nuclear status in or out of the Alliance. In 1995, this clause was extremely important for contemplating the future of a united Germany in an unstable Europe.[82]

In sum, the Johnson administration had misgivings about having failed to meet Bonn's demands concerning equality of status on the nuclear sharing issue, and its plans to now move ahead with the NPT and "bridge-building" with the Soviet Union. Such misgivings led to the Johnson administration's hesitance on many aspects of the NPT negotiations with the Soviets that threatened Bonn's interests and to its acceptance of the Allied Harmel Report of 1967 that grew out of West European demands for more control of the direction in Allied policy. Johnson's increased preoccupation with the costs and implementation of his Vietnam policy led to a decreased focus on Europe. It did not mean, however, that he had forsaken the lessons of the Wilsonian impulse and Versailles remedial; it meant that he was distracted from them.[83] Defenders at State and through powerful figures like McCloy, however, retained their focus on Bonn and Western integration.

REVISITING THE WEST GERMAN CONNECTION

On the West German domestic front, the formation of the Grand Coalition in 1966 was a milestone. The SPD finally ascended to power and became largely responsible for setting the future course of West Germany's approach to foreign policy issues. The SPD was crucial in reformulating Bonn's approach both to the German question and to the more general issue of West German security. Willy Brandt, the SPD foreign minister under the Grand Coalition, was central in leading a Western European initiative to institutionalize within the Alliance a new understanding of U.S.–Western European obligations in the security relationship. The impact of the West German and Western European thrust for greater control over Western security policy culminated in the Harmel Report of 1967, wherein the political goal of detente in East-West relations became formally acknowledged as the second prong of NATO's mission, alongside that of military defense.[84]

While the SPD altered the West German position on various security issues, a great deal of continuity was maintained in Bonn's approach to the Allied relationship. As Adenauer had done in the 1950s, the SPD perceived the advantages of appealing to the Wilsonian impulse that inspired the Western security relationship in order to achieve Bonn's interests, and to the Versailles remedial that encouraged preferential treatment of the West Germans. The issue of equality of status would now be moved from the military to the political and economic arenas.

Further, the inaction of the Alliance in resolving the German question as detente proceeded invited a new legitimization of the 1954 agreements. Willy Brandt and his party would lead the way on achieving that. The SPD formulated a West German foreign policy that won more autonomy for Bonn while maintaining the multilateral Allied pledge to reunification. That the SPD perceived and intended that Ostpolitik would grant the FRG more autonomy in formulating and executing its relations with the East bloc is illustrated by a quote from Egon Bahr:

Behind the considerations at that time was the conviction that the FRG was grown up enough to pursue its own interests, just as the other states did. It concerned carrying out every component of detente, those that only the FRG could execute, and doing so with full loyalty to the partners in the Alliance.[85]

As the Adenauer-Dulles "policy of strength" approach eroded, the ascendancy of the SPD's position embracing detente appeared to coincide with, but also influenced, changing U.S.–Allied approaches to the East-West relationship. The SPD's "German Plan" of 1959 already had envisioned German unification as occurring within a framework of detente and arms control. While it was shelved in 1960 due to the worsening of East-West relations, it is clear that the thinking behind the "German Plan" influenced later SPD foreign policy and in fact foreshadowed SPD initiatives into the 1980s for a European collective security system. Late in 1959, Helmut Schmidt articulated a security approach that was influenced by the thinking of the "German Plan" but relegated the unification question to a long-term goal and accepted indefinite West German and East German membership in their respective alliances. But, as Haftendorn states, "one of the purposes of arms reduction was to afford points of departure for progress on the German question, just as it did not appear possible to gain a lasting world peace without eliminating the political sources of tension in Europe." The new formulation of the SPD plan was detente- and arms control–oriented, envisioning a Central European arms control zone. By the mid-1960s, this new concept became the Eight-Point Program, and was instrumental in the forging of the Grand Coalition in 1966, wherein "international detente is in the interest of Germany."[86]

Thus, West German leaders such as Kurt Kiesinger, CDU chancellor during the Grand Coalition; Willy Brandt, SPD foreign minister under the Grand Coalition and then chancellor in 1969; and Helmut Schmidt, SPD defense minister under the Brandt government and later chancellor, began to cut a new path for West Germany in the tumultuous mid- to late 1960s.

However, their insistence on Allied adherence to the principles of equal rights, equal status, and nondiscriminatory practices among sovereign Allies, as well as on the Allied pledge to support German unification, maintained the legacy left by Adenauer.

Brandt and other SPD leaders, like Adenauer before them, played directly to the Wilsonian heart of U.S. postwar security policy, that of creating a stable and democratic Europe within an Atlantic community. Echoing Adenauer's position in approaching the Allies, Brandt reiterated the importance of NATO as a political as well as a military alliance. Beyond being what Brandt called a "military assignment," he noted that "NATO was supposed to be simultaneously an instrument of political cooperation and of an understanding between governments that shared the same fundamental convictions."[87] Such a description invokes directly the image of the security community as a shared culture.

Brandt and the SPD also followed in Adenauer's footsteps by linking West German loyalty to and membership in the Western Alliance to the 1954 pledge wherein the FRG renounced force regarding the border issue and the production of nuclear weapons in its territory in return for membership based on equality and the assumption of Allied responsibility for solving the German question. In reaffirming Bonn's renunciation of nuclear weapons and West German loyalty to the West, Brandt stated in 1968:

In short, we have sought a firm anchoring of the Federal Republic of Germany in the Western Alliance. We have closely linked our destinies to the alliance and to the Western European union that is being formed under its protection. This affiliation was all the easier for us because our allies accepted our legitimate national objective: the right of self-determination for our nation and a peace treaty that would enable the Germans to live under the roof of a single state.[88]

Like Adenauer, Brandt and the SPD considered the issue of German unification fundamentally linked to any movement in East-West disarmament and detente. Brandt reaffirmed in 1968 a statement he made in 1964 concerning this linkage:

We must make it clear beyond all doubt that Germany has an interest in detente and not in the maintenance of tension. But for any detente worthy of the name what is required are just those measures that will help to overcome the political causes of the tension. And here the German question cannot be by-passed.[89]

Although the issue of nuclear status was not as important to SPD leadership as it had been to Adenauer, the centrality of West German claims to equality of status remained. In a speech delivered in 1963, for example, Willy Brandt stated concerning the importance of European integration on the nuclear matter that

Atlantic partnership and the process of European union are simultaneous aims of equal status. The one may not wait for the other. . . . The same applies to the topical and in any case lively discussed question of nuclear armament. Let me say this here. It is right and necessary for Europe to have important influence on nuclear strategy and full access to the peaceful utilization of nuclear energy.[90]

There were also important differences between Brandt and Adenauer in their approaches to the nuclear issue and the German question. Adenauer and the CDU/CSU sought to hold open the nuclear option for the FRG both as a bargaining chip with the USSR on reunification and as an "equality of status" issue within the Alliance. As a matter of fact, as I discussed earlier, Adenauer threatened reclaiming West German sovereignty on the nuclear issue to force Allied attention to Bonn's claims to equality of status and Western responsibility for the German question. Brandt and the SPD discontinued this posture. The issue of nuclear modernization had been divisive in the FRG throughout the early 1960s. All along, Brandt and the SPD viewed nuclear modernization in West Germany as presenting an obstacle to achieving German unity, as it would naturally threaten the Soviet Union and discourage Moscow from considering reunification.

Further, the SPD, unlike the CDU/CSU, had long supported mutual troop reductions in the East-West relationship as a means of moving closer toward an international environment conducive to German reunification. Thus, although there still remained strong preferences within the CDU/CSU and to a lesser extent within the SPD for holding open the nuclear option for the FRG,[91] the ascendancy of the SPD to power under the Grand Coalition lessened the former stridency of this position and reduced fears among the Allies concerning West German demands on the nuclear issue.

The creation of two new committees in NATO, the Nuclear Defense Committee and the Nuclear Planning Group (NPG), further alleviated the nuclear situation as the NPG gave Bonn direct and permanent representation in Allied nuclear strategy and planning discussions. The creation of the committee was proposed by McNamara in 1965 and again in December 1966, when it actually came into being.[92] Such representation for the FRG had been advocated for some time by some West Germans, particularly by members of the SPD.[93] The NPG was a significant step forward in granting nonnuclear members of the Alliance a voice in NATO nuclear strategy. It was not a "hardware" solution as MLF would have been, and it did not grant the FRG a "hands-on" nuclear role. However, the West Germans and the Italians, along with the United States and UK, had permanent seats on the committee and part of its function was to "develop criteria for the use of nuclear weapons assigned to NATO."[94] Jonathan Dean states in his study, *Watershed in Europe*, that the creation of the NPG "tackled the coupling problem as it should have been handled, on the political level."[95]

Although the creation of the NPG was greeted with skepticism by some members of the CDU, was seen by some as an easy way out of the MLF project by the Americans,[96] and was greeted with outright disdain by the Gaullists, it was interpreted by most as at least an entrance to nuclear decision making for Bonn.[97] In fact, by 1966, Seaborg claims, the seriousness with which Washington approached the committee became apparent and "word spread about the benefits of taking part in the group."[98] Its creation actually fit quite nicely into the SPD's conception of how best to achieve West German security interests without surrendering the claim to equality of status. With permanent membership on this nuclear planning committee, demands for equality of nuclear status were at least partially met without allowing the East bloc an opportunity for raising the specter of a nuclear and therefore threatening FRG, fears that were consistently voiced by the Soviets during the MLF episode.

The SPD and Unification

A definite revision made by the SPD concerned the Allied approach to German unification. As stated above, the SPD continued Adenauer's policies of linking the German question to movement in East-West security relations and of emphasizing Western responsibility for resolution of the issue. However, unlike Adenauer, the SPD was prepared to demand more West German sovereignty in pursuing the German unity question. Whereas Adenauer consciously tied West German claims concerning unification to the collective Allied relationship in order to impede progress on detente and recognition of the postwar status quo, Brandt followed a different path. While still emphasizing Allied responsibility for the unification question, Brandt sought to increase West German maneuverability in dealing with the issue without disturbing the Allied security relationship.

Quite clearly, Western lack of success in achieving progress in this area gave Bonn an opening for demanding more autonomy. Thus, the SPD policy was at once to reaffirm its loyalty to the Alliance based on the diffuse reciprocity of the 1954 agreements and, using the relationship as a springboard, to break free from the failures it had produced in solving the German question. Brandt stated in 1968: "We must maintain our security, our partnership with the West, and our freedom. As part of this, to be sure, there must also be the knowledge that German policy has become more independent."[99]

This comparison of the SPD and CDU/CSU approaches to security issues is significant in supporting my argument that the Alliance evolved along the lines of a Wilsonian security community as well as a traditional military pact. Although Adenauer and Brandt disagreed on specific military and defense issues and over the means by which unification might be achieved, they clearly agreed on the importance of continuing to tie that fundamental national interest to the Western security relationship. Both advocated stressing Allied responsibility for the German question as the linchpin of West German loyalty to the West, and both pursued these aims by demanding equality of status and nondiscrimination in Allied relations. The continuation of Adenauer's legacy by the SPD helped maintain a sensitive audience in Washington. As will be shown in my discussion of the Harmel Report of 1967, the SPD leadership redirected the thrust of Bonn's claim for equality of status away from the issue of nuclear status toward one of political equality concerning the pursuit of detente and, thereby, the German question.

The West Germans and the Harmel Report

By 1966, de Gaulle's initial Western lead in forging ahead with a French detente policy with the Soviets was on the wane.[100] British assertiveness in Western detente efforts had likewise subsided by the mid-1960s, in part due to frustration with the hesitancy of Washington to act against the wishes of the FRG, as happened for so long with the nonproliferation issue.[101] Of the major Western European allies, it was Bonn, led by the SPD, that would step in and basically set the future pace of detente and push to institutionalize within the alliance framework the necessary foundations for West German Ostpolitik. Philip Williams observes in an article on British detente policy:

Although detente in Europe began largely through the efforts of Paris, it was not until Bonn made a clear commitment to normalizing relations with its Eastern European neighbors that it started to move rapidly. The Federal Republic's Ostpolitik was the key to detente in Europe. It was important not only because it coincided with the Soviet desire to get West German acceptance of the status quo in Europe but also because it helped to galvanize the Nixon administration into formulating its own detente policy.[102]

Further, by the mid-1960s, Western European publics were growing restive with the Alliance in its role as a military pact, questioning the reasoning behind continued membership in an age in which U.S. and Soviet military parity had been achieved, and thus wherein the American nuclear guarantee was cast in doubt. As Leon Sloss, a pivotal American participant in the Harmel Exercise, notes, "The most important objectives of the Harmel report were to restore a sense of solidarity and purpose in the Alliance, and to gain public support for the Alliance at a time when people began to question whether a military alliance still was required."[103] Rather than ending in crisis, however, this period turned out to be one of transition for the Western security relationship, and one in which the United States was receptive to West European initiatives advocating a reevaluation of the Western approach to East-West security issues. Sloss observes: "It was recognized in Washington that NATO needed a 'new face' because the Europeans demanded it."[104] In assuring that the trans-Atlantic tie was still vital, the nonmilitary aspects were emphasized—those that I have called the community-building aspects.

The result of the renewed quest for Western solidarity in the Alliance was the Harmel Report. Initiated in 1966 by Belgian Foreign Minister Pierre Harmel, the Harmel Report was formally endorsed by the Allies in 1967. The purpose of the exercise was to "study the future tasks which face the alliance, and its procedures for fulfilling them in order to strengthen the alliance as a factor for durable peace."[105] A year of inter-allied consultation followed, in which the West Germans played a central role, and members of the State Department were the major U.S. players.[106] The final report of 1967 stated that "military security and a policy of detente are not contradictory but complementary."[107] The report explicitly promoted the achievement of stability in Europe through "the use of the alliance constructively in the interest of detente."[108] Important in the Harmel Report was this inclusion of detente as the second prong of Western security, thereby explicitly embracing the political aspects of East-West relations as being an essential element of Western security.

Although there was some hesitation in Washington concerning the leeway that the Harmel Report established for independent action by various members, the Americans were "not unaware of the risks that this would occur" and it was viewed as "almost unavoidable," given West European demands.[109] For example, Sloss states: "There was clearly a difference about the emphasis to be placed on detente, with the U. S. concerned that the report would not place enough emphasis on the need to maintain military strength." Knowing that Harmel was significant and "would set the tone of the Alliance for many years to come," Sloss acknowledged that the West Europeans "wanted more emphasis on the non-military facets of NATO."[110]

Thus, the potential future resolution of such issues as German unification could now be pursued legitimately outside the context of the U.S.–Soviet strategic relationship and could include the active participation of all Allied members. As will be recalled from above discussions of SPD strategy and policy objectives, the results of the Harmel exercise fit in perfectly with the party's agenda. The result of Harmel was that detente-oriented policies would now play a central and legitimate role in achieving West German interests. The SPD was free to pursue the peaceful resolution of the German question while maintaining Allied support and responsibility for it.

The findings of the Harmel Report made Bonn more influential both within the Western camp and in the East-West relationship. Two aspects of the report emphasized the increased potential for West German influence. First, the Allied responsibility for resolution of the German question was officially reiterated and given a central place in detente.[111] Second, it was recognized in the wording of the report that independent detente efforts by member states were compatible with joint actions taken by the Alliance as a whole:

Ministers again emphasized that the peaceful settlement of the German question on the basis of the free expression of political will by the German people was an essential factor for a just and lasting peaceful order in Europe. . . .They welcomed the efforts by the Federal Government to increase human, economic and cultural contacts between both parts of Germany, and were agreed that this internal German process was to be considered an important contribution to the search for a detente in Europe.[112]

As I discussed above, Brandt, like Adenauer, linked detente and German unification, the difference being that Brandt embraced detente in order to achieve eventual unification while Adenauer had attempted to thwart detente efforts without prior action on the German question. To reiterate, Adenauer refused to recognize the postwar status quo in light of the unsolved German question. The SPD policy, on the other hand, was to recognize the status quo in order to overcome it. Continued inaction by the Alliance concerning its responsibility for the German question enabled Brandt and the SPD to demand more autonomy in pursuing resolution of the issue through detente. The Harmel Report essentially gave them the green light. In his memoirs, Brandt explicitly acknowledged his influence with Harmel and the 1967 report that bore his name.[113] Regarding the importance for Bonn of this finding, Brandt stated:

Bilateral steps are useful for gradually leading East and West together in Europe. . . . It goes without saying that the relationship of the NATO states to the Soviet Union and its allies will never be uniform, nor would that even be desirable. At the Luxemburg NATO conference [June 1967] and on other occasions I have made the point that our policy vis-à-vis the East should be agreed on but must remain elastic. What will be decisive for its success is for each NATO member to keep the alliance in his mind, to defend his allies, and to make their political path easier.[114]

In the case of Bonn, it was recognized in Washington that the new coalition government intended to take the matter of German unification more into its own hands, given the failure of past Allied policy on the issue. At least until Kissinger and the Nixon administration, this development appears to have been viewed with some relief.[115] In an NSC background paper from 1966 it was observed that

Frustration marked by disappointment is the dominant mood today in Germany. Twenty-one years after the war, Germany's foreign policy—backed by its allies—

has brought neither reunification nor complete restoration of world respectability to the FRG. . . . On the positive side, there is a more mature official attitude and a more realistic German public opinion regarding the speed with which reunification can be obtained. At a time when the new government is trying out its legs, it is important to note the growing feeling in Germany that, if reunification is to come about at all, the FRG will have to play a major role in achieving it.[116]

In sum, as had happened with the MLF, Washington supported the Harmel Report out of concern for political cohesion in the Alliance and due to the particular sensitivity for West Germany.[117] From 1967 onward, then, Western Europe, led by Bonn, would play a much more direct role in setting the East-West security agenda. Whereas Adenauer had directly influenced Western security policy by thwarting movement in East-West relations, Bonn would now take an active role in leading much of the Western approach, particularly after the SPD assumed leadership under Brandt in 1969. With the Allied endorsement of the Harmel Report, West German interests were codified into the Allied agenda and, as future American presidents would learn, West German leaders would be able to refer back to the report and the equality of status it afforded them in their pursuit of Ostpolitik. Thus, although West Germany remained militarily dependent on the United States and NATO, the Harmel Report ensured that Western security was now compartmentalized into military and political components. I will deal in detail in the next chapter with the effect of the Harmel Report on Allied policy and West Germany's increased influence thereupon in setting the East-West security agenda.

The SPD, Wilsonianism and Revisionism

Once the SPD came to power, its leaders did not passively hop aboard the peace train engineered by the United States and the Soviet Union, nor did they view detente as accepting the status quo.[118] The SPD had already supported detente measures as far back as the 1950s. But for them, detente represented a means of overcoming the status quo by first recognizing it.[119] In other words, Ostpolitik was revisionist in its objectives. The innovation over Adenauer's previous policy was to make Bonn more free in pursuing unification, with more independence and with the blessings of the Alliance.

In an article from 1969, Walter Hahn noted of Egon Bahr and the SPD's Ostpolitik: "Bonn has made it clear to the Soviet Union that, more than an acceptance of the status quo in Europe, West Germany's Ostpolitik is aimed at changing the status quo in order to achieve the ultimate objective of West German policy the reunification of Germany."[120] Embracing detente and disarmament measures therefore meant seeking to overcome peacefully the division of Europe and thereby the division of Germany. That has been the formal SPD position since the Bad Godesberg program of 1959. Fritz Erler, one of the SPD's security experts during the 1950s and 1960s, remarked in the late 1950s that, "disarmament and reunification were two sides of one problem."[121] As mentioned above, in 1959, at its Party Congress in Bad Godesberg, the SPD developed a *Deutschlandplan*, or Germany Plan. The plan called for a European collective security system, to be achieved by gradual military disengagement from Europe by the two blocs.[122] This could only be accomplished through detente measures. The eventual goal was the establishment of both a nuclear free zone in Central Europe and a collective security system, to include the United States and USSR, guaranteeing the invulnerability of the participating nonnuclear European states in that region.

The vision is seemingly Wilsonian in its call for a collective security community whose principles are to be guaranteed through political procedures. Further, central to Wilsonianism and the Deutschlandplan is the rejection of balance of power politics. A Wilsonian collective security community, as opposed to a traditional defense pact, requires the membership of all great powers, rather than the creation of adversarial alliances constructed around the great powers. The SPD blueprint for a collective security community seemed to reflect Wilsonianism in its advocacy of U.S. and Soviet membership in the community. The popular concept of a European Common House during Gorbachev's tenure in Moscow could in fact be traced back to this SPD idea.

The SPD would successfully use this Wilsonian concept after Allied endorsement of the Harmel Report in expanding the political boundaries of the Western Allied understanding eastward and thereby overcoming the postwar status quo to bring about unification. Throughout the 1960s, the SPD envisioned increased detente as promoting possibilities for a certain convergence between the blocs that would eventually bring about German unity. Bahr called this *"Wandel durch Annaeherung,"* or "change through rapprochement."[123] In 1963, Bahr outlined the concept, stating that "the zones must be transformed with Soviet approval. Once we are that far, we will have made a large step toward reunification."[124] Extremely controversial over the next two decades was the relationship that Ostpolitik led the SPD to engage in with East bloc regimes.[125]

Despite the period of promoting the convergence of East and West in his Wandel durch Annaeherung, Egon Bahr and many in the SPD came to accept the divergence of systems. In fact, as written up in 1989 in the CDU–Soviet-signed Bonn Declaration, the SPD's vision from the 1960s was maintained and not surprisingly praised by Egon Bahr. In it, Europe was to be brought together "irrespective of different social systems."[126] More the SPD–, but also the CDU–led governments, showed themselves willing to sacrifice their support of reform movements in the East bloc and the human rights issues that accompanied them to further the cause of West German interests.[127]

It is important to note the many differences between the Wilsonian impulse, one historically linked to a specifically American orientation to the world, and the Wilsonian appearances of the SPD's blueprint. The latter, at the level of theory and practice, leans closer to the traditional European great power balance system than at first is apparent. Interestingly, the West German scheme fits more closely the modern European concert model discussed by Charles and Clifford Kupchan than a Wilsonian community.[128] The SPD's plan, later largely accepted by the CDU when it returned to power in the 1980s, does not require the development of democracy, common values, and common culture as called for by the American Wilsonian impulse.

Also important to Bahr's understanding of a future peace order in Europe, the SPD vision called for an eventual withering of the Alliance system. In other words, under the SPD's plan, the end goal was not the hybrid NATO—the American Wilsonian compromise—it was a European concert of great powers that would outgrow NATO.

Finally, obviously missing was the leading role of the United States, obligatory in the Wilsonian scheme. The SPD plan was to use the Alliance relationship strategically in order to overcome the need for the Alliance. Through this process, the national goal of unification would be accomplished, and a united Germany would take its place among the great powers.

CONCLUSIONS

American sensitivity to West German claims for equality of status and to the Allied responsibility for resolving the German question returned during the Johnson administration. Under Johnson, Wilsonians like McCloy wielded much influence, as did his allies at State. West German demands for equality on the nuclear status issue had motivated the introduction of the MLF by Washington in the early 1960s and dissuaded the Johnson administration from completely dropping the issue long after it clearly disrupted U.S. relations with Great Britain, France, and the Soviet Union. MLF remained a live issue in Western and East-West relations until Bonn backed away from it in 1966. Only then did Washington move seriously to pursue the NPT, an issue that was extremely important to Johnson.

The resuscitation of the Wilsonian impulse and the Versailles remedial thus reestablished the American commitment to the active pursuit of building a community in the trans-Atlantic area while maintaining NATO's defense mission. By the end of the Johnson administration, however, the two goals were coming into conflict. To alleviate increasing Allied frustration on military security issues, the Harmel Report was accepted in 1967. Thereafter, Washington allowed Western security policy to become bifurcated in order to satisfy the political pressure for equality of status among the Allies, especially Bonn, and to renew the Western pledge for German unification.

As the SPD assumed power in Bonn, it refocused West German claims concerning equality of status and nondiscrimination away from the nuclear status issue to the political/economic realm of East-West relations. The new direction reflected the SPD's conviction held since the Kennedy administration that German unification could only be accomplished by first recognizing the postwar status quo in order to overcome it.[129] In this way, the SPD maintained Adenauer's linkage between the German question and progress in East-West relations, but enhanced Bonn's ability to pursue unification more independently. The institutionalization of detente into the Alliance as the second prong of Western security alongside military defense greatly facilitated Bonn's interests in pursuing unification, and in realizing it twenty years later.

As will be seen in the next chapter, Bonn's pursuit of Ostpolitik, initiated with Allied blessings, would have a tremendous impact on international relations. While many have argued that the radical international changes of 1989 are best understood as either the consequences of successful American policy under Reagan, or conversely, as the result of domestic change in the Soviet Union under Gorbachev, my perspective offers a different interpretation. Through its continued, if uneven, adherence to the Wilsonian impulse and the Versailles remedial, the United States allowed its goal of bipolar balancing to be subverted by its objective of creating an Atlantic community. American acceptance of the Harmel Report in 1967 reflected the commitment to assure equality of status but meant as well that Washington again embraced the openly revisionist West German claim regarding unification, this time sanctioning Bonn's open pursuit of that goal. By doing that, the Johnson administration unwittingly undercut America's dominant role in East-West relations.

NOTES

1. Frank Ninkovich, *Modernity and Power: A History of the Domino Theory in the Twentieth Century* (Chicago: University of Chicago Press, 1994), p. 283.

2. Ibid., p. 286.

3. Frank Costigliola, "Lyndon B. Johnson, Germany, and the 'End of the Cold War,'" in *Lyndon Johnson Confronts the World: American Foreign Policy 1963–1968*, ed. Warren I. Cohen and Nancy Bernkopf Tucker (New York: Cambridge University Press, 1994), pp. 173–210; quote on p. 177.

4. Costigliola, "Lyndon B. Johnson, Germany, and the 'End of the Cold War,'" p. 181. He identifies the "theologians" as those individuals at State committed to European integration, and connects them directly to John J. McCloy's role in the Johnson administration. I identify McCloy as a prominent Wilsonian braintruster.

5. Glenn H. Seaborg with Benjamin S. Loeb, *Stemming the Tide: Arms Control in the Johnson Years* (Lexington, Mass.: Lexington Books, 1987), p. 175.

6. Thomas Alan Schwartz, "Victories and Defeats in the Long Twilight Struggle: The United States and Western Europe in the 1960s," in *The Diplomacy of the Crucial Decade: American Foreign Relations During the 1960s,* ed. Diane B. Kunz (New York: Columbia University Press, 1994), p. 134.

7. See discussion by Costigliola, "LBJ, Germany, and 'the End of the Cold War,' " p. 182.

8. For an excellent examination of McCloy's importance in U.S.–German relations, see Thomas Alan Schwartz, *America's Germany: John J. McCloy and the Federal Republic of Germany* (Cambridge, Mass.: Harvard University Press, 1991).

9. Eugene Rostow, Oral History by Paige Mulhollan, December 2, 1968, LBJ Library, Container, 74-72; Folder: Eugene Rostow AC 74-72, p. 29. Rostow was under secretary of state for political affairs, 1966–68, and was himself sympathetic to McCloy's position versus that of McNamara and the Defense Department.

10. Paper by J. J. McCloy to Eugene Rostow "on the matter of force levels," February 9, 1967, LBJ Library, Papers of LBJ as President, 1963–1969, National Security File, National Security Council History, Trilateral Negotiations and NATO, 1966–67, Container: 50, Folder: Trilateral Negotiations and NATO '66–'67 Book 2, Tabs 45-52A, p. 6.

11. "Memorandum for the Chairman," January 8, 1965, by John McCloy. Declassified and Sanitized Documents from Unprocessed Files (DSDUF)—General, Container: 1; Folder: Committee on Nuclear Proliferation.

12. John J. McCloy, quoted in Schwartz, *America's Germany,* p. 155.

13. McCloy Memorandum, 1/8/65, on nonproliferation (Box 6), LBJ Library, p. 4.

14. Seaborg, *Stemming the Tide,* p. 129; Schwartz, "Victories and Defeats," pp. 134–38; Jonathan Dean, *Watershed in Europe: Dismantling the East-West Military Confrontation* (Lexington, Mass.: Lexington Books, 1987), p. 10.

15. Ninkovich, *Modernity and Power,* p. 284.

16. Costigliola, "LBJ, Germany, and 'the End of the Cold War,' " p. 187.

17. In a conversation held that month with George Ball, British Prime Minister Wilson, who was unsympathetic to the MLF, reported that Ball took a particularly hard line, insisting that the British support the project. See Seaborg, *Stemming the Tide,* p. 123.

18. Costigliola, "LBJ, Germany, and 'the End of the Cold War,' " esp. pp. 184–92; quote on p. 190.

19. McCloy Memorandum, 1/8/65, on nonproliferation (Box 6), p. 2. MacArthur was relating a discussion he had held with Henri Spaak at the American embassy in Brussels concerning the MLF.

20. See Mary N. Hampton, *The Empowerment of a Middle-Sized State: West Germany, Wilsonianism, and the Western Alliance* (Los Angeles, UCLA Press, 1993), esp. ch 4.

21. McGeorge Bundy, quoted in Seaborg, *Stemming the Tide,* p. 129.

22. Ninkovich, *Modernity and Power,* p. 285.

23. Incoming Telegram to State Department from John Leddy, October 27, 1965, p. 1, LBJ Library, Collection: National Security File, Country File, Europe and USSR, Germany, Container: 182, 183, 186, 190, 191, Folder: Germany Cables Vol. 9 7/65–1/66.

24. McCloy Memorandum, 1/8/65, on nonproliferation (Box 6), pp. 2–4.

25. Dr. Kurt Birrenbach, "Memorandum of Conversation," November 8, 1965, p. 2, LBJ Library, mandatory review item, Subject: Collective Nuclear Arrangements in NATO.

26. Ibid., p. 3.

27. Dean Rusk, in "Memorandum of Conversation," p. 3.

28. Ibid., p. 4.

29. Ibid., pp. 6–9.

30. Ibid., pp. 9–10. On p. 10, Rusk did then finally state that Washington wasn't "wedded to the precise proposals put forward in the MLF. We need to look at new arrangements and see what is best." All in all, the conversation reveals a continued timidity on the part of Washington in rejecting MLF outright.

31. Seaborg, *Stemming the Tide*, p. 106. See also George Quester, *The Politics of Nuclear Proliferation* (Baltimore, Md.: Johns Hopkins University Press, 1973), pp. 42–43.

32. Seaborg, *Stemming the Tide*, p. 103. See also Catherine McArdle Kelleher, *Germany and the Politics of Nuclear Weapons* (New York: Columbia University Press, 1975), pp. 246–50. De Gaulle's protestations and admonishments to Bonn were quite often harsh. Kelleher cites the ominous tone of one such French threat made to a West German: "I was told that unless we gave up the MLF, France would make common cause with those East European states that feared a nuclear Germany in form," p. 250.

33. Seaborg, *Stemming the Tide.*, p. 126. See also Kelleher, *Germany and the Politics of Nuclear Weapons*, p. 254.

34. Seaborg, *Stemming the Tide*, p. 126.

35. Kelleher, *Germany and the Politics of Nuclear Weapons*, pp. 246–54.

36. Ninkovich, *Modernity and Power*, p. 284.

37. Telegram to State Department from American Embassy, Bonn. LBJ Library, Subject: German Attitudes on Participation in Alliance Nuclear Defense, October 11, 1965, p. 2, Collection: NSF, Subject File, Container: 25, 36, 38, 48, Folder: MLF; Mr. Bundy: For 6:00 meeting Monday, 18 October.

38. See his "LBJ, Germany, and 'the End of the Cold War,' " pp. 189–90.

39. Seaborg, *Stemming the Tide*, pp. 106–7.

40. Quester, *The Politics of Nuclear Proliferation*, pp. 42–43.

41. Kelleher, *Germany and the Politics of Nuclear Weapons*, p. 256.

42. Seaborg, *Stemming the Tide*, p. 129.

43. Ibid., p. 158, Rusk on p. 159. In discussing a sharp response he planned to send to the British, McGeorge Bundy recommended that Rusk use "milder language that he hoped might appease the Germans and still be acceptable to the U. K. Rusk asked Bundy if his language would permit the MLF and Bundy responded that it would. Rusk thought Germany still was not ready to give up on the MLF."

44. Seaborg, *Stemming the Tide*, p. 125. Seaborg also cites in a memo from Bundy to Johnson from December 6, 1964, that Eisenhower was no "better than neutral and could be opposed" to MLF. Seaborg then states that Rusk claimed Eisenhower's support for MLF. This seems to be corroborated in a document from January 1964. In a discussion between Ambassador Merchant, General Eisenhower, Admiral Claude V. Ricketts, Lt. General Andrew Goodpaster (Joint Chiefs of Staff) and Gerard C. Smith (State Department), the original reasoning for American sponsorship of MLF is reiterated and supported by the group. For example, Good-

paster gives the position of the JCS at the time: "although not an ideal weapons system from a strictly military point of view, the MLF would have military utility and substantial political importance in terms of its potential for allied cohesion."

45. Letter written to Johnson by eight senators (Joseph Clark, Eugene McCarthy, Lee Metcalf, Maurine Neuberger, George McGovern, Gaylord Nelson, Phillip Hart and Gale McGee) on September 7, 1964, quoted in Seaborg, *Stemming the Tide*, p. 124.

46. "Memorandum of Conversation; November 8, 1965," pp. 5, 8. Of course, Birrenbach's response reveals the basic reasoning behind MLF: "He agreed that a collective nuclear force would not add to the total nuclear power of the West, but the real purpose of the collective force was not military but political—it was to bring Germany and other participating European nations as close as possible to the process of nuclear decision-making. . . . If German desires are irrelevant, he wondered why these proposals had been made by the United States."

47. James Warburg was outspoken on this theme as far back as the Eisenhower administration, and he and others continued to lobby Congress to challenge any move toward making NATO a "fourth nuclear power." See the Personal Papers of James Warburg in the JFK Presidential Library, esp. Box 72.

48. Kelleher, *Germany and the Politics of Nuclear Weapons*, p. 254. Kelleher quotes a West German during this national election period as saying of the public discussion in the FRG concerning MLF, "the silence was deafening."

49. Memorandum of Conversation, July 6, 1965, "Subject: German Attitudes Toward the MLF, Non-proliferation, and Arms Control," LBJ Library Mandatory Review, Case #NLJ88-10, Document #184, p. 1.

50. Outgoing Telegram from Department of State, July 9, 1965, LBJ Library, Collection: NSF; Country File: Europe and USSR: Germany, Container: 182,183, 186, 190, 191, Folder: Germany Cables Vol. 9 7/65–1/66. During the visit, the ambassador voiced West German nervousness at the perceived proclivity of Washington to falter on security issues important to Bonn, such as the MLF and nonproliferation, p. 1. See also Kelleher, *Germany and the Politics of Nuclear Weapons*, pp. 254–55. On the Erhard government quieting domestic discussion of the MLF before the September elections, Kelleher states on p. 255: "There must be no new opportunity . . . for public confrontation with de Gaulle and thus for a further dramatic split within the barely united CDU/CSU electoral coalition."

51. Kelleher, *Germany and the Politics of Nuclear Weapons*, p. 254.

52. Intelligence Note, to the Secretary of State from INR (Thomas L. Hughes), October 19, 1965. LBJ Library, "Subject: Current German and British Attitudes Toward the ANF/MLF," p. 3, Collection: NSF, Subject File, Container: 25, 36, 38, 44, Folder: MLF: Mr. Bundy: for 6:00 meeting, Monday, 18 October.

53. Wolfram Hanrieder, *Germany, America, Europe: Forty Years of German Foreign Policy* (New Haven, Conn.: Yale University Press, 1989), p. 47. Also see entire discussion on pp. 46–49. In passing, Stephen F. Szabo makes a similar observation in *The Diplomacy of German Unification* (New York: St. Martin's Press, 1992), p. 7. He states that "Lyndon Johnson's detente policies strained German-American relations once again."

54. Kelleher, *Germany and the Politics of Nuclear Weapons*, p. 254.

55. Schwartz, "Victories and Defeats," p. 136.

56. I posed this question to McGeorge Bundy in 1988. His response was that he did not know and never really thought much about it.

57. Seaborg, *Stemming the Tide*, p. 183.

58. Quester, *The Politics of Nuclear Proliferation*, p. 43. Quester observes that the SPD "had been opposed in principle to nuclear weapons for Germany. The new government in Bonn could thus come off the MLF limb onto which it had been coaxed by the United States."

59. That interpretation is open regarding the death date of the MLF is reflected, for example by Mason Willrich in *Non-Proliferation Treaty: Framework for Nuclear Arms Control* (Charlottesville, Va.: Michie Company, 1969), p. 77. He cites as the dates during which the United States and "certain of its NATO allies" backed away from MLF as "during 1966 and 1967."

60. For example, on p. 278 of *Modernity and Power*, Ninkovich observes that LBJ's experience of the Cuban Missile Crisis convinced him that nuclear detente policies were extremely important.

61. Bill Moyers, quoted in Ninkovich, *Modernity and Power*, p. 285.

62. Georges Fischer, *The Non-Proliferation of Nuclear Weapons* (London: Europa, 1971), pp. 198, 199.

63. Seaborg, *Stemming the Tide*, p. 177. For the full wording and a discussion of Johnson's message, see pp. 176–77.

64. Ibid., p. 183.

65. Ibid., pp. 189–91.

66. Ibid., p. 194.

67. Ibid., pp. 195–96.

68. Telegram to State Department from Bonn, March 5, 1967, LBJ Library, "Subject: McCloy's Meeting with Kiesinger—Trilateral Talks," Collection: Papers of LBJ; 1963–69, National Security File: National Security History, The Trilateral Negotiations and NATO: '66–'67, Container: 50, Folder: Trilateral Negotiations and NATO: 1966–67, Book 2, Tabs 53–71. In his conversation with McCloy, Kiesinger basically rescinds the public statement he made about the NPT representing U. S. Soviet duplicity. He states that he had made the comment "smilingly" (p. 2). The comment had stirred the ire of Johnson and many in Washington.

69. Gatzke, *Germany and the United States: A "Special Relationship?"* (Cambridge, Mass.: Harvard University Press, 1980), p. 216. See also Kelleher, *Germany and the Politics of Nuclear Weapons*, pp. 298–99. Adenauer's comment was not overlooked in Washington. During the conversation between McCloy and Kiesinger cited in footnote 82 and on page 2, McCloy refers deploringly to Adenauer's comment that "NPT was the Morgenthau Plan squared." Kiesinger assured him that he also strongly disapproved.

70. Kelleher, *Germany and the Politics of Nuclear Weapons*, p. 298.

71. See discussion in Willrich, *Non-proliferation Treaty*, pp. 178–79. Willrich discusses the benefits the NPT would have in improving relations between the FRG and the USSR. Much in keeping with the SPD design for the creation of a European collective security system, Willrich observes on page 179 that: "By providing a firm basis for a non-nuclear weapon Germany, the Non-Proliferation Treaty could be a step toward settlement of the German problem. . . . The treaty can properly be viewed as a long-term asset in the construction of a stable European system with a non-nuclear Germany at the center."

72. Willy Brandt, *A Peace Policy for Europe* (New York: Holt, Rinehart and Winston, 1969), p. 176.

73. Ibid., pp. 182–83. Brandt expressed this positively in stating: "We understand our renunciation of national control over nuclear weapons, which is an integral part of our policy, as a German contribution to a detente in Europe, and not as discrimination."

74. Seaborg, *Stemming the Tide*, p. 291. Seaborg discusses continued West German obstruction through the end of 1967, and the continued resistance of the State Department to lean on Bonn.

75. Ibid., p. 300.

76. John McCloy, "Memorandum to the President, Subject: Force Levels in Europe," LBJ Library, February 23, 1967, p. 1, Papers of LBJ, 1963–1969: NSF, NSC History, Trilateral Negotiations and NATO, 1966–67, Container: 50, Folder: Trilateral Negotiations and NATO, '66–'67, Tabs 45-52A.

77. See discussion in Fischer, *The Non-proliferation of Nuclear Weapons*, pp. 75–76.

78. See discussion in Seaborg, *Stemming the Tide*, pp. 196–97. In concluding his analysis of the interchange between the United States and the Soviets that finally left open the possibility of such a future development, Seaborg states on p. 197 that "one must ask how it was that the Soviet Union tacitly consented to a treaty interpretation that allowed for the possibility of a united Western European force, something the Soviets certainly would not welcome. They did so, in all likelihood, because they regarded such a united force as being a possibility so remote that, to gain the nonproliferation treaty, it was a chance worth taking."

79. Eugene Rostow, in an interview by Paige Mulhollan, LBJ Library, December 2, 1968, p. 20, Collection: Oral History, Eugene V. Rostow, Container: AC 74-72, Folder: Eugene Rostow AC 74-72.

80. Ibid., pp. 20–21. Also see Brandt, *A Peace Policy for Europe*, p. 182. Brandt sets out quite accurately the vague aspects of the NPT: "The treaty as submitted to the United Nations General Assembly formulates only what is prohibited: everything else is and remains permitted. . . . On the basis of what we and our other partners in the alliance were assured of on the American side, the non-proliferation treaty will not hamper the internal regulation of the Atlantic alliance."

81. Quester, *The Politics of Nuclear Proliferation*, p. 176.

82. See John Mearsheimer's provocative discussion of and prescription for a nuclear Germany in "Back to the Future: Instability in Europe After the Cold War," *International Security* 15 (Summer 1990), 5–56.

83. My reading of this chapter in history is supported by observations made by important players at the time, such as those made by the U.S. ambassador to West Germany at the time, George McGhee. See his memoirs, *At the Creation of a New Germany: From Adenauer to Brandt: An Ambassador's Account* (New Haven, Conn.: Yale University Press, 1989), esp. p. 199. For example, he notes that Johnson and those around him were shocked when the Erhard government fell in 1966. Despite the fact that the Johnson administration had become increasingly insensitive to Erhard's exposed position domestically, it appears that Johnson's distraction with Vietnam more than any manipulative objectives toward Erhard's government explains much of his behavior in 1966.

84. Dean, *Watershed in Europe*, p. 102. Dean actually identifies Brandt and Egon Bahr as the initiators of the Harmel Report.

85. Egon Bahr, *Zum europaeischen Frieden: Eine Antwort auf Gorbatschow* (Berlin: Wolf Jobst Siedler Verlag, 1988), p. 41. My translation. In a background interview

with Bahr conducted in April 1985, he went so far as to say that if nothing else, Ostpolitik was important in assuring that freedom of maneuver for Bonn.

86. Helga Haftendorn, *Security and Detente: Conflicting Priorities in German Foreign Policy* (New York: Praeger, 1985), p. 58. See discussion on pp. 53–58. Interestingly, part of this scheme called for reduction of foreign troops and the withdrawal of tactical weapons.

87. Brandt, *A Peace Policy for Europe*, p. 89.

88. Ibid., p. 88.

89. Ibid., p. 79. Interestingly, in his 1964 speech that I have quoted here, Brandt was supporting Kennedy's "comprehensive attempt to change the relationship between East and West without illusions." As I argued in the preceding chapter, however, it was the Kennedy administration that first overtly contemplated the separation of the German question from the larger U.S.–Soviet context.

90. Willy Brandt, "We Must Struggle For Europe," lecture delivered to the Friedrich Ebert Stiftung, October 1963, in Willy Brandt, *Peace: Writings and Speeches of the Nobel Prize Winner, 1971* (Bonn-Bad Godesberg: Verlag Neue Gesellschaft, 1971) pp. 29–30.

91. Fischer, *The Non-Proliferation of Nuclear Weapons*, p. 76. Fischer cites Gerhard Schroeder, CDU foreign minister under Erhard, as maintaining in 1965 that the FRG "would not give up the idea of acquiring nuclear weapons as long as Russia would not agree to German reunification."

92. Fischer, *The Non-Proliferation of Nuclear Weapons*, p. 71.

93. Telegram, "German Attitude on Participation in Alliance Nuclear Defense," from American Embassy, Bonn, Oct. 11, 1965, LBJ Library, Collection: NSF, Subject File, Container: 25, 36, 38, 44; Folder: MLF: Mr. Bundy: For 6:00 meeting, Monday, Oct. 18, p. 3. "Although it has not yet been widely discussed, support might grow in Germany for a high level alliance group with greater influence over decision making, nuclear strategy, targeting and weapon development. Some SPD leaders have already indicated that they would support this approach. . . . They did not consider it, however, a permanent solution. A political group of this kind could in theory be developed out of the Special Committee if the latter were to be broadened to allow for the participation of Foreign Mins." This is quite close to what developed with the creation of the Nuclear Planning Group.

94. Dean, *Watershed In Europe*, p. 10. See also Haftendorn, *Security and Detente*, p. 102. Citing its many functions, Haftendorn states that "the NPG has become one of the most important organs in the alliance. All in all, the German government has assessed its work positively."

95. Dean, *Watershed in Europe*, p. 10.

96. Seaborg, *Stemming the Tide*, pp. 172–74. West German suspicions that the committee idea represented Washington's hedging on the MLF were raised when McNamara proposed it to the NATO defense ministers at a meeting in May 1965. McNamara's proposal was actually the result of a suggestion by Bundy that alternatives to the MLF regarding inter-Allied nuclear coordination be examined since Bundy was increasingly of the opinion that the MLF was "never going to be the right next step for the necessary number of nations at the same time." Bundy quoted by Seaborg, p. 172.

97. Kelleher, *Germany and the Politics Of Nuclear Weapons*, p. 219.

98. Seaborg, *Stemming the Tide*, p. 174.

99. Brandt, *A Peace Policy For Europe*, p. 144.

100. Kelleher, *Germany and the Politics of Nuclear Weapons*, p. 295.

101. Philip Williams, "Britain, Detente and the Conference on Security and Co-operation in Europe," in *European Detente: Case Studies of the Politics of East-West Relations*, ed. Kenneth Dyson (New York: St. Martin's Press, 1986), pp. 224–25. On page 225, Williams notes of Great Britain's "low profile" in detente during the 1960s and 1970s that it is "somewhat surprising and puzzling because Britain in the 1950s had been a leading proponent of the argument that it was necessary to search for a less hostile relationship with the Soviet Union." As I have shown, however, the British had been frustrated in many of their detente efforts by the American refusal to lean on Bonn, or by an American willingness to allow Bonn, often in cahoots with de Gaulle, to stymie such efforts; one need only recall disarmament efforts during the early 1960s, MLF, and finally the nonproliferation issue. It is not surprising, then, that "As a result, British policy was pragmatic and reactive in a period when other states were taking major initiatives. . . . Britain was 'marginalized.'"

102. Williams, "Britain, Detente," p. 225.

103. Background written interview with Leon Sloss, 1987.

104. Ibid.

105. "Annex to Communiqué," in Richard P. Stebbins, *The United States in World Affairs, 1966* (New York: Harper and Row, 1967), p. 110.

106. Dean, *Watershed in Europe*, p. 102. Also, the central role of the West Germans was confirmed in my written interviews. Leon Sloss states that "the Germans played a very active role once the study got underway. They were certainly among the more active members."

107. "Annex to Communiqué," in Stebbins, *Documents, 1966*, p. 110.

108. *Ibid.*, pp. 110–11.

109. Written interview with Leon Sloss in 1987. Sloss responded to my question concerning Bonn using the Harmel Report to justify forging ahead with its own Ostpolitik by stating: "I do not recall specific examples of the FRG using the Harmel Study to justify Ostpolitik. However, I think you reach a valid conclusion. However, it is clear that each country arrived at its own interpretation of the report."

110. Sloss interview, 1987.

111. Brandt, *A Peace Policy for Europe*, p. 93.

112. Stebbins, *Documents, 1967*, p. 102.

113. Willy Brandt. *My Life in Politics* (New York: Viking, 1992), p. 165.

114. Brandt, *A Peace Policy for Europe*, p. 90.

115. Background written interview, George McGhee. He stated: "Washington was always divided about Brandt's Ostpolitik; however, Kennedy [Johnson?] and Rusk generally supported it, as did I. Real concern developed under Nixon, with Kissinger as the leading skeptic."

116. Background Paper, "Berlin, Germany, and German Reunification," December 7, 1966, pp. 1–2, LBJ Library, NSF, International Meetings and Travel File, Container: 35, 36, Folder: NATO: NATO Ministerial Meeting, Paris, December, 1966. Another background paper from June 14, 1967, "Berlin, Germany and German Reunification," reiterates this position on p. 1: "A major change in German thinking regarding reunification has taken place since the Kiesinger-Brandt gov-

ernment came into power. Today Germans speak less of allied responsibility for reunification and more of reunification as a problem to be solved over a period of time, primarily by Germans working together."

117. Position Paper, "Belgian Proposal for Study on Future of NATO," Paris, December 14–16, 1966, pp. 1–2, LBJ Library, Collection: NSF, International Meetings and Travel File, Container: 35 and 36, Folder: NATO: NATO Ministerial Meeting, Paris, December, 1966. Here it is recommended that the United States "maintain a flexible attitude, particularly on timing and on aspects of the problem that may have to be sorted out among European members of the Alliance. . . . Any new study should concentrate on political and non-military problems."

118. A brilliant contribution to the literature concerning the SPD's Ostpolitik and detente policies is Timothy Garton Ash's *In Europe's Name: Germany and the Divided Continent* (New York: Random House, 1993).

119. Brandt, *A Peace Policy for Europe*, pp. 117–39. For example, on page 122, Brandt states: "We must start from the status quo. What else is there to start from? But it would be against nature and against reason to renounce any desire for future development. . . . We wish to eliminate the source of mischief—the division of Germany—by means of peaceful understanding and once again to give to our own people their peace with themselves and with the world."

120. Walter F. Hahn, "West Germany's Ostpolitik: The Grand Design Of Egon Bahr," *Orbis* 16, no. 4 (Winter 1973), p. 874. Hahn goes on the state that " 'reconciliation' with the countries of the East is simply the precondition and starting point for an active West German strategy designed to set in motion, and subsequently to shape, a complex and far-reaching process of change in Europe that will lead, at some as yet indeterminate point, to the restoration of the German nation," pp. 874–75.

121. Fritz Erler, quoted in Haftendorn, *Security and Detente*, p. 53.

122. The SPD's conception of a collective security system had actually been evident since the early 1950s, when Schumacher advocated such a development. The concept went through various manifestations before its 1959 version was endorsed. See Haftendorn, *Security and Detente*, pp. 50–53.

123. Egon Bahr, "Wandel Durch Annaeherung," *Deutschland-Archiv*, 8/1973, p. 862.

124. Bahr, "Wandel Durch Annaeherung," p. 862.

125. See especially Ash, *In Europe's Name*, esp. chs. III–VI.

126. The Bonn Declaration, cited in Ash, *In Europe's Name*, p. 114. Ash's discussion of the SPD and CDU regarding Ostpolitik and its meaning for East-West history is excellent, particularly chs. 2, 3.

127. Ash, *In Europe's Name*, addresses this issue in a detailed and systematic way.

128. Charles Kupchan and Clifford Kupchan, "Concerts, Collective Security, and the Future of Europe," *International Security* 16 (Summer 1991): 114–61.

129. Kelleher, *Germany and the Politics of Nuclear Weapons*, p. 294. She puts it in the following way: "The aim must be to maximize Germany's current national freedom of maneuver, while eventually undermining the status quo through its acceptance."

FROM OSTPOLITIK TO UNIFICATION: THE LEGACY OF THE WILSONIAN IMPULSE AND THE VERSAILLES REMEDIAL

I will trace Allied relations from 1967 forward in this chapter. The Harmel Report represented a sea-change in these relationships. First, the base upon which change in East-West relations evolved was now expanded from the U.S.–Soviet strategic relationship to a less rigidly defined political-economic-diplomatic framework. From 1967 onward, West German leaders would enhance Bonn's influence in East-West relations by employing these latter components of detente and then eventually relinking them to military-security issues. The Harmel era therefore not only assured greater West German influence and autonomy within the Western security relationship, it reflected the SPD method of using the Wilsonian approach to include the East-West context and thereby guarantee greater West German influence in that relationship. The evolution of East-West security relations since the Harmel Exercise in fact largely reflected the goals expressed in the SPD blueprint discussed in the last chapter, and was adopted with modifications by the CDU throughout the 1980s.

In the meantime, American policymakers found it increasingly difficult to implement a policy that encouraged community-building and defense in the Alliance. The reasons are several. First, the tensions between the two goals increased through the 1970s and 1980s. Because of that, the lens through which German behavior was viewed tended to vary from administration to administration, although the State Department maintained the institutionalization of the Wilsonian impulse and the Versailles remedial to a great extent.

Second, and related, as U.S. power waned relative to others, but especially after American policymakers acknowledged the gains in Soviet military capabilities and then strategic parity toward the end of the 1960s, Washington's attention became more riveted to the bipolar strategic relationship, as Kennedy had attempted to do earlier. Western Europeans, and especially Bonn, became increasingly wary of American unilateralism on East-West strategic issues. As the consequences of the Harmel Exercise became clear, the Western Europeans were in fact extremely successful in delimiting America's exclusionary hold on interbloc relations through various detente initiatives and policies.

Third, the very success of the Wilsonian impulse and Versailles remedial lessened the urgency for employing them in U.S. policy toward Western Europe over time. Interestingly enough, when presidents Jimmy Carter and Ronald Reagan attempted to follow the Wilsonian impulse in other contexts, West European leaders became uneasy. When Carter tried to apply the community-building aspects of the impulse globally, especially to the developing world, he created problems in relations with Western Europe.[1] When Reagan underwent his transformation regarding the Soviet Union, he dedicated himself to finding ways to include the former adversary into the Western community of nations. He, like Carter, and revisiting the Eisenhower stance, even raised anew the notion of abolition of nuclear weapons. Reagan also brought back the idea of nuclear sharing with the Soviets. His Wilsonian ways left many in Western Europe and in his own administration unsettled.

Finally, the very meaning of community-building itself became the subject to debate in the West as the West Germans, led by the SPD, developed their own collective security scheme for Europe. As I discussed in the last chapter, their approach sounded Wilsonian, with its emphasis on self-determination, equality of status, and nondiscrimination, but it was definitely not Wilsonian in its assumption that community-building among unlike social and political systems was both possible and desirable. Unlike the Wilsonian goal of creating a common culture, this version reverted to a more traditional European understanding of great power cooperation, or to the concert concept. Thus, as West Germans used Western multilateralism for their own purposes and began extending their version of community-building eastward to facilitate achieving reunification, Bonn's behavior became more suspect to many in the West.[2]

All of that is not meant to suggest that the Wilsonian impulse and Versailles remedial disappeared. They did not. They remained institutionalized at the U.S. State Department and in the Alliance. The result was a great deal of dissonance in American foreign policy and in Allied behavior. The Alliance became bifurcated, especially evident during the early

Reagan administration. As Washington attempted to regain control of the East-West relationship by remilitarizing it, Western Europe, led by Bonn, maintained insistently the legitimacy of detente and Harmel.

DETENTE AND OSTPOLITIK: WASHINGTON VS. BONN

Since Willy Brandt and the West German SPD began the "step-by-step" detente process whose eventual goal was the dissolution of the postwar Cold War bloc system that enforced the division of Europe and therefore of Germany, American and Western European approaches to East-West security issues diverged significantly at times. When one takes a long, sweeping glance at East-West relations from the 1970s until the present, one is struck by the success with which Bonn influenced outcomes in those relations. On the one hand, American dissatisfaction with detente by the mid-1970s led policymakers in Washington to emphasize increasingly the military competition between the United States and the USSR as being once again the center of East-West relations. On the other hand, success with Ostpolitik and Deutschlandpolitik led West German policymakers to an opposite conclusion regarding East-West relations: The emphasis on detente and cooperation, rather than on a renewed military competition between the superpowers, would best serve West German interests.

In this chapter, I will examine the divergent West German and American assessments of detente. What becomes clear is that throughout this period, the American inclination to remilitarize the East-West relationship eventually yielded to West German demands that the Harmel understanding, which underwrote continued West German loyalty to the Alliance after 1967, not be sacrificed on the altar of the renewed U.S.–Soviet arms race. In other words, despite expressed interests to the contrary, the legacy of the Wilsonian impulse and Versailles remedial continued to impact on and entrap American policy.

The American interest in detente under Nixon and Kissinger was from the beginning military and strategic in nature. America's community-building objective in Western Europe corresponded with its bridge-building scheme for East-West relations under Johnson, Carter, and Reagan in his second term, but not as conceived by Nixon and Kissinger. The latter arose from Washington's concern with defense and balancing in the traditional sense. Kissinger is insightful on this point: "Because American thinking on foreign policy had been shaped by liberal ideas ever since Woodrow Wilson, there was no ready constituency for Nixon's style of foreign policy." He goes on to say that "diplomatic results . . . were emerging from principles that were anathema to the liberal tradition, such as emphasis on the national interest and the balance of power."[3] In his book on American foreign policy and Wilsonianism, Tony Smith does not include a chapter on the Nixon and Kissinger years.[4]

While there is evidence that economic motives played a role among certain U.S. groups for promoting detente at this time, these aspirations were essentially defeated by the mid-1970s.[5] For the West Germans, on the other hand, economic motives were central in pursuing detente, as was the vital political goal of addressing the German question in an environment of reduced military tensions. The economic success of the export-dependent FRG in its relations with the East is a well-known and often-cited fact. The political objective placed a premium on improving German-German relations and relations with the East bloc, especially with the Soviets. Increasingly, events during the 1970s would reveal the basically different American and West German interests in detente, and thereby the contrary assessments that would inevitably be made of the process. What resulted was a bifurcation in Allied relations, with the West Europeans, led by West Germany, continuing to pursue detente, and the United States attempting to remilitarize the East-West relationship once its perception of detente proved negative. Significantly, Washington's attempt at Western retrenchment failed.

Related to this diverging view of detente in West-West relations during the 1970s was the growing discrepancy in perceptions of the Soviet threat among the Allies. While the perceived threat of the USSR decreased dramatically in Western European countries, notably in the FRG, it did so less starkly and less quickly in the United States. For example, polls taken in the FRG reveal that public perception of the Soviet Union as a threat went from a high of 81 percent in 1954 to 47 percent in 1983. Correspondingly, perceptions of the USSR as presenting no threat rose from 19 percent in 1954 to 53 percent in 1983.[6] Alongside the perceived decrease of the Soviet threat was the increased perception that the United States posed as much "a danger to world peace" as did the USSR.[7] A poll conducted in 1987 comparing Reagan and Gorbachev revealed that 49 percent of West Germans found Soviet leader Gorbachev "more concerned about the securing of peace and disarmament," while only 9 percent placed Reagan in this category; 30 percent answered both.[8]

On the other hand, American public perception of the Soviet threat increased between the years 1978 and 1983, although a majority still believed in the importance of arms control.[9] This phenomenon attests to the bifurcation in Allied relations that evolved since the 1970s. The divergence not only affected individual Allied attitudes toward defense spending and readiness, it also had repercussions in an array of political/economic issues.[10] The Western Europeans, and particularly the West Germans, increasingly viewed the Soviet Union as a status quo power in Europe, while the United States under Carter, but especially in Reagan's first term, perceived the Soviets as a security threat. In truth, of course, it was West Germany that was the revisionist power.

Ostpolitik: Undermining the Status Quo

After the SPD assumed power in 1969, the party forged ahead with a rapid succession of detente policies intended to overcome the status quo and lead eventually to a reunited Germany. Despite reservations by Allies, West German Ostpolitik continued and Bonn could claim legitimacy based on the principles now enshrined in the Alliance with the Harmel Report. From Ostpolitik's inception onward, Bonn would be able to act directly on East-West security issues. As noted in Chapter Three, the building of the Berlin Wall revealed to SPD leaders like Brandt the lack of Allied success in overcoming the postwar division through reliance on military force and its associated rhetoric. As early as 1963, Brandt claimed the following for the FRG and Western Europe concerning detente: "We are prepared to help, whenever it is a question of a realistic rapprochement and detente, but just as obviously we must insist on our inviolable rights."[11] The "inviolable" rights to which he referred clearly sprung from the Wilsonianism underwriting the Allied relationship and included the rights of equality of status and self-determination of sovereign states.

With the "political purpose" of the Alliance now explicitly formulated, or the *politicization* of the East-West security relationship formally acknowledged,[12] Bonn rapidly set in motion a series of far-reaching, bilateral, detente-oriented policies with the Soviet Union and the East bloc. More important for this study is its direct link to the German question of reunification. As I have discussed throughout, much of the history of East-West detente has been centered on the German question. From the Cold War era of the 1950s straight through to 1990, the unachieved goal of unity allowed Bonn to focus the West, and particularly the United States, on West German concerns. From the frustrations of the Kennedy administration in decrying Adenauer's "virtual veto" over American security policy under the Eisenhower administration to Acheson's lament about Brandt's "mad race to Moscow," to Kenneth Adelman's complaint that "the Germans, as always, were the big problem,"[13] to Stanley Hoffmann observing Germany's "run" to reunification in 1990,[14] Bonn has been instrumental in shaping the Western approach to Western and East-West security issues through its continued demand for progress on the German question. For example, in discussing Bonn's changed position on detente, intra-German affairs, and the East-West question, Brandt stated in his memoirs:

Our allies fully grasped that this heralded a policy which was prepared to abandon old positions—but only given a Western consensus and the other side's willingness to talk. This was why I deliberately associated the "German question" with an all-European peace settlement at the NATO meeting at Reykjavik in June 1969.[15]

To achieve that goal, Bonn began actively promoting policies that sought eventual military disengagement in Central Europe, another long-term objective that had been expressed in the 1950s. The enhanced role of the Alliance as a political tool of Western security and East-West detente, and the Allied endorsement of independently pursued but collectively co-ordinated detente policies, greatly increased the direct political influence and the maneuverability of Bonn in beginning to realize these goals.

In order to overcome American dominance in East-West matters, the SPD also began relinking detente to progress in the strategic relationship. Although they were not as successful here, the Conference on Security and Cooperation in Europe (CSCE) and the Mutual Balanced Force Reductions (MBFR) talks should be seen in this light.[16] Both were actively promoted by West German SPD leaders, and both tension reduction processes were explicitly linked by Brandt.[17]

The security vocabulary in the last wave of preunification East-West de-tente was fundamentally influenced by West German ideas. The now-famous "zero option" pursued in arms control that led the Reagan administration down the path to the Reykjavík summit and then to the In-termediate Nuclear Forces (INF) treaty was West German in origin.[18] The call for mutual conventional and tactical troop reductions reflected SPD security policy thinking from the early 1960s. The "security partnership" to which Gorbachev stylishly referred was a concept the SPD conceived and had been promoting for some time, as was the concept of the "Euro-pean peace order." During interviews with over twenty-five SPD analysts and policymakers during 1985–86, the idea of the "security partnership" between Western Europe and the Soviet bloc was raised time and time again as an alternative cooperative conception of East-West relations to Reagan's competitive notions of East-West relations.

The "European peace order" was one of the most frequently mentioned concepts to which West German foreign policy was linked in my interviews with SPD, CDU, FDP, and Foreign Office respondents. Although there was a wide spectrum of definitions and descriptions of that order, this does not detract from the fact that they all included a vision of a European commu-nity, including East and West, in which Germany was united in some form. The concept presupposed, therefore, an overcoming of the postwar status quo and therefore the political conditions of German disunity. That most re-spondents also discussed pursuit of a "European peace order" as occurring within the contours of Alliance policy reflected the legitimization given to revisionist Ostpolitik in the Allied agenda during the Harmel Exercise.[19]

In sum, the slow but perceptible progress toward political and then mil-itary disengagement by the superpowers in Central Europe, or the process of politicization of the East-West relationship, has been steadily advocated and pursued by West Germany since the Harmel Report of 1967, and by both the SPD and CDU once Brandt's Ostpolitik forged a domestic con-

sensus in the FRG. That succeeded, however, because of the historical opportunities opened earlier by American Wilsonians and West German
leaders who helped legitimize the Wilsonian impulse to further their interests while aiding the Western integration process.

Ostpolitik and the Alliance

Was it necessary for Bonn to seek the legitimacy granted by the Harmel
Report when formulating its own Ostpolitik? The evidence suggests that it
was—that grounding Ostpolitik within the Alliance context was largely
responsible for Bonn's success in the policy.[20] Western historical memory
still recalled Germany's collusion with Russia in the 1922 Rapallo agreement. Not only was the fear of another Rapallo still a reality faced by Germans, the fact that the German question was still open continued to give
the FRG's neighbors and allies cause for concern.

While some have viewed Brandt's Ostpolitik as a short-range, pragmatic
West German readjustment to the systemic confines of the period, his "step-
by-step" detente formula for gradually transforming the postwar system
through negotiation and enhanced political and economic cooperation was
clearly revisionist. In a presentation to the West German Bundestag in November 1968, Brandt recounted the renewed Allied responsibility for the
German question as formulated in the Harmel Exercise. He also noted that
the FRG's future endeavors to achieve German unity through detente efforts and the concomitant policy of seeking closer intra-German ties were
solidly backed by the Allies and based on agreed-upon Allied policy.[21]
Brandt further cited Allied endorsement of the Harmel Exercise as proof
that the attempts of the Soviet Union and East Berlin to convince Bonn's allies of the hopelessness of the FRG's goal of German unity were fruitless.[22]
Brandt thereby sought not only domestic approval for his Ostpolitik, but
also sent a strong message both to Western capitals and to the Soviet Union
that West German detente was earnestly concerned with overcoming the
postwar status quo. Through Allied backing for his revisionist goals, Brandt
could then assert that the Federal Republic was pursuing a policy designed
to substitute a European peace settlement for the balance of terror—it was
a reasonable alternative.[23]

Clearly, many of the FRG's allies were hesitant about Bonn's new role as
detente supporter and activist. For this reason alone, it was important that
Brandt and the SPD ground their Ostpolitik in Western Allied policy. As
Timothy Garton Ash observes of this "tactical" SPD position, it was essential for the SPD to "gain and retain the support of Germany's Western
partners," and "not to be seen to put those Western ties in question. On the
contrary, she must redouble her insistence on their importance."[24]

The revisionist element of Ostpolitik contrasted directly with the mostly
status quo–seeking detente aspirations of other states. The Soviets were

explicit in using detente to confirm the postwar status quo in Europe. Goergey Laszlo has observed:

Genuine relaxation meant for Moscow and most of the satellites, the perpetuation of the status quo. It was to be equivalent to legalizing the results of World War II. . . . Moreover, in France, with or without de Gaulle, the settlement of the German problem was not understood to be identical with the re-establishment of a unitary German state. Indeed, relaxation for the French was envisaged as a reduction of tensions between West Germany and the East made possible by the prior acceptance of Germany's division by Bonn, a step that neither Kiesinger, nor Brandt nor Wehner were willing explicitly to undertake.[25]

The goals of France and other of Bonn's allies in containing West German revisionist objectives were often implicit. However, distrust of Ostpolitik was evident in London and even more so in Paris during the latter 1960s and early 1970s, although Brandt was able to enlist Western Europe's support for his policies.[26] With all the uneasiness concerning Bonn's Ostpolitik, it is illuminating that no one in the West was eager to challenge it openly. In fact, between 1969 and 1972, Bonn proceeded to complete an almost dizzying number of agreements with the Soviet Union and the East bloc, including historically significant meetings with the leadership of the GDR, culminating in 1972 with the Basic Agreement between the two Germanys.[27]

In this welter of activity, Bonn's allies continued to offer their explicit support while remaining for the most part quietly anxious. In many ways the phenomenon foreshadowed Western response to Kohl's rapid push for reunification in 1989–90. I will deal below with the American response in particular. A State Department Research Memorandum written in 1965 illustrates the potential dilemmas for the FRG relative to others in pursuing detente, and was extremely relevant to the political situation in 1989:

Unlike its Western European neighbors . . . the FRG is clearly, in the terminology of the interwar years, not a status quo but a revisionist state, in the sense that it has political-territorial aspirations going beyond preserving what it has. . . . No West European country need risk its relations with the FRG at the present time by expressing reservations about the merits of reunification because the prospects for unity seem remote. But all of these governments find themselves in the somewhat paradoxical position of favoring an East-West "detente" which many observers believe may present the most promising approach in the very long run, for developing a basis for German reunification. . . . But should prospects for reunification improve, the intra-West European political system which has emerged since the late 1940s would, at the least, face its most serious test to date.[28]

That recent Allied support for West German Ostpolitik has still been predicated on Bonn's role as an Alliance member can be gleaned from many sources. From a French perspective, for example, Henri Froment-Meurice states in his book, *Europa als eine Macht*, "The Germans are obliged to prove that their efforts to overcome the division of Germany won't set in motion a nationalistic process, but rather will remain consistent with the obligations of Western security and European unification."[29]

Most important for Brandt was that Harmel, like the 1954 agreement, promised not only nondiscrimination and equality of status among Allies, principles upon which Bonn could and did claim legitimacy for its Ostpolitik, it invoked anew Allied responsibility for resolution of the German question. Thus, by firmly planting Ostpolitik within the Allied framework, Bonn could claim legitimately that its future goal of peaceful resolution of the German question through detente-oriented policies was part and parcel of the Allied understanding upon which depended West German loyalty. Bonn thereby guaranteed that although there might be much suspicion in the West regarding the rapidity with which it pursued Ostpolitik and its inevitably revisionist objectives, the West German claim to legitimacy for its actions had been preapproved by the Wilsonian principles underwriting the Western security relationship.

The West German Domestic Debate

Brandt's ability to legitimize Ostpolitik further by casting it as an Allied-backed policy in the aftermath of Harmel not only reinforced his leverage over the Allies but also enhanced his domestic position vis-à-vis the opposition. If Ostpolitik was controversial abroad, it was even more so within the FRG. From the narrow margins with which the SPD/FDP coalition government assumed power in 1969 to the even narrower margins by which Brandt's Eastern treaties were finally ratified, the early years of Ostpolitik were highly contentious domestically. The issues of Ostpolitik and Deutschlandpolitik caused internal dissension within the parties, especially within the CDU/CSU, as well as among the parties, and the right fought ferociously against the SPD/FDP coalition policy. Allegations against the SPD and Ostpolitik ranged from accusing Egon Bahr, often cited as the architect of Ostpolitik, of pro-Soviet leanings, to chastising the SPD and its Eastern policies as selling out the interests of the FRG and the Alliance. A number of highly critical analyses inferred from it an appeasement of the Soviet Union by major SPD leaders or major weakness in SPD reasoning.[30] In an article from 1973, Walter Hahn was highly critical of Brandt's Ostpolitik, and particularly of Bahr:

We should not . . . fall victim to one grave error namely, the comforting judgment that Egon Bahr seems to be pursuing illusion. History has proven that, to the extent that it drives policy, illusion creates its own kind of reality.[31]

One CSU member, Graf von Huyn, voiced the misgivings of many on the far right in stating that

The concessions made to Moscow remind us in a painful way of Chamberlain's policy of appeasement towards Hitler. The success can be anticipated. The dictator is made stronger and remains implacable. . . . The members of the Federal Parliament who will vote for the treaty, must be aware that by the ratification of the Moscow treaty in its present form they would, according to the Kremlin's intentions, at the same time turn the first sod in digging the grave for the freedom of Germany and of Europe.[32]

Brandt's Ostpolitik policies spawned a number of defections from the coalition FDP Party to the opposition CDU Party. By April 1972, Ostpolitik and the domestic political turmoil it unleashed resulted in the first motion of no confidence to be seriously brought in FRG history. Led by Rainer Barzel, contender for the Chancellor's seat should the CDU return to power, the CDU hoped to gain a majority in the Bundestag for its motion of no confidence. This did not occur.[33] The final votes on the treaties with the Soviet Union and Poland were narrowly won in May. After Brandt deliberately lost a vote of confidence in Parliament that same month, new elections were held in the autumn of 1972. In these elections, Brandt hoped to achieve a safe majority in Parliament in order to continue unimpeded with Ostpolitik. In the elections, the SPD/FDP coalition finally won a majority, and the stage was set for completing the most important of the Eastern policies—the Basic Agreement with the GDR, which was signed on December 21, 1972.

The problem for the opposition at this point was that with the Harmel Exercise completed and the initial phases of Ostpolitik having been spawned during the CDU/SPD Grand Coalition, the CDU/CSU could no longer return to the policy of thwarting Western detente initiatives by linking them negatively to movement on the German question. Brandt had assured the demise of such linkage strategies. Thus, the CDU's alternatives were the following: accept Ostpolitik as defined by the SPD; pursue an active Eastern policy that would be differentiated from the SPD version by moving away from the CDU's former reactive role in thwarting movement in East-West detente to an active one; or raise the specter of Bonn one day pursuing its reunification goal through a unilateral nationalist policy outside the Alliance framework. Gerhard Schroeder and Helmut Kohl advocated unreserved reliance on American deterrence and active engagement in Eastern Europe. Rainer Barzel and Gerhard Stoltenberg called for hard-line negotiations with NATO for increases in individual commitments and strict reciprocity in dealings with Eastern Europe, and Franz Josef Strauss and Baron von Guttenburg of the CSU pressed for a reduced U.S. military presence and creation of a European nuclear deterrent and no concessions to Eastern Europe.[34] In light of these possibilities, it is understandable that the Allies, including Washington, believed they had little recourse but to accept Brandt's lead in Ostpolitik and his forging ahead with East-West detente.

One thing is clear: Whichever domestic position attained salience in Bonn, movement on the German question in some form or another would be high on the agenda. The domestic debate inside the FRG had reached a point where innovating on accomplishing movement toward that goal was deemed essential and was driven by the SPD. The West German proclivity to manipulate earlier Western inaction to Bonn's advantage had succeeded, and Adenauer had for years thwarted Western attempts at pursuing detente. Brandt now provided the main engine for detente.

Thus, the watershed in West German and in Allied policy fostered by Ostpolitik and legitimated by the Harmel Exercise was not so much the result of Bonn responding to international constraints; it was the manipulation by Bonn of international constraints and opportunities in the name of national interest. Hanrieder counters:

Dynamic as Brandt's Ostpolitik was in many ways, it was nonetheless fundamentally a policy of resignation, designed not so much to bring about changes for a foreseeable future as not to foreclose possibilities for an unforeseeable future. Even so, by attuning West German foreign policy to the dynamics of detente—the outstanding foreign policy aim of most members of the Warsaw Pact as well as of the Atlantic Alliance—Bonn kept pace with developments.[35]

From my perspective, the point is that Bonn set the pace and attuned the as yet undefined and vague impulses toward detente to West German interests. Brandt correctly observed of the active rather than reactive nature of Ostpolitik:

What really mattered was to create a climate in which the status quo could be changed—in other words, improved—by peaceful means. I was unjustly accused, both then and later, of 'bowing to realities.' I was, and still am, of the opinion that realities can be influenced for the better only if they are taken into account.[36]

The tumultuous domestic situation left Bonn's allies little room to maneuver in attempting to influence Brandt's course. Their backing of Ostpolitik was partially explained by the fear that the alternatives to Brandt might be worse and might appear even more conducive to a new German nationalism or disruptive policy. The recurring theme from the early years of Adenauer's tenure should be noted: Either help and back the seemingly moderate demands of the current regime or risk something perhaps worse. The Versailles remedial was still potent.

The United States and Detente

The election of Richard Nixon corresponded with the formation of the SPD/FDP coalition in Bonn, led by Brandt and FDP Foreign Minister Walter Scheel. While Woodrow Wilson was Nixon's boyhood idol, his major foreign policy player, Henry Kissinger, was a student of Metternich and German realism.[37] From his perspective, international order depended upon ensuring stability, which was preserved "through artfully tending to balances of power."[38] Kissinger subscribed to classical realism. In this way, he opposed what he saw as the Wilsonian idealist strand of American foreign policy, although he clearly understood it and was sensitive to it in domestic political terms.[39] Walter Isaacson quotes him as once presenting his view of international relations with a paraphrase of Goethe: "If I had to choose between justice and disorder, on the one hand, and injustice and order on the other, I would always choose the latter."[40] As I have argued throughout the study, the Wilsonian impulse included both.

Having said that, Kissinger was actually extremely receptive to the Versailles remedial and thus to West German special interests. This sensitivity, however, often collided with his instincts for approaching international relations from a particularistic American perspective that focused on the balancing of power between the two superpowers. The two instincts remained in conflict throughout his term, although, as Kennedy experienced earlier, American policy continued to be ensnared by West German interests through the influence of the Wilsonian impulse at State.

Nixon and Kissinger were immediately distrustful of Brandt and Ostpolitik.[41] Although West German Ostpolitik was formally underwritten by Allied policy, Kissinger voiced a widely held cautionary note:

It seemed to me that Brandt's new Ostpolitik, which looked to many like a progressive policy of quest for detente, could in less scrupulous hands turn into a new form of classic German nationalism. From Bismarck to Rapallo, it was the essence of Germany's nationalist foreign policy to maneuver freely between East and West. By contrast, American (and German) policy since the 1940s had been to ground the Federal Republic firmly in the West, in the Atlantic Alliance and then the European Community.[42]

Interestingly, while still maintaining a position wherein he thought the United States could unilaterally constrain and guide Ostpolitik through its bilateral relationship with the FRG and its power over Allied relations with the Soviet Union, Kissinger acknowledged the reality of Allied relations:

That I thought Ostpolitik was more likely to lead to a permanent division of Germany was irrelevant. The Brandt government was asking not for our advice but for our cooperation in a course to which its principal figures had long since been committed. . . . It seemed to me important to work with Brandt rather than against him; opposing him would earn us the opprobrium of all the Germans of both parties who believed that Bonn deserved a chance. Moreover, Brandt's course was supported by all allies with the possible exception of France, which was, however, unwilling to make its opposition explicit.[43]

In his efforts to see that the United States maintained an element of control over Bonn's pursuit of Ostpolitik, Kissinger sidestepped the State Department and established a White House "backchannel" with Egon Bahr.[44] Kissinger revealed through this action not only his dislike for the bureaucratic and Wilsonian State Department, but also his predilections to try and rationalize foreign policy by controlling it, and his predisposition to diplomatic secrecy.[45]

Interestingly, however, while Brandt and Bahr kept Kissinger informed on the series of negotiations that Bonn quickly opened with the Soviets and East Europeans, and Washington did maintain influence on the rapidity with which negotiations progressed by linking Ostpolitik to other Allied issues such as Berlin, the impetus was clearly with Bonn.[46] Kissinger's depiction of Brandt's communication style with Washington during this time sounds like de Gaulle's reaction to American behavior to the Allies during the Cuban missile crisis, although Brandt did his part to assuage anxiety by keeping in close touch: "To be sure, the new German government informed rather than consulted. They reported progress; they did not solicit advice."[47] The situation also foreshadowed the events of 1989, when it would be the West German chancellor, not the American president, who through an amazingly adroit series of diplomatic and political moves achieved German unification in the course of one year.

What is curious about this era of Allied history is the seeming role reversal of Bonn and Washington vis-à-vis East-West relations. Whereas Adenauer and the CDU–led Bonn government sought to retard American and Western detente efforts in order not to legitimize the postwar status quo, and thus continuously linked such progress to the German question and security issues, Kissinger and the White House similarly sought to restrain West German efforts and maintain more influence for Washington in controlling the course of East-West relations.

Washington eventually attempted to regain its influence by reemphasizing the military-strategic element of the East-West relationship, and thus the defense element of the Allied relationship, where it still enjoyed preeminent power. By this point, however, the defense-detente, or military-political components of the Alliance were irrevocably linked through the Harmel Exercise, and a certain bifurcation developed in the relationship. This phenomenon was alluded to by Kissinger when he observed in 1982 that "I do not believe in divisible detente in the sense that one side does the defense and the other side does the negotiating . . . that Europe should have a monopoly on detente and America on defense."[48] Professor Martin Hillenbrand observed of Kissinger and his position regarding Allied detente policy: "His view, I would imagine, derives from a belief that the superpowers must be the essential creators of detente, and that a military alliance should stick to its original purpose of defense against possible Soviet aggression."[49]

The continued ability of Bonn to set the detente agenda was striking. While Kissinger goes to great lengths in his memoirs to stress the final veto power the United States had over Ostpolitik due to Bonn's continued reliance on Washington to pressure the Soviets for an agreement on Berlin,[50] it was Bonn that set the agenda and the parameters by which the United States would bring its continued influence to bear. Nixon was furious in 1971 that Brandt had taken the Western lead in detente by signing the important Warsaw Treaty with Poland while the United States and the other Allies watched "on the sidelines."[51] Once the treaty was signed, Brandt urged Washington to "step up the pace of their own negotiations" on Berlin.[52] Only at this point did Brandt accept Kissinger's idea of linkage between ratification of the treaty and the completion of a Berlin Agreement. While Kissinger interpreted this development as the United States reining Brandt in, the fact is that Brandt had made U.S. pressure to achieve a swift agreement on Berlin certain, and wanted a Berlin agreement, particularly for the reason that it would grant domestic credibility to Ostpolitik.[53] Despite his insistence that Washington's role was pivotal in the Ostpolitik process, Kissinger concedes that the United States was captive to Ostpolitik:

We could abort his Ostpolitik only by massive intervention in German internal politics, the alienation of our allies, and (as President Pompidou feared) the refashioning of NATO into a German-American alliance for the liberation of Eastern Europe. And we had no alternative to offer. It was their fear of a German "liberation policy" that had caused Pompidou and Harold Wilson to endorse Brandt's approach publicly and to press us privately to follow suit.[54]

Allied acquiescence to the "inevitable" reveals the legacy of the Wilsonian impulse and Versailles remedial. Interestingly, regarding the latter, it is quite clear from the historical record that Kissinger took Allied responsibility for German unification seriously. First, Kissinger, like many American policymakers before him, stood firm against recognition of the GDR, which he felt "would cause serious disillusionment in the Federal Republic."[55] Further, in his book, *Kissinger: Portrait of a Mind*, Stephen R. Graubard states that Kissinger believed:

The West had to support German unification, whatever its misgivings, if it did not want to see the establishment of "a militant, dissatisfied power in the center of the

Continent." The West might be compelled to acquiesce in the continued division of Germany, but it ought not to agree to it, and it certainly ought not to advocate it.[56]

Kissinger's support of German unification does not make him less a realist. As I stated earlier, realists and Wilsonians could superficially find agreement there. Yet, as I have discussed, the point is that the Brandt-led government had assured West German independence through Ostpolitik by legitimizing it in the Harmel Exercise of 1967. The ability of the United States to control East-West relations was thereby diminished. Kissinger grudgingly acknowledged that fait accompli in 1982: "In 1968, at Reykjavik, NATO developed the theory—which I believe is totally wrong—that the alliance is as much an instrument of detente as it is of defense. . . . NATO is not equipped to be an instrument of detente."[57]

The Decline of American Detente

Already by 1976, U.S. interest in detente was waning, spurred mainly by domestic anxiety and frustration over strategic considerations. The Soviets, it seemed, were reaping more advantage from arms control than was America. After President Ford's 1975 Vladivostok "understanding" with the Soviets, another episode along the way to a SALT II agreement, American detente took a nose-dive. With Kissinger having already launched a domestic political debate to "sell" detente, the adversaries of SALT and detente were on the offensive.[58] Led by conservatives such as Ronald Reagan, the attack against Kissinger's policies of detente culminated with the deletion of the term from Ford's 1976 presidential campaign. Reagan is quoted as having stated: "Under Kissinger and Ford, this nation has become Number Two in a world where it is dangerous—if not fatal—to be second best."[59] Instead, Ford campaigned on a "peace through strength" platform. Kissinger himself all but rejected detente after leaving office and remained a critic of many detente-oriented Allied policies.[60]

President Jimmy Carter's Wilsonian persuasion was evident. As one author observes, Carter exerted "efforts to promote a cooperative, global community."[61] The Wilsonian goals of creating "a new political and international order that is truly more participatory and genuinely more responsive to the global desire for greater social justice, equity, and more opportunity for individual self-fulfillment" harkened back to the Wilsonian concept of building a global security community.[62] His rejection of the balance of power scheme in international relations was obvious by his purposeful downgrading of the bipolar competition. His linkage of a variety of global issues was meant to help the global community evolve.[63]

Carter's attempt to move the Wilsonian impulse to the global level meant a lesser role in U.S. foreign policy not just for the American-Soviet competition, but for the European connection as well. In this way, Carter threatened the tenets of the Western community as it had evolved, and it certainly left little room for the Versailles remedial. Benign neglect of those relationships left many West Europeans unhappy. His relationship with West German Helmut Schmidt was sour for many reasons, but his global Wilsonianism certainly did not improve it.

Further, although he advocated arms control, Carter preferred disarmament initiatives. His advocacy of disarmament gave him serious trouble with Western Europeans and his perceived naivete in Allied politics generally provoked the wrath of important American allies, particularly Schmidt.[64] Bilateral disarmament initiatives between Washington and Moscow hardly addressed the West German interest of keeping East-West relations focused on Bonn. Carter's moves on arms negotiations with the Soviets were constantly met with demands from Bonn that West European interests be taken into account.[65] At one point, when progress on SALT II was stalled due to American domestic politics, Schmidt actually consulted with Brezhnev and then Carter about serving as an outside personal emissary with Moscow. Carter's national security advisor, Zbigniew Brzezinski "warned against using the Germans."[66]

Toward the end of the Carter administration and after the Soviet invasion of Afghanistan, the President's community-building scheme gave way to a refocusing on bipolar competition. At that point, Carter rejected the global Wilsonian impulse and opted for the realist paradigm of Munich. West German impatience grew as the United States increasingly attempted to recapture control of East-West relations generally through strategic arms control talks.[67]

Thus, alongside the well-known personal animosity between Carter and Schmidt was Schmidt's constant maneuvering to sustain the East-West detente process codified through Harmel and to keep it centered on European, or German, interests while not sacrificing Western defense efforts. Once again, in 1977, Schmidt actually suggested to Carter that Schmidt be appointed Carter's secret intermediary between Washington and Moscow, and thus make the West more responsive to the "good Brezhnev who is promoting detente and who needs our help."[68] The tension between Washington and Bonn reached its height after a 1980 summit meeting of the Allies in Venice following the Soviet invasion of Afghanistan. Not only did Schmidt resist the American call for sanctions against the Soviets, but immediately following the summit the West German chancellor flew to Moscow for a private meeting with Brezhnev to discuss, among other items, Afghanistan. The U.S. president had opposed this visit.[69] The real Allied crisis produced during Carter's and Schmidt's tenures, however, was the INF issue, on which much has already been written.[70]

Finally, when Carter attempted to apply his Wilsonian community-building policies to the European context, he ran into the emerging West German blueprint. The two concepts clashed many times, but the differences were particularly reflected in the contrasting approaches to detente and especially to the continuing CSCE, or Helsinki, process. Whereas Carter emphasized democratization and human rights as central to measured progress in East bloc politics, the West Germans tended to measure progress according to the increase of human, economic, and political contacts across the East-West divide that met their own goal of inching toward unity.[71]

What made Carter's position even more untenable was the fact that the domestic mood in the United States had become stridently negative toward detente, and therefore toward arms control and especially toward disarmament. This made him an easy target in the rising domestic backlash against detente, which the Soviet invasion of Afghanistan brought to a head. Unlike in Western Europe, then, detente had become the bogeyman of American domestic politics by the end of the 1970s.

The Unexpected Wilsonianism of Ronald Reagan

The United States was now ready for the tough talk of Cold Warrior Ronald Reagan. William Schneider observes of the American domestic mood that "what motivated the surge of international assertiveness in 1980 was a sense of military vulnerability and anti-Soviet hostility. Americans suddenly realized that it was in their own interest to fortify the anti-Soviet military alliance."[72] What is remarkable about the Reagan presidency is not that it took the administration four years to come around once again to detente-oriented goals, but rather that it came around at all and, when it did, with such passion. Ronald Reagan in fact turned out to be the most committed disarmer of them all and a Wilsonian, much to the surprise of his closest advisors[73] and of the newly mobilized social conservatives and Christian right forces, whom he recruited to defeat the "evil empire."[74]

Much has already been written about the Reagan-Gorbachev breakthrough on detente II, including explanations ranging from the personality traits of Reagan and Gorbachev to the domestic politics of the USSR, to the positive payoff of Reagan's get-tough arms race approach to the Soviets, to the old adage that only a committed anti-Communist could really bring about a successful agreement with the Soviets.[75] Noticeably lacking in the wealth of studies concerning Reagan's stunning success in reopening channels to Moscow is an adequate analysis of the central role played by Western Europe, notably the FRG, in stimulating that phase of Washington-Moscow engagement. The problem with many security analyses of East-West security relations is that they proceed from a priori assumptions regarding how the United States and the Soviet Union set their security agendas. Typically, it was assumed that when it came to the important area of strategic issues confronting the two superpowers, the Western Europeans were only marginally significant. This study has shown that reality was different from these assumptions.[76]

As discussed above, Allied relations with the East bloc became bifurcated during the late 1970s and early 1980s. Reagan domestically lambasted the "evil empire" and oversaw a great increase in the American defense budget. An important element of America's retrenchment during the late 1970s and early 1980s was the inherent unilateralism of such behavior. Yet, on close examination, Reagan's reactions reveal that the United States was not willing to sustain abrogation of the Allied position in the face of West European resistance. He responded positively when pressured by the Western Europeans. Robert W. Tucker notes that,

Given the indisposition of Europe to surrender to a reassertive America, the Reagan years seemed to promise a chronic crisis in the alliance. Yet what came to pass was quite different. . . . The fear of the Europeans, that this administration would break from its predecessors in a determination to act unilaterally, did not materialize. When the administration did act unilaterally, it did so in matters that were peripheral to Europe's security.[77]

The West Germans led Western Europe in the continuation of detente and prodded a reluctant Washington into maintaining and institutionalizing open channels to the East. Strategic arms control was now one area of a much larger detente process, a process that since the end of the 1960s had been slowly redefining the context of East-West interaction. Almost all NATO Reviews from the late 1970s or early 1980s reiterated the Harmel obligations of all Western states to pursue simultaneously military security and decreased tensions vis-à-vis the East bloc. The West Germans, including Helmut Kohl, constantly invoked Harmel, usually intended for their American audience.

Aside from Allied pressure, Reagan increasingly met domestic resistance to continued military arms racing with the Soviets. Public opinion, easily comforted, had returned to a pro–arms control stance by the end of Reagan's first term. Also, the influence of the State Department served to reinforce calls for a return to detente-oriented policy.[78]

Despite the arguments used by analysts and policymakers alike that the Reagan strategy of increasing American defense spending and awareness was what brought the Soviets under Gorbachev back to the bargaining table, the evidence is not entirely convincing. Not only did Reagan's strategic and defense goals often remain vague, they quite often failed.[79]

Further, by the end of his tenure, Reagan had come to embrace an orientation reflective of the Wilsonian impulse. In fact, I will highlight the issue of the Strategic Defense Initiative (SDI), often raised to prove that Reagan's get-tough approach to the Soviets brought them back to the bargaining table, to make my case. Whatever the evidence concerning SDI's influence on the Soviet concerns about military spending, I posit that SDI showed something much more interesting about Reagan and the American approach to security—that Reagan's SDI venture suddenly recalled the Eisenhower presidency.

As will be remembered, Eisenhower suggested during his tenure in office that international or multinational organizations be formed to control nuclear weapons. To the dismay of many of his advisors and supporters, Reagan similarly advocated sharing SDI technology with the Soviet Union at Reykjavik in 1986. In fact, Kenneth Adelman recalls of Reagan's idea:

Why not, he asked this time, develop the idea of sharing SDI technology, combine it with the total elimination of nuclear weapons, and do this through an international body? That way, SDI would exist for everybody, not just for us and the Russians. No one would want or need nuclear weapons anymore.

After a surprised Adelman advised Reagan that nuclear weapons had kept the peace for forty-odd years, the president responded that "it wasn't clear that nuclear weapons had kept the peace. Maybe other things, like the Marshall Plan and NATO, had kept the peace."[80] Adelman ruminated that he "did not sense the depth of the President's passion for a nuclear-free world, or its tenacity, until Reykjavik."[81] I raise these points because they reveal the embedded Wilsonianism of postwar American security thinking. The notion that security collectively managed by international organizations could serve national security interests was explicitly held by both Eisenhower and Reagan. The idea that the Soviets could be rehabilitated and included in the Western community of nations upon their rejection of Soviet communism harkened back to the Wilsonian view concerning adversaries. John Foster Dulles had even on occasion discussed the day when the Soviet Union would be integrated with the West.

In all, certainly Reagan's defense posture and policies played some role in leading Gorbachev to the path of reform. However, more important was the continued opening to the West left open by Bonn and Western Europe and sanctified by the Harmel Report that Gorbachev walked through. Given the opportunities made available through many years of opened East-West channels, it made more sense for the Soviets, with their extremely ailing economy, to save money and gain in prestige and economic opportunity by themselves embracing the detente process. In the end, Reagan, too, returned to the process of unraveling East-West tensions, and in doing so changed relations rapidly by seeking to rehabilitate the Soviet Union in the Wilsonian tradition of encouraging its democratization and potential membership in the Western community of nations.

The relatively rapid return of the United States to the Harmel fold led many of the conservatives who applauded Reagan's anti-Soviet rhetoric and his goals of regaining American military superiority during the period of retrenchment to become critics of his detente policies. It is clear as well that the Reagan administration's security objectives were most successful when they realigned with the Harmel goals of the Alliance. By eventually opting for that path himself, Reagan went from seeking the "peace-keeper" MX to being proclaimed the "peace-maker" president.

In sum, American foreign policy took many turns in the 1970s and 1980s. There was less consistency regarding America's policies toward Europe and the Soviet Union than earlier. However, even after American leaders had determined to downplay Wilsonian goals in Europe in order to fulfill basic security interests, or to downplay the Alliance in favor of a more global Wilsonian vision, the legacy of earlier success, institutionalized in the State Department and then in the Alliance itself through Harmel, brought Washington back around. Europe was on its way to German reunification.

U.S. Foreign Policy and German Unification

As in the 1950s, so too in the 1980s and in 1990, American foreign policy was beholden to West German claims to reunification. With all the hesitation that transpired over the decades regarding how to achieve that goal, Washington remained sincere in its desire to see it occur. The Versailles remedial guaranteed that. Once Gorbachev's policies of openness, encouraged by Harmel's detente legacy, released the unraveling of the Soviet order, German reunification became possible. West Germans and other Westerners were not prepared for the rapidity with which that revisionist goal of the Alliance became achievable.

However, once it became clear in 1989 that the Berlin Wall and the order that ruled behind it were on the verge of collapse, Chancellor Helmut Kohl followed in the footsteps of Konrad Adenauer and Willy Brandt. Seizing the historic moment, he tied his quest for unity to the Allied relationship and the reciprocal understanding that undergirded it. Just as Acheson complained of Willy Brandt's "mad race" to Moscow in 1969, many voices in the West in 1989 complained of Kohl's mad race to reunification.[82]

However, as with previous examples, U.S. foreign policy supported West German efforts, and much of the support emanated from the State Department. In fact, echoing earlier American foreign policy under Eisenhower, there developed quickly in the Bush administration a near consensus that anticipated and backed German reunification.[83] Top aides in the State Department warned of not heeding signs in Germany that change was needed.[84] Echoing earlier American leaders on the U.S. position, Bush told West German Foreign Minister Hans-Dietrich Genscher "that Bonn must take the lead on the national issue, saying that the German question was a 'matter for the Germans.' . . . The only condition that the American President placed on his support was that German unification occur peacefully."[85] Again, as in earlier times, Bush "was not prepared to . . . use its superpower status to interfere with the politics of German unity."[86]

In short, the 1954 reciprocal agreement held firm for Washington. It had been institutionalized at State and in the Alliance, and was now coming to fruition. The Versailles remedial had worked. The Wilsonian impulse had also worked. A democratic Germany now continued in the footsteps of its West German predecessor by maintaining its institutionalized, interdependent position in the Western community.

In anticipating a new sea-change in international relations, James Baker, the former American secretary of state, reiterated an early Allied understanding in West Berlin in November 1990, that NATO was a political community as much as it was a military organization. Addressing the Berlin Press Club, Baker proposed that NATO be transformed from a military organization "to a political alliance." Of course, as I have shown throughout the study, NATO was already both from its inception. In this speech, Baker further stated that

As Europe changes, the instruments for Western cooperation must adapt. Working together, we must design and gradually put into place a new architecture for a new era. This new architecture must have a place for old foundations and structures that remain valuable—like NATO—while recognizing that they can also serve new collective purposes. . . . And the new architecture must build up frameworks . . . that can overcome the division of Europe and bridge the Atlantic Ocean.[87]

Baker went on to say:

NATO should also begin considering further initiatives the West might take . . . to build economic and political ties with the East. . . . Finally, NATO may have its greatest and most lasting effect on the pattern of change by demonstrating to the nations of the East a fundamentally different approach to security. . . . The reconciliation of ancient enemies, which has taken place under the umbrella of NATO's collective security, offers the nations of Eastern Europe an appealing model of international relations.[88]

In his speech, Baker restated the Wilsonian vision in Europe. What is depicted here is the possible extension of the Allied security community eastward. Just as Washington brought West Germany into the fold in the immediate postwar period, so now the former Soviet areas might also be rehabilitated and given entry. Such was the optimistic assessment read through the lens of the Wilsonian assumptions underlying Baker's words as secretary of state, assumptions that continue to have resonance.

On a less positive note, there were and are many differences between the two situations. In the current post–Cold War era, the pressures toward change or even dissolution of the Western Alliance have multiplied. First, because the Allied relationship was from the beginning one that wedded the objectives of defense against a threat with community-building, it is not clear that the latter can stand without the former. Related, as I have argued throughout, the Wilsonian impulse and Versailles remedial were specifically formulated to deal with the West and Germany. How successfully it might be extended eastward, or even globally, as Carter tried, is an open question.

Further, and extremely significant, the role of Germany itself is now less clear than heretofore. This study has shown that much of the support for the Alliance from West German leaders resided in the fact that West Germany gained in influence by helping to shape East-West relations through its Allied membership. Throughout, one of the main objectives was reunification. The very success of West German efforts in 1990, the resolution of the German question through peaceful means, necessarily means that the reciprocal understanding regarding German unity between West Germany and the West, particularly the United States, became irrelevant.

Thus, one of the major community-building blocks is gone. The quandary is reflected by Michael H. Haltzel's observations of 1987:

What can Germans and Americans do to prevent West German Absonderung or going its own way? First, the United States should do nothing to indicate a backing down from its commitment to an eventual, peaceful German reunification. To do otherwise would violate not only treaty obligations but also the American commitment to the right of self-determination.[89]

That has now been accomplished. What happens now to maintain mutual commitments is less clear.

That opens new questions about German and American intentions concerning the Western Alliance and about the Allied relationship generally. NATO continues to have many supporters. If the Alliance has truly become a Western security community, then the Allied relationship will weather current and future changes in Europe and the international system. Even if so, its future is unclear. If not, then it will wither if and as the Russian threat retreats.

CONCLUSIONS

In sum, the success of the Wilsonian order and of West German policy therein, indeed of formal Allied policy, that culminated in German unification now presents the West with a conundrum. The seeds for a Europe-wide collective security community in which a united Germany would be a member were planted within the contours and according to the principles of the Wilsonian impulse. That was accomplished within the historical process unleashed during the moment of American hegemonic creativity that allowed the United States to project abroad its own domestic vision of international relations.

The legacy of the Wilsonian impulse and its influence in defining Western relations are substantial. The recasting of Allied relations in the mid-1960s helped bring about the sea-change in East-West relations that began in 1989. Since then, with the collapse of the Soviet Union and the unification of Germany, Western elites have been scrambling to ensure continued public support for NATO by again emphasizing the political rather than the military rationale for the relationship, just as had been done during the time of the Harmel Report.[90]

The pressures to rerally the West around NATO as a community increased, as did the growing nervousness about the German question in the post-1989 period. One must return to the dual purpose of American and Allied postwar security goals to understand why. Even if, or even as, the Russian military threat to Western Europe wanes, the second goal of the Alliance may remain relevant. Because the Alliance is the political vehicle through which German aspirations and Western communal obligations have been expressed and institutionalized, the importance of that relationship during current systemic change has become central.

However, the loss of the Soviet threat means that galvanizing the impulse into action and into a coherent set of policies will be difficult. Further, the peaceful unification of Germany has rendered the Versailles remedial obsolete, and left Germany as a potentially global power that may well develop ordering principles of its own. For German policymakers since the late 1960s, the influence of the American Wilsonian impulse was definitely of instrumental value in pursuing Ostpolitik, but having achieved unification, Germany's orientation today demands redefinition. U.S.–German relations will remain the key to success in the trans-Atlantic relationship, and there is good reason to expect that those relations will remain positive. However, it is also possible that competition between American and German prescriptions for order in Europe will occur, as happened beginning in the 1970s.

Similarly, the ability and/or willingness of America to lead in the post–Cold War period remains an open question. Since an important premise of the Wilsonian impulse has been U.S. leadership, it is unclear that the impulse can be galvanized again.[91] For American policymakers, the Wilsonian impulse retains influence and continues to have an impact on the American approach to European and international security, but in a less systematic way. President Bush's call for a "new world order" was at base Wilsonian, where he called for a "partnership based on consultation, cooperation, and collective action, especially through international and regional organizations."[92] President Clinton has sounded Wilsonian themes as well: "It is time for America to lead a global alliance for democracy as united and steadfast as the global alliance that defeated communism."[93] But it is uncertain whether the community aspects of the trans-Atlantic security relationship will survive the absence of the Soviet threat, the presence of a united Germany, and the erosion of U.S. Cold War authority.

Finally, is community-building in fact possible when unaccompanied by the objective of defense against an external threat? Assuming that community-building does remain valid for the recast NATO and trans-Atlantic relations, whose community-building scheme will be applied to incorporate the former East bloc? These are central questions that must be answered in the coming years.

NOTES

1. For an account of Carter's global efforts, see Jerel A. Rosati, *The Carter Administration's Quest for Global Community: Beliefs and Their Impact on Behavior* (Columbia: University of South Carolina Press, 1987).

2. Timothy Garton Ash states that even McCloy was skeptical of Brandt's Ostpolitik; see *In Europe's Name: Germany and the Divided Continent* (New York: Random House, 1993), p. 82. Also see Henry Kissinger, *Diplomacy* (New York: Simon and Schuster, 1994), pp. 733–37.

3. Kissinger, *Diplomacy*, p. 743.

4. Tony Smith, *America's Mission: The United States and the Worldwide Struggle for Democracy in the Twentieth Century* (Princeton, N.J.: Princeton University Press, 1994).

5. James R. Kurth, "The Political Consequences of the Product Cycle," *International Organization* 33, no. 1 (Winter 1979), p. 32. Kurth notes that industrial and financial sectors in the United States that supported detente in the late 1960s, such as the automobile industry, lost interest by 1975.

6. Hans Rattinger, "The Federal Republic of Germany: Much Ado About Nothing," in *The Public and Atlantic Defense*, ed. Gregory Flynn and Hans Rattinger (Totowa, N.J.: Rowman and Allanheld, 1985), p. 118.

7. Gebhard Schweigler, "Anti-Americanism in German Public Opinion," in *America's Image in Germany and Europe* (Washington, D.C.: Friedrich Ebert Stiftung, 1985), p. 21.

8. Forsa Institute poll cited in "Gorbachev Outpolls Reagan in West Germany," *New York Times*, May 17, 1987, p. 18.

9. William Schneider, "Peace and Strength: American Public Opinion on National Security," in *The Public and Atlantic Defense*, ed. Gregory Flynn and Hans Rattinger (Totowa, N.J.: Rowman and Allanheld, 1985), p. 327. On page 361, Schneider observes of American attitudes that "what motivated the surge of international assertiveness in 1980 was a sense of military vulnerability and anti-Soviet hostility. Americans suddenly realized that it was in their own interest to fortify the anti-Soviet military alliance."

10. Jonathan Dean, *Watershed in Europe: Dismantling the East-West Military Confrontation* (Lexington, Mass.: Lexington Books, 1987), p. 87. The author cites the divergent approaches taken toward the Soviet invasion of Afghanistan, the declaration of martial law in Poland, and the issue of economic sanctions.

11. Willy Brandt, "We Must Struggle for Europe," lecture at the Friedrich Ebert Stiftung concerning "European Community in the Atlantic Area," Berlin, October

1963, in Willy Brandt, *Peace: Writings and Speeches of the Nobel Peace Prize Winner, 1971* (Bonn-Bad Godesberg: Verlag Neue Gesellschaft, 1971), p. 31.

12. Professor Horst Ehmke, a long-time SPD Parliament member and close associate of Brandt, first gave me this notion of Ostpolitik having *politicized* the East-West security relationship. Background interview, Bonn, 1985.

13. Kenneth L. Adelman, *The Great Universal Embrace: Arms Summitry—A Skeptic's Account* (New York: Simon and Schuster, 1989), p. 208.

14. Stanley Hoffmann, "The Case for Leadership," *Foreign Affairs* 81 (Winter 1990–91), p. 20.

15. Willy Brandt, *People and Politics* (Boston: Little, Brown, 1979), p. 186.

16. For discussions of CSCE, see Henry Kissinger, *White House Years* (Boston: Little, Brown, 1979), pp. 414, 415; Richard J. Barnet, *The Alliance, America-Europe-Japan: Makers of the Postwar World* (New York: Simon and Schuster, 1983), p. 295; Helmut Schmidt, *Men and Powers: A Political Retrospective* (New York: Random House, 1989), p. 38; for a discussion of the CSCE three baskets, see Carl C. Krehbiel, *Confidence- and Security-Building Measures in Europe* (New York: Praeger, 1989), esp. ch 1.; Dean, *Watershed in Europe*, esp. p. 99. On MBFR, see Dean in *Watershed in Europe*, esp. p. 102, pp. 153–71; Brandt, *People and Politics*, esp. p. 188; Jean Klein, "Current Aspects of Security and Arms Control in Europe," in *Arms Control and International Security*, ed. Roman Kolkowicz and Neil Joeck (Boulder, Colo.: Westview Press, 1984), esp. p. 103; John Newhouse, *War and Peace in the Nuclear Age* (New York: Alfred A. Knopf, 1989), p. 236; Barry Blechman and Cathleen Fisher, eds., *The Silent Partner: West Germany and Arms Control* (Cambridge, Mass.: Ballinger, 1988), pp. 139, 174; Helga Haftendorn, *Security and Detente: Conflicting Priorities in German Foreign Policy* (New York: Praeger, 1985), esp. p. 143; Ash, *In Europe's Name*.

17. See Ash, *In Europe's Name*, p. 83.

18. See Thomas Risse-Kappen, *The Zero Option: INF, West Germany and Arms Control* (Boulder, Colo.: Westview Press, 1988), pp. 45–47. The term and substance of the "zero option" was first raised by the West German SPD in 1979 during intraparty debates on INF. Risse-Kappen then states on page 78 that it was Schmidt and the SPD/FDP that were "mainly responsible for getting the zero option accepted by NATO and the United States, where it was backed by those who used it to block the INF talks."

19. Among others, Dr. Heinrich Vogel, then director of the Bundesinstitut fuer Ostwissenschaftliche and internationale Studien, in Cologne, FRG, was extremely helpful to me in his discussion of the "European Peace Order" during an interview on July 22, 1986.

20. Catherine McArdle Kelleher, *Germany and the Politics of Nuclear Weapons* (New York: Columbia University Press, 1975), p. 296. Kelleher's assessment of the policy is similar: "In the face of continuing American carping, European suspicion, continuing bureaucratic sabotage, and debilitating party defections, the stance has been firm and skilled."

21. Willy Brandt, "Erklaerung der Bundesregierung zur Sicherheits- und Buendnispolitik," 29. November 1968, Fuenfte Wahlperiode, 200. Sitzung, in Brandt, Willy, *Bundestags Reden* (Bonn: Pfattheicher & Reichardt, 1972), p. 106.

22. Ibid., p. 106.

23. Brandt, *People and Politics*, p. 190.

24. Ash, *In Europe's Name*, p. 81.

25. Goergey Laszlo, *Bonn's Eastern Policy, 1964–1971* (Hamden, Conn.: Archon Books, 1972), pp. 84–85, quote on p. 84.

26. Allied response to Ostpolitik was indeed complex and also entangled with the West European debate on British entry to the EC. See various discussions in Kissinger, *White House Years*, pp. 416, 422–24; Brandt, *People and Politics*, pp. 250, 260; Mary N. Hampton, *The Empowerment of a Middle-Sized State: West Germany, Wilsonianism and the Western Alliance* (Los Angeles: UCLA Press, 1993), ch. 5.

27. For a brief and concise discussion of the various agreements and Ostvertraege completed between 1969 and 1972, see Hans W. Gatzke, *Germany and the United States: A Special Relationship* (Cambridge, Mass.: Harvard University Press, 1980), pp. 223–29. Also, for an English translation of the texts of the Eastern treaties, including the controversial Bahr Paper of 1970, see Lawrence L. Whetten, *Germany's Ostpolitik; Relations Between the Federal Republic and the Warsaw Pact Countries* (London: Oxford University Press, 1971), pp. 217–31.

28. Research Memorandum, August 6, 1965, LBJ Library, "Subject: Western Europe Looks at Germany," pp. 1, 3–4, Collection: NSF, Country File: Europe and USSR, Germany, Container: 182, 183, 186, 190, 191, Folder: Germany Memos vol.9, 7/65–1/66.

29. Henri Froment-Meurice, *Europa als eine Macht.* (Cologne: Verlag Wissenschaft und Politik, 1986), p. 166. Translation mine. See his discussion of the "unavoidable German question" on pp. 160–67.

30. Walter F. Hahn, "West Germany's Ostpolitik": The Grand Design of Egon Bahr," *Orbis* 16, no. 4 (Winter 1973), esp. pp. 872–74.

31. Ibid., p. 880.

32. Hans Graf Huyn, quoted from his book, *Ostpolitik im Kreuzfeuer* (Stuttgart: Seewald Verlag), in "Congressional Record—Senate," February 17, 1972, p. 2033. Graf Huyn also includes with his testimony to Congress a chart that reveals the identical positions of Moscow, East Berlin, and the Brandt-Scheel government on issues such as recognition of postwar borders and equality of status and recognition for the GDR, p. 2034.

33. Gatzke, *Germany and the United States*, pp. 225–27.

34. Whetton, *Germany's Ostpolitik*, pp. 94–116.

35. See Wolfram Hanrieder, "West German Foreign Policy, 1949–1979: Necessities and Choices," in *West German Foreign Policy, 1949–1979*, ed. Wolfram Hanrieder (Boulder, Colo.: Westview Press, 1980), esp. pp. 28–30.

36. Brandt, *People and Politics*, p. 168.

37. On Nixon, see William E. Leuchtenburg, *In the Shadow of FDR: From Harry Truman to Bill Clinton* (Ithaca, N.Y.: Cornell University Press, 193), ch. 5. He cites Garry Wills's *Nixon Agonistes: The Crisis of the Self-Made Man* (New York: New American Library, 1971). The best source for understanding Kissinger is still his memoir, *White House Years*.

38. Walter Isaacson, *Kissinger* (New York: Simon and Schuster, 1992), p. 75.

39. Ibid., discussion on pp. 654–57. Also see Kissinger's discussion of Wilsonianism in his *Diplomacy* (New York: Simon and Schuster, 1994), esp. ch. 9.

40. Isaacson, *Kissinger*, p. 76.

41. Kissinger, *White House Years*, pp. 408, 416.

42. Ibid., p. 409.

43. Ibid., p. 411. Kissinger reiterates these positions in *Diplomacy*, esp. pp. 733–37.

44. On the lengths Kissinger went to in bypassing State and dealing directly with Brandt and Bahr, see Isaacson, *Kissinger*, pp. 322–24.

45. Ibid., p. 557.

46. Kissinger, *White House Years*, p. 412.

47. Ibid., p. 530.

48. Henry Kissinger, quoted in Richard J. Barnet, *The Alliance, America-Europe-Japan: Makers of the Postwar World* (New York: Simon and Schuster, 1983), p. 409.

49. Professor Martin Hillenbrand, background written interview, May 1987.

50. Kissinger, *White House Years*, pp. 530–34.

51. Barnet, *The Alliance*, p. 292.

52. Ibid., p. 294.

53. Kissinger, *White House Years*, p. 534. Kissinger seems to overstate the role of Washington in claiming that "we had harnessed the beast of detente, making both a European Security Conference and ratification of Brandt's treaties dependent upon a Berlin agreement that met our objectives." In fact, both pressure from the Western Allies and the State Department for a European Security Conference, and pressure from Brandt to reach an agreement on Berlin revealed the fact that Washington was indeed obliged to reach a Berlin agreement because of the distance Brandt had already gone in binding Bonn to the Eastern treaties.

54. Kissinger, *White House Years*, p. 530.

55. Stephen R. Graubard, *Kissinger: Portrait of a Mind* (New York: W. W. Norton, 1974), p. 142.

56. Ibid., p. 143. Graubard states further of Kissinger's view of German unification: "While entertaining no illusions about the possibilities for achieving German unity, he continued to believe that it mattered very much whether or not the Western Allies supported Bonn in its call for unification."

57. Henry Kissinger, *For the Record* (Boston: Little, Brown, 1982), p. 243.

58. Newhouse, *War and Peace in the Nuclear Age*, pp. 246–63.

59. Ibid., p. 262.

60. Ibid., p. 265.

61. Rosati, *The Carter Administration's Quest for a Global Community*, p. 40.

62. Carter, quoted in ibid., p. 42.

63. Ibid, p. 49.

64. For a general discussion of Carter's naivete in foreign policy matters, particularly those concerning East-West relations and Allied policy, see Newhouse, *War and Peace*, ch. 11.

65. On West German and British persistence that progress be made on SALT, see Zbigniew Brzezinski, *Power and Principle: Memoirs of the National Security Advisor, 1977–1981* (New York: Farrar, Straus, Giroux, 1985), p. 165.

66. Ibid., p. 176.

67. Ibid., p. 292–95. In a revealing anecdote on page 293, Brzezinski says of a meeting with Schmidt; "without any further ado, he lit into me, announcing that he was tired of the U.S. supported Radio Free Europe operating on German soil, that its presence was contrary to detente, and that he would like to get it out of Germany."

68. Ibid., p. 307.

69. Ibid., pp. 462–63.

70. For one of the best discussions of this, see Risse-Kappen, *The Zero Option*.

71. See discussion in Ash, *In Europe's Name*, esp. pp. 262–66.

72. Schneider, "Peace and Strength," p. 361.

73. On Reagan's view of a nuclear free world, see Adelman, *The Great Universal Embrace*, p. 69. Adelman, Reagan's director of the U.S. Arms Control and Disarmament Agency, revealingly observes again the embedded Wilsonian vision that influenced those views: "His talk about arms control would often leap into unbridled idealism, the kind more often associated with advocates of Esperanto as a global language and with World Federalists . . . than with a conservative Republican." On Reagan's Wilsonianism, see Tony Smith, *America's Mission*, esp. ch. 10.

74. See discussion in Sara Diamond, *Roads to Dominion: Right Wing Movements and Political Power in the United States* (New York: Guilford Press, 1995), esp. pp. 216–25.

75. Among many, see Paul Johnson, "Europe and the Reagan Years," *Foreign Affairs: America and the World 1988/89* 68, no. 1 (1989), pp. 34–35. Johnson states, for example, on page 35 that Gorbachev's interest in detente and striking new arms control agreements revealed "once again the importance of will in politics. For the Reagan Administration's decision to rearm was essentially an act of will." For another interesting interpretation, see Ash, *In Europe's Name*, pp. 118–20.

76. See Risse-Kappen, *The Zero Option*, pp. 13–17. He cites the direct interference of the West Europeans during U.S.–Soviet negotiations on Salt I and Salt II.

77. Robert W. Tucker, "Reagan's Foreign Policy," *Foreign Affairs: America and the World 1988/89* 68, no. 1 (1989), p. 18.

78. For an example of the continued influence of the State Department position, see Elizabeth Pond, *Beyond the Wall: Germany's Road to Unification* (Washington, D.C.: The Brookings Institute, 1993), esp. pp. 166–67.

79. On the vagueness and incoherence of Reagan defense policy, see Barry R. Posen and Stephen Van Evera, "Defense Policy and the Reagan Administration: Departure from Containment," *International Security* 8, no. 1 (Summer 1983), pp. 3–45. See also Robert A. Hoover, "Strategic Arms Limitation Negotiations," in *Technology, Strategy, and Arms Control*, ed. Wolfram F. Hanrieder (Boulder, Colo.: Westview Press, 1986), pp. 108–9. See also Marvin Leibstone, "Fiscal Year 1987—U. S. Defense Budget," in *NATO'S Sixteen Nations* 31, no. 8 (December 86/January 87), pp. 72–78. The ideas of limited nuclear war and nuclear war winning strategy also became popular among some analysts and policymakers early in Reagan's first administration, but for rather obvious reasons that were fueled by the rhetoric of its proponents, the idea failed to win a sympathetic audience in Western Europe. See David P. Calleo, *Beyond American Hegemony: The Future of the Western Alliance* (New York: Basic Books, 1987), pp. 72–73.

80. Adelman, *The Great Universal Embrace*, p. 318.

81. Ibid., p. 69.

82. See Stanley Hoffmann, "The Case for Leadership," p. 20.

83. See discussion of Bush administration policy in Stephen F. Szabo, *The Diplomacy of German Unification* (New York: St. Martin's, 1992), esp. ch. 2.

84. See Szabo's discussion on p. 11 of Robert Zoellick's papers prepared for Secretary of State Baker regarding changing circumstances in Germany that required new initiatives.

85. Szabo, *The Diplomacy of German Unification*, p. 41.

86. Ibid.

87. James Baker, quoted in "Baker, in Berlin, Outlines a Plan to Make NATO a Political Group," *New York Times*, Wednesday, December 13, 1989, pp. A1, A10.

88. Ibid., p. A10.

89. See Michael H. Haltzel, "The Two Germanies and Bonn-Washington Relations," *Atlantic Community Quarterly* 24, no. 4 (Winter 1986–87), p. 344.

90. This has been, for example, a central theme of CDU and conservative policies in the FRG, or as Philipp Borinski puts it, "to recast the debate about allies and adversaries in terms of Western political core values." See Philipp Borinski, "Report on Germany," *Atlantic Community Quarterly* 24, no. 4 (Winter 1986–87), p. 272.

91. Kissinger offers an interesting discussion of these points in *Diplomacy*, esp. ch. 31.

92. George Bush, cited in Kissinger, *Diplomacy*, p. 804. See also Tony Smith's discussion of Bush as a Wilsonian in *America's Mission*, esp. ch. 11.

93. Bill Clinton, quoted in Smith, *America's Mission*, p. 320.

Chapter 6 ⸻⸻⸻⸻⸻⸻⸻⸻

CONCLUSIONS

I have shown that the U.S. interest in balancing against the Soviet threat explains only a part of the American push to create the Western Alliance. Preceding that interest was a Wilsonian view of the world that included an important set of beliefs about how to approach Western security. This set of beliefs and their galvanization upon emergence of the Soviet threat constituted the Wilsonian impulse. The evolution of West-West and East-West relations was directly influenced by it.

Because the Wilsonian impulse included a set of objectives and assumptions separate from American balancing behavior against the Soviet Union, the Western Alliance evolved differently from previous alliances. The Alliance evolved as a hybrid between a traditional defense pact that targeted an external threat, as typical of the realist assessment of alliances, and a Wilsonian security community, wherein the trans-Atlantic community evolved and West Germany reaped great advantage through the Versailles remedial.

The set of Wilsonian ideas that were legitimized by the history of World War I and the interwar years confirmed the Wilsonian expectations of key postwar American foreign policy players and influenced directly the policy alternatives they perceived as available to them. Even after the Eisenhower presidency, which was the last administration in which the Wilsonian elite consensus existed among the president, the secretary of state, and the State Department, the effects of the impulse were maintained. Early on, the Wilsonian impulse and Versailles remedial were institutionalized into the American foreign policy process at State, and into the Alliance through the Charter of 1949, the Paris Accords of 1954, and the Harmel Report of 1967. For these reasons, the Wilsonian impulse was causally significant.

West Germany's speedy integration into the Western Alliance was an American foreign policy success story. Because of the ordering principles established for American policymakers by the Wilsonian impulse, the United States was not willing to use coercive power as a hegemon to socialize West Germany into the Western fold. Most important for the integration of West Germany into the West was the set of principles, rules, and objectives directed toward building a security community. These were at the heart of the Western security relationship and enabled Bonn to proceed swiftly with rehabilitation after the war. In fact, the Versailles remedial made certain that West Germany would enter the West on highly advantageous terms. Bonn became adept at appealing to the lessons of Versailles and reinforcing the active influence of the Wilsonian impulse.

Participation in the Alliance constructed West German foreign policy choices in unique ways. Most important was that Bonn accepted the diffuse reciprocal agreement made by the Allies in 1954 wherein they assumed responsibility over the long run for achieving peaceful German unification. That West German leaders accommodated themselves to this approach regarding a central security interest was a major sign that the Wilsonian political culture was being accepted by West Germans. It revealed that long-term expectations based on Western cooperation constructed fundamental national security concerns in a distinct way. By 1969, the West Germans determined to undermine from within the Alliance the Cold War order that froze German division. This they did legitimately by continuing to appeal to the 1954 convention and by institutionalizing the goal further in the Alliance.

By the 1970s and 1980s, U.S. foreign policy had become dissonant because of the tension that had grown between its dual Allied goals of thwarting the Soviet threat and building a Western community. Bifurcation occurred in American foreign policy and in Allied policy. However, even as U.S. power waned relatively and conditions changed at the strategic and domestic levels, the Wilsonian impulse maintained a decisive impact in Allied relations because it was institutionalized in the U.S. State Department and in the Alliance.

In 1990, the tumultuous changes in international politics presented Bonn with the historic moment in which to reunite. While great skepticism and fear existed among its neighbors and allies regarding its "rush to unity," Kohl could and did legitimize his moves through the Allied understanding. In fact, the Bush administration was supportive, especially its

State Department, and alluded to the Allied Wilsonian bargain struck with West Germany.

The study raises important issues regarding how we should now think about NATO and its future. First, the dual mission of the Alliance must be carefully considered. The resiliency of NATO can be only partly understood in light of its role as a continued insurance policy against Russian backsliding, or because of its collective defense mission. It is also still sought after largely due to its potential as the nucleus of a broadly stroked collective security community. The community-building aspect of the Alliance has been highly successful, and thus could serve as the model for a trans-Atlantic and Europe-wide security community.

However, several problems now confront the Alliance on that level. The case of Russia illuminates a current dilemma of purpose facing the community-building aspects of the Alliance. For one thing, it is evident that enlarging the Allied community eastward but short of Russia raises the real possibility that Moscow will respond precisely as if the action implies a renewed Western threat. Some, such as John Mearsheimer, would maintain NATO as long as it is needed as insurance against the Russians.[1] Others who advocate expanding NATO to the Central and East European states but not to Russia are redrawing a line in Europe for many different reasons. One could propose such a scheme in order to maintain NATO as a hybrid—to expand the community to East and Central European states, while still maintaining defense against an unstable Russia.[2]

From the Wilsonian perspective as identified in this study, the case could be made that the logic of courting Russia now resembles that employed in the courtship of West Germany during the early 1950s—to coopt former adversaries into the West by offering them favorable terms as members of the Western liberal community. Reagan was actually not far from this position. If American leaders are to be as sensitive to the domestic vulnerabilities of Russian reformers as they were of Adenauer's in the immediate postwar years, then enlarging NATO short of Russia is a rather self-defeating proposition, just as it would have been then.

On the other hand, it is very unclear that the security community component of the Allied relationship can be maintained successfully without the threat that accompanied it. Admitting Russia to NATO promptly would necessarily undermine the collective defense understanding of the Cold War at a time when agreement on the principles and rules of a potentially expanded collective security community remain elusive. Bosnia and other recent crises reveal that there is not yet widespread agreement among Allies and potential allies concerning the terms of internal monitoring and intervention that would necessarily accompany a broadly defined collective security community that focused only on internal threats. The Bosnian NATO intervention of 1995 may or may not help define the NATO mission. Particularly troublesome is the fact that even in its heyday the Alliance helped settle the internal community rivalry of France and West Germany, an immense accomplishment, but it failed in dealing effectively with the long-standing and continuing dispute over Cyprus between Allies Greece and Turkey.[3]

Equally important is the role to be played by the united Germany. Fundamental to the Western community was the diffuse reciprocal agreement with Bonn concerning West German reunification and the Allies, led by the United States. In exchange for the Allied guarantee of equality and of promoting its eventual unification, Germany integrated into the West. The result was that for the first time in modern history, Germany unified in peace. The influence of the Wilsonian impulse and the accompanying Versailles remedial was substantial in accomplishing that task. The West Germans were able to subvert peacefully and legitimately through the Alliance the order that divided them. Thus, the Alliance purposefully accommodated the peaceful major revision of the international system by one of its members.

Germany has now reunified as a democratic state, and therefore attained the vital security interest that wedded it so loyally to the West. It continues at this time to uphold its place in Western institutions. The indication is therefore that a strong Western community has arisen. However, such indicators are premature. The united Germany is questioning anew its rightful place in post–Cold War Europe and reassessing its national interests.[4] How much effort the new Germany devotes to continuing the community-building institutions that brought it to this point remains to be seen.

Therefore, whether the trans-Atlantic community will continue to play a constructive role in managing the issues raised by German unity and Soviet disintegration remains to be seen. Whatever becomes of the Western Alliance, I have argued that the impact of the Wilsonian impulse on Western security relations has been largely responsible for the peaceful devolution of the historic European and East-West confrontations. The study offers another explanation for the "long postwar peace" that John Lewis Gaddis and others have addressed.[5] I have explained how a set of ideas that guided American and West German foreign policy, and that were separate from bipolar considerations, contributed immensely to that peace. Those ideas were fundamental to the American-led order. The political legitimacy of the Alliance as a Wilsonian security community was decisive in maintaining the Western security bond, in enhancing the role of the FRG and underwriting its reunification, and in promoting the peaceful devolution of East-West tensions.

NOTES

1. John Mearsheimer, "Back to the Future: Instability in Europe After the Cold War," *International Security* 15 (Summer 1990), pp. 5–56.

2. See, for example, the argument made by Ronald D. Asmus, Richard L. Kugler, and F. Stephen Larrabee in "Building a New NATO," *Foreign Affairs Agenda 1994*, pp. 201–13. They claim to be wanting to bring the East and Central European states into the Western fold as the West did West Germany, but it is clear that so doing would send definite messages to Moscow.

3. For an excellent examination of the issue, see Montague Stearns, *Entangled Allies: U.S. Policy Toward Greece, Turkey, and Cyprus* (New York: Council on Foreign Relations Press, 1992.)

4. There are countless books and articles that address the identity of the new Germany and its orientation to foreign policy. In this regard, see Wolfgang Schaeuble, *Und der Zukunft zugewandt* (Berlin: Siedler Verlag, 1994); Joschka Fischer, *Risiko Deutschland: Krise und Zukunft der deutschen Politik* (Cologne: Verlag Kiepenheuer and Witsch, 1994); Heinz Brill, *Geopolitik Heute: Deutschlands Chance?* (Berlin: Ullstein, 1994); Timothy Garton Ash, "Germany's Choice," *Foreign Affairs* (July/August, 1994), pp. 65–81.

5. See John Lewis Gaddis, *The Long Peace: Inquiries into the Cold War* (New York: Oxford University Press, 1987). A number of books and articles on the subject followed.

BIBLIOGRAPHY

MANUSCRIPTS AND DOCUMENTS

Dwight D. Eisenhower Library, Abilene, Kansas

Eisenhower Papers as President: Ann Whitman File

DDE Diary Series. Boxes 19, 49, 53.
International Series. Boxes 13, 14, 15.
International Meetings Series. Box 3.

Papers of John Foster Dulles

Telephone Calls Series. Boxes 6, 7, 12.
Subject Series. Box 4.

Lyndon B. Johnson Library, Austin, Texas

Papers of LBJ, 1963–1969. Container 4.
Papers of LBJ as President, 1963–1969.
National Security File: Subject File. Container 24.
National Security File: National Security Council History; Trilateral Negotiations
    and NATO, 1966–67. Container 50.

Oral Histories

Rostow, Eugene. Oral History by Paige Mulhollan. December 2, 1968. Containers
    74–72.
David K. Bruce. Oral history by Thomas H. Baker. Containers AC 73–39.

NSF Collection

NSF Agency Files. Container 12.
International Meetings and Travel File. Containers 35, 36.
Country File. Europe and USSR; Germany. Containers 182, 183, 186, 190, 191.
Subject File. Containers 25, 36, 38, 44, and 48. Folder: MLF; Mr. Bundy: For 6:00
    meeting Monday, October, 18, October 11, 1965, p. 2.
Committee File. Committee on Nuclear Proliferation. Containers 1–2.

Mandatory Review

Case #NLJ88-10. Document #184. July 6, 1965, p.1.

Declassified and Sanitized Documents from Unprocessed Files (DSDUF)

General. Container 1.

John F. Kennedy Library, Boston, Massachusetts

NSF

Subject File. Containers 25, 36, 38, 44.
National Security File—Countries. Boxes 52, 75–81, 82, 117.

NEWSPAPERS AND PERIODICALS

The New York Times.
The Salt Lake Tribune.
Der Spiegel.
Stuttgart Zeitung.
The Week in Germany.

INTERVIEWS: 1985–87, 1990

Germany

Egon Bahr, Dr. Rainer Barzel, Dr. Alfred Blumenfeld, Boege, Dr. Willy Brandt, Mr.
    Brueckmann, Dr. Peter Corterier, Freimut Duve, Dr. Horst Ehmke, Felenski,
    Dr. Paul Frank, Klaus Francke, Dr. Eugen Gerstenmaier, Dr. Wilhelm
    Grewe, von dem Hagen, Hans Juergen Hoppe, Dr. Hoyer, Dr. Herbert
    Hupka, Hans Graf Huyn, Kaul, Petra Kelly, Dr. Hans Klein, Dr. Kliesing,
    Oskar Lafontaine, Dr. Karl Lamars, Dr. Ekard Luebkemeyer, Peter Maen-
    ning, Alfred Mechtersheimer, Wolfgang Mischnick, Dr. Wolfgang Pfeiler,
    Dr. Gert Poettering, Volker Ruehe, Alfred Sauter, Dr. Walter Scheel,

Schnappertz, Dr. Schierbaum, Dr. Schoenfelder, Dr. Eberhard Schultz, Soelen, Dr. Lutz Stavenhagen, von Studnis, Dr. Juergen Todenhoefer, Dr. Guenther Verheugen, Dr. Heinrich Vogel, Karsten Voigt, Ambassador Wieck, Juergen Wischnewski.

Brussels

Simon Lunn, Jamie Shea.

U.S.A.

Dr. Martin Hillenbrand, George McGhee, Leon Sloss.

ARTICLES

Aron, Raymond. "Macht, Power, Puissance." In *Power*, edited by Steven Lukes, 253–77. New York: New York University Press, 1986.

Ash, Timothy Garton. "Germany's Choice." *Foreign Affairs* 17, no. 4 (July / August, 1994) 65–81.

Asmus, Ronald D., Richard L. Kugler, and Stephen E. Larrabee. "Building a New NATO." In *Foreign Affairs Agenda 1994*: 201–13.

Auton, Graeme P. "Conventional Arms Control in Europe: Beyond MBFR and CDE." In *Arms Control and European Security*, edited by Graeme P. Auton, 95–109. New York: Praeger, 1989.

Bahr, Egon. "Wandel durch Annaeherung." *Deutschland-Archiv* (8 / 1973): 860–63.

Borinski, Philipp. "Report on Germany." *Atlantic Community Quarterly* 24, no. 4 (Winter 1986–87): 272–77.

Burley, Anne-Marie. "Regulating the World: Multilateralism, International Law, and the Projection of the New Deal Regulatory State." In *Multilateralism Matters: The Theory and Praxis of an Institutional Form*, edited by John Gerard Ruggie, 125–56. New York: Columbia University Press, 1993.

———. "Restoration and Reunification: Eisenhower's German Policy." In *Reevaluating Eisenhower: American Foreign Policy in the 1950s*, edited by Richard A. Melanson and David Mayers, 220–40. Urbana: University of Illinois Press, 1984.

Cooper, Jr., John Milton. "Wilsonian Democracy." In *Democrats and the American Idea: A Bicentennial Appraisal*, edited by Peter B. Kovler, 203–27. Washington, D.C.: Center for National Policy Press, 1992.

Costigliola, Frank. "Lyndon B. Johnson, Germany, and the 'End of the Cold War.'" In *Lyndon Johnson Confronts the World: American Foreign Policy 1963–1968*, edited by Warren I. Cohen and Nancy Bernkopf Tucker, 173–210. New York: Cambridge University Press, 1994.

Cox, Robert W. "Social Forces, States and World Orders." In *Neorealism and Its Critics*, edited by Robert O. Keohane, 205–54. New York: Columbia University Press, 1986.

de Waart, Jules. "Alliance Security and the Military Balance." In *The State of the Alliance 1986–1987*, edited by John Cartwright, 95–154. Boulder, Colo.: Westview Press, 1987.

Doyle, Michael. "Liberalism and World Politics." *American Political Science Review* 80, no. 4 (December 1986): 1151–69.

Dunn, Keith A. "NATO's Enduring Value." *Foreign Policy* 71 (Summer 1988): 156–75.

Elbrick, C. Burke. "American Policy and the Shifting Scene." *Department of State Bulletin* 35, no. 890 (July 16, 1956): 108–13.

Falk, Richard. "Superseding Yalta." In *Dealignment: A New Foreign Policy Perspective*, edited by Mary Kaldor and Richard Falk, 28–51. New York: Basil Blackwell, 1987.

Friedmann, Bernhard. "The Reunification of the Germans as a Security Concept." *Atlantic Community Quarterly* 25, no. 2 (Summer 1987): 118–22.

Gaddis, John Lewis. "The Unexpected John Foster Dulles: Nuclear Weapons, Communism, and the Russians." In *John Foster Dulles and the Diplomacy of the Cold War*, edited by Richard Immerman. Princeton: Princeton University Press, 1990.

George, Alexander. "The 'Operational Code': A Neglected Approach to the Study of Political Leaders and Decision-Making." *International Studies Quarterly* 13 (1969): 190–222.

Goldstein, Judith, and Robert O. Keohane. "Ideas and Foreign Policy: An Analytical Framework." In *Ideas and Foreign Policy: Beliefs, Institutions and Political Change*, edited by Judith Goldstein and Robert O. Keohane, 3–30. Ithaca, N.Y.: Cornell University Press, 1993.

Grabbe, Hans-Juergen. "Konrad Adenauer, John Foster Dulles, and West German–American Relations." In *John Foster Dulles and the Diplomacy of the Cold War*, edited by Richard Immerman, 109–32. Princeton, N.J.: Princeton University Press, 1990.

Hahn, Walter F. "West Germany's Ostpolitik: The Grand Design of Egon Bahr." *Orbis* 16, no. 4 (Winter 1973): 859–80.

Haltzel, Michael H. "The Two Germanies and Bonn-Washington Relations." *Atlantic Community Quarterly* 24, no. 4 (Winter 1986–87): 338–44.

Hampton, Mary. "Die deutsche Vision von einer sich wandelnden Welt." In *Deutschland's Einheit und Europas Zukunft*, edited by Bruno Schoch, 301–24. Frankfurt: Suhrkamp Verlag, 1992.

Hanrieder, Wolfram. "West German Foreign Policy, 1949–1979: Necessities and Choices." In *West German Foreign Policy, 1949–1979*, edited by Wolfram Hanrieder, 15–36. Boulder, Colo.: Westview Press, 1980.

Hoffmann, Stanley. "The Case for Leadership." *Foreign Policy* 81 (Winter 1990–91): 20–38.

Hoover, Robert A. "Strategic Arms Limitation Negotiations." In *Technology, Strategy, and Arms Control*, edited by Wolfram F. Hanrieder, 93–114. Boulder, Colo.: Westview Press, 1986.

Huyn, Hans Graf. *Ostpolitik im Kreuzfeuer*. In "Congressional Record—Senate" (February 17, 1972): 2032–34. Stuttgart: Seewald Verlag.

Ikenberry, G. John. "Creating Yesterday's New World Order: Keynesian 'New Thinking' and the Anglo-American Postwar Settlement." In *Ideas and Foreign Policy: Beliefs, Institutions and Political Change*, edited by Judith Goldstein and Robert O. Keohane, 57–86. Ithaca, N.Y.: Cornell University Press, 1993.

Ikenberry, G. John, and Charles A. Kupchan. "Socialization and Hegemonic Power," *International Organization* 44 (Summer 1990): 283–315.

Immerman, Richard H. "Introduction." In *John Foster Dulles and the Diplomacy of the Cold War*, edited by Richard H. Immerman, 3–20. Princeton, N.J.: Princeton University Press, 1990.

Joffe, Josef. "Europe's American Pacifier." *Foreign Policy* (Spring, 1984): 64–82.

———. "The Foreign Policy of the Federal Republic of Germany." In *Foreign Policy in World Politics*, 6th ed., edited by Roy C. Macridis, 72–113. Englewood Cliffs, N.J.: Prentice-Hall, 1985.

Johnson, Paul. "Europe and the Reagan Years." *Foreign Affairs: America and the World 1988/89* 68, no. 1 (1989): 28–38.

Kaiser, Karl. "The New Ostpolitik." In *West German Foreign Policy: 1949–1979*, edited by Wolfram Hanrieder, 145–56. Boulder, Colo.: Westview Press, 1980.

Kennedy, John F. "Appeasement at Munich: The Inevitable Result of the Slowness of Conversion of the British Democracy from a Disarmament to a Rearmament Policy." Harvard Senior Paper. JFK Library, March 15, 1940.

Klein, Jean. "Current Aspects of Security and Arms Control in Europe." In *Arms Control and International Security*, edited by Roman Kolkowicz and Neil Joeck, 102–18. Boulder, Colo.: Westview Press, 1984.

Krasner, Stephen D. "United States Commercial and Monetary Policy: Unraveling the Paradox of External Strength and Internal Weakness." In *Between Power and Plenty: Foreign Economic Policies of Advanced Industrial States*, edited by Peter J. Katzenstein, 51–87. Madison: University of Wisconsin Press, 1978.

Kupchan, Charles, and Clifford Kupchan. "Concerts, Collective Security, and the Future of Europe." *International Security* 16 (Summer 1991): 114–61.

Kurth, James R. "The Political Consequences of the Product Cycle." *International Organization* 33, no. 1 (Winter 1979): 1–34.

Lake, David A. "International Economic Structures and American Foreign Policy, 1887–1934." *World Politics* 34, no. 4 (July 1983): 517–43.

Lebow, Richard Ned. "Generational Learning and Conflict Management." *International Journal* 40, no. 4 (Autumn 1985): 555–85.

Leibstone, Marvin. "Fiscal Year 1987—U. S. Defense Budget." *NATO'S Sixteen Nations* 31, no. 8 (December 86/January 87): 72–76.

Lenski, Gerhard. "Power and Prestige." In *Power*, edited by Steven Lukes, 243–52. New York: New York University Press, 1986.

Link, Arthur S. "Wilson: Idealism and Realism," in *Woodrow Wilson: A Profile*, edited by Author S. Link, 163–77. New York: Hill and Wang, 1968.

Mearsheimer, John. "Back to the Future: Instability in Europe After the Cold War." *International Security* 15 (Summer 1990): 5–56.

Merchant, Livingston T. "Fundamentals of U.S. Foreign Policy." *Department of State Bulletin* 35, no. 889 (July 9, 1956): 56–60.

Migone, Gian Giacomo. "The Decline of the Bipolar System, or a Second Look at the History of the Cold War." In *The New Detente*, edited by Mary Kaldor, 155–182. London: Verso, 1989.

Mueller, John. "The Essential Irrelevance of Nuclear Weapons: Stability in the Postwar World," in *The Cold War and After: Prospects for Peace*, edited by Sean Lynn-Jones and Steven Miller, 45–69. Cambridge, Mass.: MIT Press, 1993.

168   Bibliography

Osgood, Robert E. "Woodrow Wilson, Collective Security, and the Lessons of History." In *The Philosophy and Policies of Woodrow Wilson*, edited by Earl Latham, 187–98. Chicago: University of Chicago Press, 1958.

Posen, Barry R., and Stephen Van Evera. "Defense Policy and the Reagan Administration: Departure from Containment." *International Security* 8, no. 1 (Summer 1983): 3–45.

Preussen, Ronald. "The Predicaments of Power." In *John Foster Dulles and the Diplomacy of the Cold War*, edited by Richard H. Immerman, 21–45. Princeton, N.J.: Princeton University Press, 1990.

Putnam, Robert D. "Diplomacy and Domestic Politics: The Logic of Two-Level Games." *International Organization* 42 (Summer 1987): 427–61.

Rattinger, Hans. "The Federal Republic of Germany: Much Ado About Nothing." In *The Public and Atlantic Defense*, edited by Gregory Flynn and Hans Rattinger, 101–74. Totowa, N.J.: Rowman and Allanheld, 1985.

Roper, John. "European Defense Cooperation." In *Evolving European Defense Policies*, edited by Catherine McArdle Kelleher and Gale A. Mattox, 39–57. Lexington, Mass.: D. C. Heath, 1987.

Ruggie, John G. "International Regimes, Transactions, and Change: Embedded Liberalism in the Postwar Economic Order." *International Organization* 36, no. 2 (Spring 1982): 379–416.

———. "Multilateralism: The Anatomy of an Institution." In *Multilateralism Matters: The Theory and Praxis of an Institutional Form*, edited by John G. Ruggie, 3–47. New York: Columbia University Press, 1993.

Scheider, William. "Peace and Strength: American Public Opinion on National Security." In *The Public and Atlantic Defense*, edited by Gregory Flynn and Hans Rattinger, 321–64. Totowa, N.J.: Rowman and Allanheld, 1985.

Schwartz, Thomas Alan. "Victories and Defeats in the Long Twilight Struggle: The United States and Western Europe in the 1960s." In *The Diplomacy of the Crucial Decade: American Foreign Relations During the 1960s*, edited by Diane B. Kunz, 115–48. New York: Columbia University Press, 1994.

———. "Eisenhower and the Germans." In *Eisenhower: A Centenary Assessment*, edited by Guenter Bischof and Stephen E. Ambrose, 206–21. Baton Rouge: Louisiana State University Press, 1995.

Schweigler, Gebhard. "Anti-Americanism in German Public Opinion." In *America's Image in Germany and Europe*. Papers of a Seminar: Friedrich Ebert Stiftung. Washington, D.C.: Friedrich Ebert Stiftung, 1985: 8–33.

Steininger, Rolf. "John Foster Dulles, the European Defense Community, and the German Question." In *John Foster Dulles and the Diplomacy of the Cold War*, edited by Richard H. Immerman, 79–108. Princeton, N.J.: Princeton University Press, 1990.

Tucker, Robert W. "Reagan's Foreign Policy." *Foreign Affairs: America and the World 1988/89* 68, no. 1, 1989: 1–27.

Wampler, Robert A. "Eisenhower, NATO, and Nuclear Weapons: The Strategy and Political Economy of Alliance Security." In *Eisenhower: A Centenary Assessment*, edited by Guenter Bischof and Stephen E. Ambrose, 162–90. Baton Rouge: Louisiana State University Press, 1995.

Weber, Steve. "Shaping the Postwar Balance of Power: Multilateralism in NATO." In *Multilateralism Matters: The Theory and Praxis of an Institutional Form*, edited by John G. Ruggie, 233–92. New York: Columbia University Press, 1993.

Williams, Philip. "Britain, Detente and the Conference on Security and Cooperation in Europe." In *European Detente: Case Studies of the Politics of East-West Relations*, edited by Kenneth Dyson, 221–36. New York: St Martin's Press, 1986.

BOOKS

Acheson, Dean. *Present at the Creation: My Years in the State Department*. New York: W. W. Norton, 1969.

Adelman, Kenneth L. *The Great Universal Embrace: Arms Summitry — A Skeptic's Account*. New York: Simon and Schuster, 1989.

Adenauer, Konrad. *Memoirs, 1945–1953*. Chicago: Henry Regnery, 1966.

———. *Erinnerungen 1955–1959*. Stuttgart: Deutsche Verlags-Anstalt, 1967.

———. *Briefe Ueber Deutschland: 1945–1951*. Berlin: CORSO bei Siedler, 1985.

———. *"Es musste alles neu gemacht werden." Die Protokolle des CDU-Bundesvorstandes 1950–1953*. Stuttgart: Ernst Klett Verlage, 1986.

Ash, Timothy Garton. *In Europe's Name: Germany and the Divided Continent*. New York: Random House, 1993.

Baehr, Peter R. and Leon Gordenker. *The United Nations: Reality and Ideal*. New York: Praeger, 1984.

Bahr, Egon. *Zum europaeischen Frieden: Eine Antwort auf Gorbatschow*. Berlin: Wolf Jobst Siedler Verlag, 1988.

Baker, Ray Stannard. *Woodrow Wilson: Life and Letters*. New York: Doubleday, Doran, 1939.

Barnet, Richard J. *The Alliance, America-Europe-Japan: Makers of the Postwar World*. New York: Simon and Schuster, 1983.

Berding, Andrew H. *Dulles on Diplomacy*. Princeton, N.J.: D. Van Nostrand, 1965.

Blechman, Barry, and Cathleen Fisher, eds. *The Silent Partner: West Germany and Arms Control*. Cambridge, Mass.: Ballinger, 1988.

Bloomfield, Lincoln P., Walter C. Clemens, Jr., and Franklyn Griffiths. *Kruschev and the Arms Race: Soviet Interests in Arms Control and Disarmament, 1954–1964*. Cambridge, Mass.: MIT Press, 1966.

Brandt, Willy. *A Peace Policy for Europe*. New York: Holt, Rinehart and Winston, 1969.

———. *Peace: Writings and Speeches of the Nobel Peace Prize Winner, 1971*. Bonn-Bad Godesberg: Verlag Neue Gesellschaft, 1971.

———. *Bundestags Reden*. Bonn: Pfattheicher & Reichardt, 1972.

———. *People and Politics*. Boston: Little, Brown, 1979.

———. *My Life in Politics*. New York: Viking, 1992.

Brill, Heinz. *Geopolitik Heute: Deutschlands Chance?* Berlin: Ullstein, 1994.

Brinkley, Douglas. *Dean Acheson: The Cold War Years, 1953–71*. New Haven, Conn.: Yale University Press, 1992.

Brzezinski, Zbigniew. *Power and Principle: Memoirs of the National Security Advisor, 1977–1981*. New York: Farrar, Straus, Giroux, 1985.

Calhoun, Frederick S. *Power and Principle: Armed Intervention in Wilsonian Foreign Policy*. Kent, Ohio: Kent State University Press, 1986.

Calleo David P. *Beyond American Hegemony: The Future of the Western Alliance*. New York: Basis Books, 1987.

Calleo, David P., and Benjamin M. Rowland. *America and the World Economy*. Bloomington: Indiana University Press, 1973.

Carr, Edward Hallet. *The Twenty Years' Crisis, 1919–1939*. New York: Harper and Row, 1964.

Cioc, Marc. *Pax Atomica: The Nuclear Defense Debate In West Germany During The Adenauer Era*. New York: Columbia University Press, 1988.

Claude, Inis L. *Power and International Relations*. New York: Random House, 1964.

Cohen, Benjamin J. *Organizing the World's Money*. New York: Basic Books, 1977.

Collier, Peter, and David Horowitz. *The Kennedys: An American Drama*. New York: Warner Books, 1984.

Cottam, Richard. *Competitive Interference and 20th Century Diplomacy*. Pittsburgh, Pa.: University of Pittsburgh Press, 1967.

Curl, Peter V., ed. *Documents on American Foreign Relations, 1954*. New York: Harper and Brothers, 1955.

Daalder, Ivo. *Divergent Needs: The United States, France, Germany and the Nuclear Controversy, 1961–1966*. Paper submitted for Masters of Letters, University of Oxford, December 1983.

Dallek, Robert. *The American Style of Foreign Policy: Cultural Politics and Foreign Affairs*. New York: Alfred A. Knopf, 1983.

———. *Franklin D. Roosevelt and American Foreign Policy, 1932–1945*. New York: Oxford University Press, 1979.

Dean, Jonathan. *Watershed in Europe: Dismantling the East-West Military Confrontation*. Lexington, Mass.: Lexington Books, 1987.

Dennett, Raymond, and Robert K. Turner, eds. *Documents on American Foreign Relations, 1949*. Princeton, N.J.: Princeton University Press, 1950.

Deutsch, Karl, et al. *Political Community and the North Atlantic Area*. Princeton, N.J.: Princeton University Press, 1968.

Diamond, Sara. *Roads to Dominion: Right Wing Movements and Political Power in the United States*. New York: Guilford Press, 1995.

Die Gruenen: The Program of the Green Party of the Federal Republic of Germany.

Doenhoff, Marion Grafin. *Deutsche Aussenpolitik von Adenauer bis Brandt*. Hamburg: Christian Wagner Verlag, 1970.

Etzold, Thomas H., and John Lewis Gaddis, eds. *Containment: Documents on American Policy and Strategy, 1945–1950*. New York: Columbia University Press, 1978.

Evans, Peter B., and Harold K. Jacobson, and Robert D. Putnam, eds., *Double-Edged Diplomacy: International Bargaining and Domestic Politics*. Berkeley: University of California Press, 1993.

Fischer, Georges. *The Non-Proliferation of Nuclear Weapons*. London: Europa, 1971.

Fischer, Joschka. *Risiko Deutschland: Krise und Zukunft der deutschen Politik*. Cologne: Verlag Kiepenheuer and Witsch, 1994.

Foreign Relations of the United States, 1949, Vol. 3. Washington, D.C.: U.S. Government Printing Office, 1974.

Foreign Relations, 1952–1954, Vol. 5. Washington, D.C.: U.S. Government Printing Office, 1974.

Frank, Paul. *Entschluesselte Botschaft: Ein Diplomat macht Inventur*. Munich: Deutscher Taschenbuch Verlag, 1985.

Froment-Meurice, Henri. *Europa als eine Macht*. Cologne: Verlag Wissenschaft und Politik, 1986.

Fromkin, David. *In the Time of the Americans: The Generation That Changed America's Role in the World*. New York: Alfred A. Knopf, 1995.

Gaddis, John Lewis. *Strategies of Containment: A Critical Appraisal of Postwar American National Security Policy*. New York: Oxford University Press, 1982.

Gatzke, Hans W. *Germany and the United States: A Special Relationship?* Cambridge, Mass.: Harvard University Press, 1980.

Goergey, Laszlo. *Bonn's Eastern Policy, 1964–1971*. Hamden, Conn.: Archon Books, 1972.

Goldstein, Judith. *Ideas, Interests, and American Trade Policy*. Ithaca, N.Y.: Cornell University Press, 1993.

Graubard, Stephen R. *Kissinger: Portrait of a Mind*. New York: W. W. Norton, 1974.

Greenstone, J. David. *The Lincoln Persuasion: Remaking American Liberalism*. Princeton, N.J.: Princeton University Press, 1993.

Grosser, Alfred. *Germany in Our Time: A Political History of the Postwar Years*. New York: Praeger, 1971.

———. *The Western Alliance: European-American Relations Since 1945*. New York: Vintage Books, 1985.

Haftendorn, Helga. *Security and Detente: Conflicting Priorities in German Foreign Policy*. New York: Praeger, 1985.

Hall, Peter. *Governing the Economy: The Politics of State Intervention in Britain and France*. New York: Oxford University Press, 1986.

Hamilton, Nigel. *JFK: Reckless Youth*. New York: Random House, 1992.

Hampton, Mary N. *The Empowerment of a Middle-Sized State: West Germany, Wilsonianism and the Western Alliance*. Los Angeles: UCLA Press, 1993.

Hanrieder, Wolfram, ed. *West German Foreign Policy, 1949–1979*. Boulder, Colo.: Westview Press, 1980.

———. *Germany, America, Europe: Forty Years of German Foreign Policy*. New Haven, Conn.: Yale University Press, 1989.

Hardin, Russell. *Collective Action*. Baltimore, Md.: Johns Hopkins University Press, 1982.

Hartz, Louis. *The Liberal Tradition in America*. New York: Harcourt, Brace, 1955.

Heller, Deane, and David Heller. *John Foster Dulles: Soldier for Peace*. New York: Holt, Rinehart and Winston, 1960.

Howard, Michael. *The Lessons of History*. New Haven, Conn.: Yale University Press, 1991.

Hull, Cordell. *The Memoirs of Cordell Hull, Volume 2*. New York: Macmillan, 1948.

Hunt, Michael H. *Ideology and U.S. Foreign Policy*. New Haven, Conn.: Yale University Press, 1987.

Ikenberry, G. John, David A. Lake, and Michael Mastanduno, eds. *The State and American Foreign Economic Policy*. Ithaca, N.Y.: Cornell University Press, 1988.

Isaacson, Walter. *Kissinger*. New York: Simon and Schuster, 1992.

Isaacson, Walter, and Evan Thomas. *The Wise Men: Six Friends and the World They Made*. New York: Simon and Schuster, 1986.

Jahn, Hans Edgar. *Die Deutsche Frage von 1945 bis heute*. Mainz: v. Hase und Koehler Verlag, 1985.

Jansson, Bruce S. *The Reluctant Welfare State*. Belmont, Ca.: Wadsworth, 1988.

Johnson, Lyndon Baines. *The Vantage Point: Perspectives of the Presidency 1963–1969*. New York: Holt, Rinehart and Winston, 1971.

Katzenstein, Peter J. *Between Power and Plenty: Foreign Economic Policies of Advanced Industrial States*. Madison: University of Wisconsin Press, 1978.

Kelleher, Catherine McArdle. *Germany and the Politics of Nuclear Weapons*. New York: Columbia University Press, 1975.

Kennan, George F. *Memoirs*. New York: Bantam Books, 1969.

———. *Memoirs 1950–1963*. New York: Pantheon, 1972.

Keohane, Robert O., ed. *Neorealism and Its Critics*. New York: Columbia University Press, 1986.

———. *International Institutions and State Power*. Boulder, Colo.: Westview Press, 1989.

Keohane, Robert O., and Joseph S. Nye. *Power and Interdependence: World Politics in Transition*. Boston, Mass.: Little, Brown, 1977.

Keynes, John Maynard. *The Economic Consequences of the Peace*. New York: Harcourt Brace, 1929.

Khong, Yuen Foong. *Analogies at War: Korea, Munich, Dien Bien Phu, and the Vietnam Decisions of 1965*. Princeton, N.J.: Princeton University Press, 1992.

Kissinger, Henry. *White House Years*. Boston: Little, Brown, 1979.

———. *For the Record*. Boston: Little, Brown, 1982.

———. *Diplomacy*. New York: Simon and Schuster, 1994.

Klunk, Brian. *Consensus and the American Mission: The Credibility of Institutions, Policies and Leadership, Vol. 14*. Lanham, Md.: University Press of America, 1986.

Knorr, Klaus. *Power and Wealth: The Political Economy of International Power*. New York: Basic Books, 1973.

Kraft, Joseph. *The Grand Design*. New York: Harper and Brothers, 1962.

Krasner, Stephen D. *Defending the National Interest: Raw Materials Investment and U.S. Foreign Policy*. Princeton, N.J.: Princeton University Press, 1978.

Krehbiel, Carl C. *Confidence- and Security-Building Measures in Europe*. New York: Praeger, 1989.

LaFeber, Walter. *The American Age: U.S. Foreign Policy at Home and Abroad Since 1896, Vol. 2*. New York: W. W. Norton, 1994.

Lake, David A. *Power, Protection, and Free Trade: International Sources of U.S. Commercial Strategy, 1887–1939*. Ithaca, N.Y.: Cornell University Press, 1988.

Larson, Deborah Welch. *Origins of Containment: A Psychological Explanation*. Princeton, N.J.: Princeton University Press, 1985.

Laszlo, Goergey. *Bonn's Eastern Policy, 1964–1971*. Hamden, Conn.: Archon Books, 1972.

Leuchtenburg, William E. *In the Shadow of FDR: From Harry Truman to Bill Clinton*. Ithaca, N.Y.: Cornell University Press, 1993.

———. *The Perils of Prosperity, 1914–32*. Chicago: University of Chicago Press, 1993.

Mandelbaum, Michael. *The Fate of Nations: The Search for National Security in the Nineteenth and Twentieth Centuries*. Cambridge: Cambridge University Press, 1988.

Marks, Frederick W., III. *Power and Peace: The Diplomacy of John Foster Dulles*. Westport, Conn.: Praeger, 1993.

McGhee, George. *At the Creation of a New Germany: From Adenauer to Brandt: An Ambassador's Account.* New Haven, Conn.: Yale University Press, 1989.

Melanson, Richard A., and David Mayers, eds. *Reevaluating Eisenhower: American Foreign Policy in the 1950s.* Urbana: University of Illinois Press, 1987.

Montague, Kern, Patricia W. Levering, and Ralph B. Levering. *The Kennedy Crisis: The Press, the Presidency, and Foreign Policy.* Chapel Hill: University of North Carolina Press, 1983.

Moresey, Rudolf, and Hans-Peter Schwarz, eds. *Rhoendorfer Ausgabe: Teegespraeche, 1950–54. Vol. 1.* Berlin: Siedler Verlag, 1984.

Nathan, James A., and James K. Oliver. *United States Foreign Policy and World Order.* Glenview, Ill.: Scott, Foresman, 1989.

Nevins, Alan, ed. *The Strategy of Peace.* New York: Harper and Brothers, 1960.

Newhouse, John. *War and Peace in the Nuclear Age.* New York: Alfred A. Knopf, 1989.

Newhouse, John, Melvin Croan, Edward R. Fried, and Timothy W. Stanley. *U. S. Troops in Europe: Issues, Costs, and Choices.* Washington, D. C.: The Brookings Institute, 1971.

Nicolson, Harold. *The Congress of Vienna: A Study in Allied Unity, 1812–1822.* New York: Viking, 1968.

Ninkovich, Frank. *Modernity and Power: A History of the Domino Theory in the Twentieth Century.* Chicago: University of Chicago Press, 1994.

Nye, Joseph. *Bound to Lead: The Changing Nature of American Power.* New York: Basic Books, 1990.

Page, Benjamin I., and Robert Y. Shapiro. *The Rational Public: Fifty Years of Trends in Americans' Policy Preferences.* Chicago: University of Chicago Press, 1992.

Poettering, Hans-Gert. *Adenauer's Sicherheitspolitik 1955–1963.* Duesseldorf: Droste Verlag, 1975.

Pond, Elizabeth. *Beyond the Wall: Germany's Road to Unification.* Washington, D.C.: The Brookings Institute, 1993.

Preussen, Ronald. *John Foster Dulles: The Road to Power.* New York: Free Press, 1982.

Public Papers of the Presidents: Dwight D. Eisenhower; 1956. Washington, D.C.: U.S. Government Printing Office, 1958.

Quester, George. *The Politics of Nuclear Proliferation.* Baltimore, Md.: Johns Hopkins University Press, 1973.

Reeves, Richard. *President Kennedy: Profile of Power.* New York: Simon and Schuster, 1993.

Richardson, James L. *Germany and the Atlantic Alliance: The Interaction of Strategy and Politics.* Cambridge, Mass.: Harvard University Press, 1966.

Risse-Kappen, Thomas. *Die Krise der Sicherheitspolitik.* Mainz: Matthias-Gruenewald-Verlag, 1988.

———. *The Zero Option: INF, West Germany and Arms Control.* Boulder, Colo.: Westview Press, 1988.

Robinson, James L. *Germany and the Atlantic Alliance: The Interaction of Strategy and Politics.* Cambridge, Mass.: Harvard University Press, 1966.

Rosati, Jerel A. *The Carter Administration's Quest for Global Community: Beliefs and Their Impact on Behavior.* Columbia: University of South Carolina Press, 1987.

Saksena, K. P. *The United Nations and Collective Security: A Historical Analysis.* Delhi: D. K. Publishing House, 1974.

Schaeuble, Wolfgang. *Und der Zukunft zugewandt*. Berlin: Siedler Verlag, 1994.

Schlesinger, Arthur M., Jr. *A Thousand Days: John F. Kennedy in the White House*. Boston: Houghton Mifflin, 1965.

Schmidt, Helmut. *Men and Powers: A Political Retrospective*. New York: Random House, 1989.

Schwartz, David N. *NATO's Nuclear Dilemmas*. Washington, D.C.: The Brookings Institute, 1983.

Schwartz, Thomas Alan. *America's Germany: John J. McCloy and the Federal Republic of Germany*. Cambridge,Mass.: Harvard University Press, 1991.

Schwarz, Hans-Peter, ed. *Konrad Adenauer: Reden, 1917–1967*. Stuttgart: Deutsche Verlags-Anstalt, 1975.

———. *Die gezaehmten Deutschen: Von der Machtbessenheit zur Machtvergessenheit*. Stuttgart: Deutsche Verlags-Anstalt, 1985.

Schwarz, Jordan A. *The New Dealers: Power Politics in the Age of Roosevelt*. New York: Alfred A. Knopf, 1993.

Seaborg, Glenn T., with Benjamin S. Loeb. *Stemming the Tide: Arms Control in the Johnson Years*. Lexington, Mass.: Lexington Books, 1987.

Slany, William Z., ed. in chief. *Foreign Relations of the United States, 1952–1954, Vol. 5, Part 2*. Washington, D.C.: U.S. Government Printing Office, 1983.

Smith, Michael. *Western Europe and the United States: The Uncertain Alliance*. London: George Allen and Unwin, 1984.

Smith, Tony. *America's Mission: The United States and the Worldwide Struggle for Democracy in the Twentieth Century*. Princeton, N.J.: Princeton University Press, 1994.

Snyder, Jack. *Myths of Empire: Domestic Politics and International Ambition*. Ithaca, N.Y.: Cornell University Press, 1991.

Sorensen, Theodore C. *Kennedy*. New York: Harper and Row, 1965.

Stearns, Montague. *Entangled Allies: U.S. Policy Toward Greece, Turkey, and Cyprus*. New York: Council on Foreign Relations Press, 1992.

Stebbins, Richard P., ed. *The United States in World Affairs, 1951*. New York: Harper and Brothers, 1952.

———. *The United States in World Affairs, 1966*. New York: Harper and Row, 1967.

———. *The United States in World Affairs, 1967*. New York: Simon and Schuster, 1968.

Stein, Arthur A. *Why Nations Cooperate: Circumstance and Choice in International Relations*. Ithaca, N.Y.: Cornell University Press, 1990.

Steinbruner, John D. *The Cybernetic Theory of Decision: New Dimensions of Political Analysis*. Princeton, N.J.: Princeton University Press, 1974.

Stern, Fritz. *Dreams and Delusions: National Socialism in the Drama of the German Past*. New York: Vintage Books, 1989.

Szabo, Stephen F. *The Diplomacy of German Unification*. New York: St. Martin's, 1992.

Talbott, Strobe. *Deadly Gambits*. New York: Vintage Books, 1985.

Truman, Harry S. *Public Papers of the Presidents of the United States: Harry S. Truman*. Washington, D.C.: U.S. Government Printing Office, 1964.

Walt, Stephen M. *The Origins of Alliances*. Ithaca, N.Y.: Cornell University Press, 1987.

Waltz, Kenneth N. *Theory of International Relations.* Reading, Mass.: Addison-Wesley, 1979.

Weidenfeld, Werner. *Der deutsche Weg.* Berlin: Siedler Verlag, 1990.

Whetten, Lawrence L. *Germany's Ostpolitik; Relations Between the Federal Republic and the Warsaw Pact Countries.* London: Oxford University Press, 1971.

Willrich, Mason. *Non-Proliferation Treaty: Framework for Nuclear Arms Control.* Charlottesville, Va.: Michie Company, 1969.

Wills, Gary. *Nixon Agonistes: The Crisis of the Self-made Man.* New York: New American Library, 1971.

Wolfers, Arnold. *Discord and Collaboration: Essays on International Politics.* Baltimore, Md.: Johns Hopkins University Press, 1975.

Zinner, Paul E., ed. *Documents on American Foreign Relations, 1956.* New York: Harper and Row, 1957.

INDEX

Acheson, Dean, 20, 24–26, 51, 68, 72, 76, 77, 80, 83, 95, 131, 146
Adelman, Kenneth, 131, 145
Adenauer, Konrad, 4, 15, 20, 22, 23, 24, 25, 27, 36–40, 43–56, 66, 69–71, 74–76, 78, 79, 86, 99, 104, 107–111, 117, 131, 137, 139, 146
Alsop, Joseph, 79
Ash, Timothy Garton, 98
Atlantic Charter, 17

Bad Godesberg Party Program of 1959, 48, 115
Bahr, Egon, 107, 114, 115, 135, 139
Baker, James, 147
Ball, George, 97, 98
Barzel, Rainer, 99, 136
Basic Agreement, 134, 136
Berlin Agreement, 140
Berlin Crisis, 44
Berlin Wall, 45, 74, 76, 82, 131
Birrenbach, Dr. Kurt, 98–100
Brandt, Willy, 46, 74, 104, 106–111, 113, 114, 129, 131–140, 146

Brentano, Heinrich von, 51, 75, 77
Bretton Woods, 18
Brinkley, Douglas, 68, 76
Bruce, David, 55, 85
Brussels Treaty Organization, 25
Brzezinski, Zbigniew, 142
Bulganin, Nikolai, 47
Bundy, McGeorge, 69, 71, 73, 74, 97, 98, 102
Bush, George, 146, 149

Carter, Jimmy, 55, 78
Challener, Richard, 36
Christian Democratic Union (CDU), 49, 53, 54, 75, 77, 82, 98, 99, 102, 104, 107, 109, 110, 115, 116, 127, 132, 135, 136, 139
Christian Social Union (CSU), 43, 53, 77, 82, 104, 109, 110, 135, 136
Churchill, Winston, 15
Clinton, Bill, 149
collective security, 36, 55, 66, 67, 95, 98, 107, 115, 128, 147, 148

Conference on Security and
  Cooperation in Europe (CSCE), 132,
  143
Costigliola, Frank, 14, 93, 97, 99, 101
Cuban Missile Crisis, 81, 139
Czechoslovakia, 103

de Gaulle, Charles, 42, 45, 74, 76–79,
  81, 82, 93, 95, 98, 99, 111, 134, 139
Dean, Jonathan, 109
Deutsch, Karl, 10
Deutschlandpolitik, 46, 114, 129, 135
Dulles, John Foster, 4, 13, 14, 15, 21, 25,
  26, 35, 37, 38, 39, 40, 41, 44, 47

Eisenhower, Dwight, 4, 8, 16, 21, 26, 27,
  35, 37, 39, 41, 43, 44, 46, 47, 49–52,
  54–56, 65–67, 69–72, 75, 78–81, 83, 84,
  95, 128, 131, 145, 146
Erhard, Ludwig, 98, 101, 105
Erler, Fritz, 115
European Defense Community (EDC),
  25, 26, 38
European Nuclear Disarmament
  Committee (ENDC), 103
"Europeanists" at State, also called
  "theologians," 14, 79, 83, 94

flexible response, 68, 80, 81–83
Ford, Gerald, 141
France, 25, 38, 40, 47, 52, 55, 70, 73, 74,
  76, 82, 83, 98, 116, 134, 139
Franco-German Treaty of Friendship,
  77, 78, 84
Free Democratic Party (FDP), 104, 132,
  135, 136, 138
Froment-Meurice, Henri, 135
Fromkin, David, 8, 14
Fulbright, William, 48, 74

Genscher, Hans-Dietrich, 146
Goldberg, Arthur, 103
Goldstein, Judith, 2, 85
Gomulka Plan of 1963, 103
Gorbachev, Mikhail, 115, 117, 130, 132,
  143–146
Grabbe, Hans Juergen, 38
"Grand Design" of de Gaulle, 76, 78

"Grand Design" of Kennedy, 65, 76, 78
Graubard, Stephen R., 140
Great Britain, 40, 47, 52, 54, 55, 67, 81,
  98, 99, 103, 116
Greenstone, J. David, 8
Griffith, William, 45
Grosser, Alfred, 45, 78

Haftendorn, Helga, 42, 107
Hahn, Walter, 114, 135
Hanrieder, Wolfram, 136, 101, 137
Harmel Report of 1967, 4, 46, 74, 94, 96,
  105, 106, 111–117, 127–129, 131–133,
  135–137, 139, 141, 142, 144–146, 149
Harriman, W. Averell, 51, 72, 84
Hassell, Kai Uwe von, 77
Helsinki process, 143
Herter, Christian, 47, 51
Higgins, Marguerite, 79
Hillenbrand, Martin, 140
Hitler, Adolph, 13
Hull, Cordell, 14, 15, 17
Humphrey, Hubert, 48
Huyn, Hans Graf von, 136

Ikenberry, G. John, 2, 3, 13, 15
International Trade Organization, 20
Isaacson, Walter, 138

Johnson, Lyndon Baines, 4, 45, 51, 55,
  75, 85, 93–99, 101–103, 105, 106, 116,
  117, 129
Joint Committee on Atomic Energy
  (JCAE), 100

Kaysen, Carl, 73, 75
Kelleher, Catherine, 69, 82, 101, 104
Kennan, George, 11, 18, 19, 41, 48, 68
Kennedy, John F., 3, 4, 41, 45, 55, 56, 57,
  65–86, 93, 94, 96, 100, 117, 128, 131, 138
Kennedy, Robert F., 70
Keohane, Robert, 2, 10
Keynes, John Maynard, 2, 68
Khong, Yuen Foong, 8, 67, 68
Kiesinger, Kurt Georg, 104, 107, 134
Kissinger, Henry, 12, 19, 20, 85, 113,
  129, 138–179
Klunk, Brian, 40

Knappstein, Heinrich, 103
Kohl, Helmut, 134, 136, 144, 146
Krasner, Stephen D., 17
Kruschev, Nikita, 42
Kupchan, Charles and Clifford, 116

Laszlo, Georgey, 134
Leddy, John, 97
Lippmann, Walter, 46, 79
Lisbon Conference of 1952, 50
London Disarmament Conference, 47

MacArthur, General Douglas, 97
Macmillan, Harold, 47
Mansfield, Michael, 79
Marshall Plan, 17, 20
massive retaliation, 51, 79, 80
McCarthy, Eugene, 100
McCloy, John J., 13, 14, 24, 51, 77,
    94–96, 97, 98, 105, 106, 116
McGovern, George, 100
McNamara, Robert, 80, 82, 83, 94, 98,
    100, 109
Melanson, Richard, 35
Metternich, 138
Moscow Conference of 1943, 18
Moyers, Bill, 102
Multilateral force (MLF), 18, 22, 27, 52,
    54, 55, 70, 75, 79, 81, 83–85, 93–103,
    105, 109, 110, 114, 116
Munich lesson, 2–4, 8, 13, 36, 56, 67, 68,
    79, 85, 142
Mutual Balanced Force Reductions
    (MBFR), 132
MX missile, 146

Nassau, 81
National Security Action
    Memorandum 40 (NSAM 40), 80
NATO (North Atlantic Treaty
    Organization), 1-5, 17, 19–22, 25, 37,
    38, 41, 44, 46–48, 50, 52–55, 66, 69, 73,
    75, 77, 79, 83, 85, 94–96, 99, 100, 103,
    105, 106, 108, 109, 112–114, 116, 131,
    136, 140, 144, 145, 147–150
Nelson, Gaylord, 100
"new look," 50, 51, 53
Nerlich, Uwe, 42, 43

Nicolson, Harold, 22
Ninkovich, Frank, 8, 9, 11, 54, 72, 74,
    76, 82, 93, 97
Nixon, Richard, 75, 85, 111, 113, 129,
    138, 140
nonproliferation treaty (NPT), 95,
    103–106, 116
Norstad, General Lauris, 44, 48, 80, 83
Nuclear Defense Committee, 109
nuclear nonproliferation, 82, 83
Nuclear Planning Group (NPG), 109,
    110
Nuclear Test Ban Treaty, 72, 84

Oder-Neisse Line, 45, 72, 73, 79
Osgood, Robert, 16
Ostpolitik, 102, 104, 105, 107, 111, 114,
    115, 117, 127, 129, 131, 132, 134–141,
    149

Paris Peace Accord of 1954, 22, 25, 36,
    37, 41, 43, 44, 46, 55, 56
Poland, 103, 136, 140
Presbyterianism, 39
Preussen, Ronald, 38

Radford Plan, 46, 50, 51
Rapacki Plan, 46, 47
Rapallo, 70, 97, 138
Reagan, Ronald, 55, 117, 128–130, 132,
    141, 143–146
Reeves, Richard, 84
Reykjavik, 131, 132, 141, 145
Roosevelt, Franklin D., 8, 14, 15, 40
Rostow, Eugene, 70, 94, 105
Rostow, W. W., 45, 70, 71, 102, 105
Rusk, Dean, 72, 77, 84, 97–99, 100

San Francisco Conference of 1945, 68
Scheel, Walter, 138
Schlesinger, Arthur M., Jr., 70
Schmidt, Helmut, 78, 107, 142
Schneider, William, 143
Schroeder, Gerhard, 136
Schumacher, Kurt, 48, 49
Schwartz, David N., 52–54
Schwartz, Thomas, 11, 83
Seaborg, Glen, 84, 99, 105

Sloss, Leon, 111, 112
Smith, Tony, 9, 11
Social Democratic Party (SPD), 42, 48,
   49, 53, 73, 74, 96, 102, 104, 111–117,
   127–129, 131–137
Sorensen, Theodore, 86
Soviet Peace Note of 1952, 49
Soviet Union, 3, 35, 36, 38, 41, 44, 66,
   67, 68, 69, 70, 72, 75–78, 84, 85, 95, 99,
   101, 105, 106, 109, 113, 114, 115, 116,
   128, 130, 131, 133–135, 138, 143, 145,
   146, 149
Sputnik, 50, 51, 69
Stassen, Harold, 21, 47
Steinbrunner, John, 83
Stevenson, Adlai, 51
Stoltenberg, Gerhard, 136
Strategic Defense Initiative (SDI), 144,
   145
Strauss, Franz Josef, 43, 53, 75, 82, 99,
   104, 136

Trilateral Negotiations, 94
Truman, Harry S., 8, 14, 15, 40
Tucker, Robert W., 144

United Nations, 19–21, 39, 68

Versailles, 1–4, 11–15, 25–27, 35–37, 39,
   44, 48, 50, 52, 56, 65–71, 74, 76, 82, 84,
   85, 94, 95, 97, 104, 106, 107, 116, 117,
   127–130, 137, 138, 140, 142, 146–149
Vietnam, 68, 94, 102, 103, 106
Voigt, Karsten, 74

Warsaw Pact, 16, 137
Warsaw Treaty, 140
Weber, Steve, 21, 66

Yeltsin, Boris, 49

About the Author

MARY N. HAMPTON is Assistant Professor of Political Science at the University of Utah. Her areas of specialization include international relations and comparative politics, and her writings have appeared in journals and edited collections devoted to these topics.

ISBN 0-275-95505-2

90000>

EAN

9 780275 955052

HARDCOVER BAR CODE